T0322640

'This is a beautifully written, thoughtful book about a subject which concerns us all. It should be required reading for everyone who cares about elephants, Africa, and the natural world.'

John Simpson, World Affairs Editor, BBC News

'Fascinating and timely. Emphasising the cultural bond between people and wild animals, Martell describes the dangers and rewards of working with local communities to save elephants and rhinos from extinction. Read it and buy copies for everyone who cares about the natural world.'

Jane Goodall DBE, founder of the Jane Goodall Institute and UN Messenger of Peace

'*Flowers for Elephants* brings to life the extraordinary coexistence and resilience of nature and people in Kenya's Northern territories over the past four decades. Martell's prose captures this intriguing true story, a must-read for those seeking to understand more about this wonderful but troubled part of the world.'

The Rt Hon. Francis Ole Kaparo, former Speaker of the National Assembly of Kenya

'This important book—by a devoted reporter, about a critical ecosystem—should be on the reading list of any Africa-bound traveller or armchair conservationist. In lucid prose, it reveals what is at stake and what can be saved through the tenacity and long-term vision of a few brave people working against the odds.'

Sophy Roberts, travel journalist and author of *The Lost Pianos of Siberia,* a *Sunday Times* Book of 2020

'A compelling story of how the power of connecting with wildlife can strengthen communities. A must-read for anyone with a love for elephants.'

Major Levison Wood FRGS, explorer, and author of *Walking the Nile* and *The Last Giants*

'*Flowers for Elephants* is a deeply reported, beautifully written homage to the natural world. Its focus is a patch of Kenyan wilderness known as Lewa, and on Ian Craig, the man who found a novel way to save Kenya's vanishing herds of elephants, its rhinos and lions and other wild animals, from certain destruction. It also tells the story of some remarkable people within the indigenous communities who have joined Craig's efforts by creating a web of conservancies to form the Northern Rangelands Trust, in which people and wildlife coexist sustainably across a broad swathe of northern Kenya. In an age when all of us fear the worst is yet to come for our planet, Martell's book provides proof that human dedication to the cause of conservation, and to one another, can still make a difference.'

Jon Lee Anderson, *New Yorker* staff writer

FLOWERS FOR ELEPHANTS

PETER MARTELL

Flowers for Elephants

*How a Conservation Movement in
Kenya Offers Lessons for Us All*

FOREWORD
by HRH The Duke of Cambridge

HURST & COMPANY, LONDON

First published in the United Kingdom in 2022 by
C. Hurst & Co. (Publishers) Ltd.,
New Wing, Somerset House, Strand, London, WC2R 1LA
Printed in Scotland.

Distributed in the United States, Canada and Latin America by
Oxford University Press, 198 Madison Avenue, New York, NY 10016,
United States of America.

A Cataloguing-in-Publication data record for this book
is available from the British Library.

ISBN: 9781787386938

This book is printed using paper from registered sustainable
and managed sources.

www.hurstpublishers.com

Printed in Great Britain by Bell and Bain Ltd, Glasgow

To the brave people of northern Kenya risking all to protect wildlife for the future. And to Robyn, for adventures past and explorations ahead, with all my love.

CONTENTS

FOREWORD

The scale of the environmental crisis facing our world can often seem overwhelming, but stories of brave groups of people who are creating positive change provide both hope and inspiration.

One of those stories close to my heart is in Kenya, where the remarkable community-led Northern Rangelands Trust (NRT) is bringing people together across vast lands to better protect their precious environment. They are using age-old knowledge about living sustainably to support themselves and their communities in a rapidly changing world.

I have had the privilege to witness their work firsthand, listening, learning and seeing how—against all the odds—the trend of declining wildlife numbers can be reversed. The NRT is an exceptional model of large-scale environmental protection that critically strengthens the land rights of the people whose ancestral home it is.

Peter Martell's *Flowers for Elephants* is an exciting, important and inspiring account of how a region once known for conflict and poaching used conservation to help build peace.

It brings back many happy memories of my time with the NRT team in Northern Kenya. I recall once wading across a flooded river with a reputation for hungry crocodiles. As the fast-flowing muddy water reached our waists, two rangers midstream leapt into the air shouting and the rest of us splashed in headlong panic to get out. Only later—to much laughter—did we realise that the 'crocodile' was only a tree branch bumping our legs.

This is a story about astonishing wildlife: how the poaching of elephants was reduced by 98 per cent in just five years, and how endangered species such as the black rhino and Hirola antelope have been rescued from the brink of extinction. But more importantly, it is a story about people and what can be achieved when we work together towards a common goal. It is a story that gives me hope.

HRH The Duke of Cambridge
November 2021

TIMELINE

1920s	Britain declares Kenya a colony. Craig family turn Lewa into a farm.
1946	Nairobi National Park opened, Kenya's first. Kinyanjui Lesderia born.
1952–60	Mau Mau war. Ian Craig born in 1952.
1963	Kenya's independence from Britain. Shifta War in northern Kenya begins.
1973	Elephant hunting banned in Kenya.
1977	Ian Craig starts running Lewa as a cattle ranch. All hunting in Kenya banned.
1983	Lewa Rhino sanctuary opens.
1989	Ivory burn in Nairobi amidst poaching wave.
1991	Fencing around Lewa begins and rhino sanctuary expands.
1995	The first community conservancy, Il Ngwesi, is formed.
2002	Meeting at Kom, and start of Sera conservancy. Several others follow.
2004	Leaders unite as the Northern Rangelands Trust.
2009	Rhino poaching crisis on Lewa begins.
2013	Lewa inscribed as a World Heritage Site.
2015	Rhino return to Sera.
2016	Reteti elephant sanctuary opens, and Kenya burns 106 tonnes of ivory.
2019	First orphaned elephants released into Sera.
2020	Coronavirus hits and tourism struggles, but the conservancies continue.

THANK YOU

This is not my story, and my many thanks to Kinyanjui and Ian, and to all the many more it includes, for entrusting me to tell it. This is dedicated to all those in the community conservancy movement working to make a change. As a small gesture of my thanks, ten percent of author profits from the sale of this book will be donated towards schools in community conservancies in northern Kenya.

PREFACE

'In a few decades, the relationship between the environment, resources and conflict may seem almost as obvious as the connection we see today between human rights, democracy and peace.'

Nobel Peace Prize award speech for Wangarī Maathai, 2004

The rattle of bullets smacked down into the soft sand on the hillside a stone's throw above. For a moment, I looked at where the tiny clouds had puffed up from the impact, and then across the valley to where the crackling gunfire was coming from. The explosions made me freeze. 'Run!' a policeman shouted at me. 'Go!' I sprinted a zig-zagging route down the slope, my heart in my throat. I threw myself down behind a pile of jumbled rocks. Overhead, an army helicopter roared down low, nearly skimming the tops of the bushes in the hot and dry valley. The thumping rotor blades threw up a cloud of stinging dust. Gunners hanging out the doors of the helicopters had been firing into the dirt to break up fighting between groups of young men. I thought about lifting my camera up, but there was another prolonged burst of gunfire. Several people had told me that the army had the day before fired mortars to keep combatants apart. I pushed myself down deeper. My body shook in fear.

I was a journalist based in Kenya, and I had caught a lift on an aid flight assessing the impact of the unrest in the far northern town of Moyale. Fighting between rival groups, the camel and cattle herding Borana and the Gabra people, had spilled into town. The first shot was fired in an argument over access to a well. Old debates over land, and who had the right to graze their livestock on the sparse patches of remaining grass as the heat of the dry season began to bite, flared once again. That led to one group stealing camels—each side blamed the other for starting it—and soon escalated into heavy fighting. Local politicians saw opportunities in the chaos to score popularity points.

They called the other group enemies, and encouraged their supporters to seize what they could from them. A clash over water that had erupted between a small group of hungry people was given the dangerous cloak of an ethnic battle. Anger boiled into hatred.

I thought the worst of it was over, and I'd expected to be reporting on the aftermath. Instead, it felt like I'd stepped into an ongoing war. Dozens of people were reported to have been killed, shot or hacked to death. Hundreds had fled for their lives. In town, where shops were torched, I heard the mourning cries as mothers wept for their dead sons. In the basic local hospital, I spoke to men with machete cuts on their arms and heads. A policeman was carried in by his comrades, shot in the thigh and shoulder in an ambush on the outskirts of town. He grimaced as comrades heaved him from a pickup onto a medical trolley, his military fatigues dark with dripping blood.

From faraway, in Kenya's capital Nairobi, the fighting hadn't seemed anything out of the ordinary; this battle was in 2013, but the violence was just one more flare up of conflict that had plagued the north for decades. Assault rifles meant that cattle raids were far more deadly than the old days of skirmishing with spears, and could spiral into revenge attacks of horrifying proportions.

Still, such clashes often only made small stories tucked away in Kenya's newspapers. In Nairobi, a swiftly growing cosmopolitan city bigger than Chicago or Berlin that echoed to the beating sounds of pumping music and constant construction, and where entrepreneurs with smartphones hustled for business, the troubles of the north seemed like a distant and untidy corner of the country that was best ignored. It was treated as if violence there was somehow the normal state of affairs.

So if, as I lay face down with the shooting all around me, someone had told me then that soon the people of the north would defy the doomsayers to come together as a community to build peace, I don't think I would have believed them for a second.

This is the story of how that apparently impossible transformation took place.

* * *

Imagine, for a moment, soaring like a bird above the great continent of Africa. Beneath your wings is a vast land of more than fifty-five countries, an area in which the USA, China and all of Europe would fit with space left over. On the eastern side, where the land juts out like a finger pointing towards the Arabian Peninsula, the waters of the Indian Ocean crash on white sand shores. Just below, lies Kenya.

The Equator divides the country neatly in two. The top half of the country spreads across an area somewhere in size between the state of New Mexico and Germany. Down below, the ground is an artist's palette, from luminous green to crackling yellow and dry burnt brown. The land shifts from lush jungle to savannah, from bush to rocky hills. Poking up high is a snow-peaked mountain top with glaciers glinting in the sun, and in the far north, the world's biggest desert lake, a jade-coloured sea surrounded by sweltering stony shores. Right through the centre runs the epic Rift Valley, a giant geological fault where the Earth's splitting tectonic plates created soaring canyon walls and wide valley floors, the birthplace of our most ancient ancestors. All of us can trace our roots back home to this great valley.

Northern Kenya is also among the very few places left where elephants still march across the open spaces in big, free-ranging populations, moving to follow the rains. Think of sweeping savannahs with umbrella-shaped acacia trees and giraffe galloping across golden grassland plains. If that sounds like a film, blame the Disney artists who animated The Lion King, because it is where they came to do their research illustrations. Pride Rock is fantasy, but its inspirations are not.

For many decades, northern Kenya had a rough reputation of being dangerous bandit country. The first time I visited, in 2005, what today is a wide tarmac highway to Ethiopia was a slow and single track of bumpy red soil through baking deserts and rugged hills. Back then, the route was too rough for all but the strongest of vehicles. To get a lift meant asking truck drivers heading north from the busy market town of Isiolo.

As I waited for a ride in the dark chill before dawn, I sipped thick coffee spiced with ginger, brewed on a brazier with fragrant frankincense crumbled on the coals. I remember watching a herd of camels and cattle cross the sandy street. They were being pushed forward by half a dozen tall and wiry young men from the Samburu people. They are cousins of the Maasai, and one of more than two dozen different groups who live across the north. Each has their distinctive culture, beliefs and language.

They wore the dramatic dress of the Samburu warrior. Denim jeans and T-shirts were easily available in the market, but the young men preferred their traditional dress: red and blue wraps around their waist, a bright tartan blanket on their shoulders like a super-hero's cape, striped football socks pulled up to their knees, intricate rolls of rainbow-coloured beaded necklaces and bracelets, and a sword in a scabbard at their belt. Their hair was braided into thin long locks, adorned in a ceremonial maroon paste made of mixed sheep fat and clay, with a punk rock headdress of long white flutter-ing feathers, and thick ivory plugs stretched into their hanging ear-lobes. They love the brightest of colours; red is a favourite because it signifies courage, danger and strength. Many Samburu say their name means 'the fierce ones'; the tough men who can handle the harshest of terrains. Their Maasai cousins look instead at their flam-boyant fashion and call them 'the butterfly people'.

As daylight broke, the call to prayer rang out over the tin-roof town from the tall mosque. It felt like a very different land from the multi-lane highways and gleaming skyscrapers of Nairobi I had come from. Eventually, a friendly Somali driver offered me a lift, clinging to the bars on the top of a cattle truck. Kind arms grabbed my hands, lifting me and my bag up high, as the sharp cow horns below knocked at the soles of my dangling boots. When the police signed the lorry out from the checkpoint, lifting the barbed-wire barrier, it was as if we were being stamped out from a frontier passport post. Yet there were still two hot days of bone-shaking drive bal-anced above the cows before we reached the Ethiopian border safely, the distance the length of England. My bouncing seat on the rollercoaster roof of the truck had outstanding all-round views, perfect for scanning for a glimpse of an elephant or a tall giraffe's head poking out of the trees—or gangs of men lying in wait. Trucks travelled in convoy with an armed guard, because highway gunmen regularly held up travellers to rob them.

The expanses of grey thorns stretched to a horizon dotted with mesa and butte hills rearing up with giant cliff faces glowing red in the dawn rays. In between, open grasslands shone almost silver. For an outsider staring out, the land looked deserted. But that is only in the eyes of a foreigner, we who are used to measuring human habitation by the scars of tarmac roads and metal power lines leading the way to a concrete collection of houses. It was no uninhabited wilderness; far from it. For the people that live there, this is home.

* * *

I am a reporter, and for years, whenever I travelled to northern Kenya, it was to cover grim stories of suffering, starvation and conflict. When the bad droughts came, in cycles every few years, I listened to the herders say that each was worse than the one before.

I saw the deep sadness of the families as they carried out the mass slaughter of their livestock. Even the camels had collapsed. Charities, rather than bringing in sacks of food aid, thought it better to pay people to kill their herds to eat before it was too late— money they could use later to buy grain. One by one, the weakest goats first, they had their throats cut. It was a last-ditch sacrifice for survival, for no one knew what would happen in the future when the animals were all gone. It was the most mournful of meals. This was no celebratory feast, but a funeral wake.

The herding life was once how almost all humans lived. We moved with livestock, following the rains, seeking grazing. Now the herders were side-lined on the edge of a changing planet. People had to respond to alarming new pressures. There were battles over water and grazing—and the land became ever more degraded. The wild animals were annihilated: antelopes for their meat, elephants for their ivory, and rhino for their horns. The old ways of authority were battered by a changing society and a flood of automatic rifles.

Sometimes battles erupted in times of scarcity, when the drought came and demands on dwindling resources increased. But some times the conflict came after the rains, in times of abundance, when people took what they could and replenished lost stock, because they feared more hard times ahead.[1] Elders said that their communities used to sleep with their shoes on, because they never knew when they might have to flee the fighting.

As a journalist, the arid lands could seem like just one more conflict to cover. Northern Kenya often appeared a place with more in common with the war-ravaged nations it bordered, South Sudan and Somalia, than with the rest of the country. Sometimes, it too felt like a land on the brink of civil war.

* * *

For more than a decade, East Africa was my home, and my reporter's beat. Conflict was never the only story—far from it. I am no war correspondent. I tried to always balance reporting violence with positive stories of progress and innovation, defiance against authoritarianism, hope and courage. Even in the gloomiest times, parents bring up their children, fulfil their dreams, aim high and achieve their best. They fall in love, worry about work, live and laugh.

Still, the nature of news means journalists go to the trouble spots, and reports all too often were of struggle and misery. I lived in South Sudan for several years, where money from oil was squandered on buying guns and battles for authority. Fights over cattle were on the scale of a war zone, leaving scores of dead in each raid and revenge attack.

In Ethiopia, I was on the streets when the police opened fire on furious demonstrators, as a growing youth excluded from power challenged the old authoritarian rulers; and I lived in neighbouring Eritrea, a dictatorship where people dared not even protest. I spent months talking over tea with rebel commanders from Sudan's war-ravaged Darfur, who described how they were driven out by bomber airplanes and government-armed militia fighters who burned their homes, stole their animals and seized their land. It wasn't, as some said, as simple as a war over water—but that played a part.

I sailed on a creaking wooden ship taking refugees fleeing Somalia across the Red Sea, then headed up into the jagged mountains of Yemen, living for a year in an ancient tower house in a land where men wear curved daggers and carry rifles slung over their shoulder. They were not to be messed with. Wars were fought between rival villages to secure a water well using machine guns and mortars.

I went often to Somalia, a land where grandparents put children on their knees to tell them tales of what life was once like when there was peace. Swathes of lands were left barren because the trees were hacked down for charcoal. Desert encroached onto grazing lands. I saw baby after baby die in a manmade famine, where drought was exploited by gunmen as a weapon of war. Offshore, fleets of foreign trawlers had taken advantage of the anarchy to wipe out fishing stocks, while international gangs had used Somalia as a dumping ground for toxic barrels, from hazardous chemicals to even alleged radioactive waste.[2] In the seaside capital Mogadishu, I interviewed notorious pirate chiefs who led murderous hijackings of ships far out into the Indian Ocean. They were no peg-leg and a bottle of rum pirates, but modern crime bosses raking in multi-million dollar ransoms from oil tankers. They blamed piracy on hungry young men who had no other chance of jobs.

I spoke to those who had fled the violence in Somalia's drylands into tight-packed refugee cities, houses of plastic bags stretched onto frames of sticks, proud people forced from their homes and made dependent on food aid handouts. I saw how desperate people without opportunities can turn in anger to believe extremist ideologies and join brutal insurgent forces. Then I went to the frontline trenches with the soldiers sent in to kill them. I camped behind sandbag emplacements and peered out from the gunner's hatch in the armoured convoys. All too often, war led not to victory and peace. It led to more war.

In rankings of countries most vulnerable to climate change, East African nations were almost all listed in the danger zone, some at the very top of the list. It is a global crisis, but they were disproportionately affected. The people who had contributed the least to causing it were those being hardest hit. They were the nations both most vulnerable to climate change—and least ready to cope with it.[3]

Such drylands on the edge act as an early warning system of what will happen elsewhere without action. As the world becomes hotter and drier—and much harder to live in—those who have lived for generations on such lands have something to teach the rest of us. The struggles there today are those that all of us will face tomorrow; coping with the impact of climate breakdown, habitat loss, growing pressures on land, decimated wildlife populations, the annihilation of species, and societies changing with population growth, migration, and conflict driven by poverty. If this was a taste of what is yet to come, it was terrifying.

* * *

As the list of conflict areas visited grew longer, the reporting blurred in repetition. Stories explained the political arguments that started a fight, but rarely went beyond those immediate triggers. I felt like I was only reporting on *how* conflict was fought, not *why*. I was missing the bigger picture that made some sense of it all.

I looked at what was common to the conflicts I had seen; how they had begun, what kept them going, and when they stopped, what had changed. Each conflict was unique in its own way, but there were also similarities. At the heart of almost every war are resources—and who controls them. That not only meant valuable minerals, metals, timber and oil; often it was the fundamentals of life itself—land and water.

Most of the lands lay beyond the reach of central government. They were out of their control—but not necessarily out of control. They were 'stateless' spaces but not un-ruled, for authority lay with the community who lived there. The strength of local institutions was a bellwether of war. When a community managed their land together, the situation was stable. They worked out solutions where all could benefit for the longer term. In tough times, people pulled together. Resource scarcity could bring people together in coopera-tion, not drive them apart into conflict.[4]

But where institutions were weak, and where power was shared unequally, or where a community was divided or broken by outside forces, trouble brewed. Its resources were stripped, and the poorest suffered disproportionately. When the structures of authority col-lapsed, people turned and fought one another for short-term gain in the greedy grab for power. Without a community structure, individuals took what they could for themselves. Outsiders picked over the bones.

Environmental reasons may not be the spark for conflict, for wars rarely begin from simple causes or single grievances. Past changes in climate have proved a poor predictor of civil wars; largescale conflict is driven by political failure, the exclusion of people and struggling economies, rather than directly from a single drought.[5] The link is not always linear; changes in climate can lead to significant increases of violence in one place but not in another—because what matters is how governments deal with the challenge.[6]

Yet environmental factors played a role in almost every stage of conflict, accelerating instability in vulnerable areas. Soldiers assessing the impacts of climate change call them 'catalysts for conflict.'[7] As the consequences of environmental change become more severe—from causing economic damage, to agricultural land loss and rising migration—many fear those drivers of conflict will be exacerbated, which will undermine the ability of local and government institutions to cope.[8] Crop failure, lack of water, natural disasters and disease are all tipping points for violence. One analysis in Somalia calculated that even a relatively small increase in the strength and length of droughts above the norm resulted in the risk of conflict rising by nearly two-thirds.[9] It was a downward spiral: failed rains ruined harvests, and that drove food prices higher. Hungry people needed to get food for their family. People were pushed into violence—and then conflict made food scarcer.[10]

Where there was conflict, destruction of the environment compounded the problem—and changes in the world's heating climate only added to that. Shifting weather patterns altered the fertility of the lands, pushing populations to move, bringing neighbours into conflict. People were caught between deadly extremes of floods or drought; and when they ran from violence, they found only the most inhospitable land left empty.

Poverty, conflict, and environmental degradation are all fundamentally connected. When our natural world is in crisis, so are we. What we do to our linked web of life, we do to ourselves.

* * *

As scientists warn our heating world is hurtling towards ecological catastrophe, with a loss of species at rates unprecedented in human history, leading voices say we must protect at least half the world's lands and oceans or the impacts will be dire.[11]

Nearly a tenth of Kenya is already protected as national parks and reserves, a gigantic area. They are clearly demarcated zones given over to wildlife, where humans are banned from living. They are rarely fenced in, but they are guarded by armed government rangers who keep people out. As settlements and farms of growing populations stretch onto new lands, such pockets of protection provide core reserves where animals are left in peace.

The conundrum is, the land now often suggested to be protected is not a wilderness empty of people, and any response for the future cannot be through the gross injustice of shutting out those whose home it is. It is not only clearly wrong, but ineffective too. Researchers across the world have shown that nature is declining less rapidly on lands where it is managed by the people who have always lived there.[12] After all, they know better than anyone how to protect their ecosystem. Their life is often called 'traditional', but that makes some see it as outdated. In fact, it is a sophisticated system of land management built up through generations of living in close cooperation with nature.

* * *

As the years passed, I realised northern Kenya had slowly shifted down my journalist's list of trouble spots to report on. It was not a sudden shift, and there was no single event I could put my finger on as a turning point. Journalism is driven by the breaking news of immediate disaster; the slower trends of gradual positive change are far harder to see.

There were still cattle raids, and heart-breaking stories of violence. Yet in other areas, security was improving. Northern Kenya shared so much in terms of the culture, ways of life and landscape of neighbouring nations, but it appeared to be taking a different path. Something, it seemed, was changing for the better. This was no 'forever conflict', after all.[13]

Those I spoke to offered many explanations for the change, but there was a common foundation—the growth of a community conservation movement. People, I was told, had come together to create an enormous network of dozens of community-owned protected areas, to manage and guard the greatest resource they had, their land. Each community had elected leaders and a council, managing land and building peace, to support old ways of living on the land as they face the new challenges of a modern world. Community members were recruited as ranger teams, helping stem conflicts. More children were going to school, and health clinics were opening. Businesses could grow. Wars have social, economic and political roots; bringing people together was the best way to tackle those grievances.

Much of the land is made up of *rangelands*, open country of wild grass and bush used for grazing. Wildlife was not something to be enclosed and contained. Some estimate that as much as two-thirds of Kenya's wildlife could be found outside the formal national parks, roaming on land owned communally by the people who live there.[14] These were no fenced off nature reserves, but places where people and wild animals co-existed alongside each other. In northern Kenya, wilderness—in terms of a separate land without humans—was a foreign concept. The people had tackled the much harder, and much more important, challenge; of finding ways to live in a respectful relationship with nature. The local inhabitants—the Borana and Gabra, Samburu and Somali, Rendille and Turkana, the Meru and Pokot, and many, many more—were the keepers of the lands far back into the past. They were pastoralist peoples, who moved their livestock on ancient routes to the same areas each year to find water and grazing. They knew every step of the ground, for the landscape was shaped by the way they moved their animals. The communities nurtured the land because their lives depended on it.

Northern Kenya's open grazing rangelands were all too often dismissed as marginal lands of little value, but that is very far from the truth. As the dire impacts of climate breakdown reverberate around the world, the work to support large-scale efforts are a vital part of the puzzle. Savannah grasslands are key sinks of carbon—at times as good as thick forests—but intact ecosystems are far more efficient at sequestering carbon than degraded ones.[15] If the land was ruined and became desert, it would have global ramifications. Rangelands, in their many forms, cover more than half the world's landmass.[16] They include the prairies and tundra of North America—including a third of the USA—to the pampas in South America, the steppes of Eurasia, to the Australian Outback. Across Africa, they cover some two-fifths of the land, providing a way of life for at least a quarter of the continent's people.[17] Understanding how to keep the rangelands healthy has an impact that matters to us all.

The community-protected lands reconnected key areas for wildlife, strengthening animal populations. Degraded grazing lands long stripped bare were being slowly restored. Elephants returned to lands they had not been seen in for decades. Across Kenya, wildlife numbers were dropping dramatically: two-thirds of animals were estimated to have been lost since the 1970s.[18] But here, at least, the frightening race towards the mass extinction of species had slowed, and even been put into reverse. Even the most heavily poached and endangered rhino were returning to lands they had long been exterminated from. Rhinos and elephants are not only beautiful animals; they are barometers of the health of the living systems needed for our survival. Communities widened their efforts to work across an immense landscape to safeguard entire ecosystems—the complex interlocking world from plants to fungi, animals, insects and birds—that make up the very fabric of life. Faced with a crisis, people united to drive for wider social, environmental and political change. If their community-protected lands were placed together, they would stretch across an area bigger than Switzerland.

* * *

Still, to be honest, based on the initial reports, I was deeply skeptical. It is easy to make things sound great in glossy brochures, but the reality was often so very different. In the midst of global gloom about the destruction of the natural world, everyone wanted to find a solution. But to look for it in the north of Kenya, a land with a long history of violence, seemed especially unlikely. People in more temperate lands often say that making a difference to the environment is too difficult. Yet if, against such odds, real change could be enacted in the hard lands of northern Kenya, then perhaps their example could inspire the rest of us.

I decided to see what was happening for myself. I stuffed a bag with clothes and food, notebooks and a camera, and grabbed a sleeping bag. I headed north.

1

KINYANJUI'S CLASSROOM
(HOW THE LESSONS WERE LEARNED)

Beneath the spreading branches of a shady tree, two old friends laugh, as they remember shared adventures from the days when they were young. They speak of journeys far across the sweeping savannahs of northern Kenya, lands dotted with graceful giraffe, and through the harsh plains where herders graze their animals on the wild grasses. There are tales of tough treks scrambling up steep escarpments to the cool green forests on the plateaus of sacred mountains, where the sweet waters flow even when the red dust deserts are baking dry down below. There are memories of secret valleys where herds of hundreds of elephants grazed in peace—until those who came to kill for their ivory found them.

Stories are told of nights in the mountains, sleeping to the sounds of the whooping hyenas prowling close by, and the dark blue sky flashing with stars arched in a bowl above. There are stories of how they followed the fearsome lions who had killed the cattle. They tell of legends of mystery, fables of spirits in the forests, and wizened men in caves deep in the hills who whispered magic and claimed to speak to rhinos. These are powers, the pair say with hesitation, that while they don't believe, they also can't explain and, it seems, might still fear.

On one side of the tree sits Kinyanjui Lesderia, dressed in his best in black leather shoes and a faded pinstripe jacket, too big despite his tall and still sturdy body. A grey-haired elder with deep sunken eyes, his dangling earlobes are stretched long by the plugs he once wore as a warrior of the Maasai people. Now he is retired, and spends his days at home, a tin-roof cottage surrounded by green fields on a small farm, with chicken scratching in the hedges, a flock of goats half-watched by his sleeping sheep dog, and a dozen prized cattle grazing beyond. But he was not always a comfortable farmer, and his weathered hands and lined face reflect a tough life of challenges. Staring out from above deep-set eyes, he holds the authority of a man used to giving orders and being obeyed. Yet his eyes also sparkle with a streak of humour, and his mouth twitches with a grin, for he is a man who finds humor even in the hardest of times.

On the other side of the tree is Ian Craig, a slim but strongly-built man dressed in a pair of sand-coloured shorts and a loose shirt, ironed with crisp creases but faded by long days in the sun. On his feet are scuffed old Converse shoes, and in leather holders on his belt, a pen-knife and compass that he uses as a pilot in the bush airplane he flies. He still looks like what he was for many years—a farmer. When he grins, his weather-beaten and deeply tanned face crinkles into lines of laughter. His passion is wildlife, and he seems happiest when tracking the great round footsteps of elephants through the forests.

Too often, these days, he is stuck in meetings and conferences, though he owns just one blazer and tie, and wears it only if he really has to. If he has a chance, he is off at dawn to join the wildlife rangers on their patrols in his tiny airplane, waggling its wings after take-off over his home to wave to his wife Jane. With cloth-covered fuselage and tyres like giant children's balloons—meaning he can bounce down to use dry riverbeds as landing strips—it looks more a magnificent flying motorbike than an airplane. Often he heads out with Jane, camping on the sand, lighting a fire to cook food—and keep hungry lions at bay.

Kinyanjui and Ian have been friends since they were boys, out exploring the remotest corners of northern Kenya. They'd pack a small rucksack, grab a rifle and a cooking pot, and head into the hills where the rhino hid. In the bush, faced with the dangers of lion, they put their lives in each other's hands.

Both men are now grandfathers. Much time has passed since those early days, so that the near misses each had when they flung themselves headfirst into bushes to dodge charging buffalos are retold with bravado, not terror. Then their voices are quieter as they recall the companions they have lost in battles with bandits in the bush, when the gunmen killing rhinos and elephants switched from wildlife to hunt the men too, the bullets thumping down beside them. They have seen so much, and there have been both good times and bad. They have supported each other through them.

Some might scoff and say their tales have been burnished in their fireside retelling over the years, but there is no reason not to believe them. They have no need to show off to each other; the two men have been friends for well over half a century. If the stories sound astonishing, then it is because they have both lived truly extraordinary lives. They have spent so much time together, from boys to old men today.

Their friendship would be the catalyst for a remarkable home-grown conservation movement for change, and set them on a course that would impact the land and wildlife far beyond the wildest of their adventures.

If you had asked them as young men if they could imagine what it would lead to, they would have laughed in disbelief. For their first small steps would be the seed for something far greater. Their role would be only one small part of a community effort, for many, many more contributed. It is a tale that includes a long list of people, who all faced overwhelming obstacles but who came together in trust, hope and courage to take action. So this is not just Ian's and Kinyanjui's story; far from it. But it is how this one begins.

* * *

For both men, home has always been the same rolling hills and rocky valleys. Ian grew up on the golden grasslands known as Lewa, and Kinyanjui comes from the tree-cloaked mountains of Il Ngwesi, bordering just beyond. They grew up exploring every step of the plains, climbing to the high tops, and looking out to where the peaks stretch far to the north.

At dawn, the jagged height of Mount Kenya rears up on the horizon. The summit slices through the wispy clouds, dreamlike, as if somehow floating and unattached. Ice and snow catch the light, shining silver directly on the line of the Equator. Some say that the holy peak—the tallest in Africa after the colossal Kilimanjaro—looks like the horns of a young rhino, and the snowy top on black rocks, like the white plumes on the black back of an ostrich. For those seeing 'The White Mountain' for the first time, it might seem more like a postcard of the Alps than the generic image of arid 'Africa' they've seen on television.[1] It feeds life-giving rivers that run far down into the hot plains.

But the land far below on Lewa is a different world. It marks a border line. Behind, to the south, are the cool highlands, where the trees hang heavy with bananas, and green farms burst with vegetables from rich dark earth. Ahead, to the north, the soil grows thin and red. The land shimmers in the blazing sun on the horizon, and the hairdryer heat of the open savannah comes in dusty waves. Huge rocky outcrops rear up high, towering over surrounding thorn forests.

In the long hard months without rains, most of the land is crackling dry. But a permanent spring rises up in the centre of the Lewa. Looking down onto the thick reeds around the water, the marshlands stand out almost neon green against buttery-yellow grasslands around. Encircling the swamp at the spring, the woods have grown thick and tangled. Flat-topped trees dot the land, and avenues of the graceful fever tree line the tracks, curling high above the tracks to meet like rafters in a cathedral. It is a damp-loving acacia, and got its name from travellers attracted to camp under the shade of its branches. They found the mosquitoes that carried malaria liked the same cool places too. At dusk, birds roost in the trees, the noisy calls echoing far out across the plains. Flocks of white and black sacred ibis settle on the branches, and flamboyant crested cranes with their headdresses of golden feathers fly in to rest.

On the plains are whistling thorn, a bush with finger-length spikes that whisper as the wind rushes through. The tree grows plum-sized hollow balls on its bark as a home for ants, which in return pour out to attack animals who come to eat the tree. From the biggest to the smallest, predator to prey, everything is connected.

* * *

To tell the story of the present requires a short step back for the story of the past—and Lewa has the most ancient of histories. The name *Lewa* comes from the Maa language spoken by the Maasai people. It means 'a clearing where the warriors meet'. People have gathered here since humans took their very first steps.

In the heart of Lewa there is a ford crossing through a shallow river, in the shadow of a steep hill with sharp cliffs of dark rock. If you have someone to show you exactly where—and someone else to guard your back so that the lions which creep with silent paws leave you alone—you can push through the tangled grass and find almond-shaped hand axes chipped out from volcanic rock. They still lie in the dirt where our ancestors dropped them. They used the sharp stone cleavers for cutting, hunting and killing. The stones are heavy in the hand, larger than both fists. If you run your finger the wrong way, some are sharp enough still to cut. Axes were cut here for thousands of centuries. Some are estimated to have been made 1.7 million years ago.[2]

So the lands were never empty of humans. It is where people came with their livestock to get water—and then stayed to talk. The waters attracted the wild animals too. Herds of elephants would stop there to drink, for Lewa lies on the marathon migration routes they march, as they move from the cool forests on the slopes of Mount Kenya to the hot scrubland north beyond. The cattle herders would push the wild animals away while their livestock drank, but when they were gone, huge herds of buffalo, zebra and giraffe all came to take their turn.

Arabs and Europeans moved from the coast ever further inland into East Africa in the late nineteenth century. It marked the start of waves of change—and destruction. One of the first—and worst—was the arrival of the deadly *rinderpest*. More simply, it was called the 'cattle plague'. It was a highly contagious virus, like measles for cattle, and deadly for any animal with a cloven hoof. It swept across the continent in 1890. Africa, south of the Sahara at least, had been shielded from the disease by that daunting desert barrier for centuries. However, it jumped the gap when invading Italian troops on Africa's Red Sea coast in Eritrea arrived with an infected cow—and the virus spread like a forest fire. The intense fever killed animals within days, decimating both domestic cattle and goats, as well as wild herds of buffalo, giraffe and antelope.[3]

'Never before in the memory of man, or by the voice of tradition, have the cattle died in such vast numbers,' wrote Frederick Lugard, a British army captain who rode across East Africa in 1890. 'Never before has the wild game suffered. Nearly all the buffalo and eland are gone. The giraffe has suffered, and many of the small ante-lope.'[4] People had learned to cope with cycles of drought and other diseases, but had never experienced anything like rinderpest. The virus spread on all the way south to Cape Town, leaving in its path near total destruction.[5]

'Through all this great plain we passed carcasses of buffalo; and the vast herds of which I had heard, and which I hoped would feed my hungry men, were gone,' Lugard wrote. 'The breath of the pestilence had destroyed them as utterly as the Winchesters of Buffalo Bill and his crew and the corned-beef factories of Chicago have destroyed the bison of America.'[6]

Livestock were people's entire livelihoods, and their death sparked famine. 'The loss of their cattle meant death,' Lugard added. 'Everywhere the people I saw were gaunt and half-starved, and covered with skin diseases.' Hard on the tail of rinderpest came other diseases, including smallpox. One estimate suggests that as many as a third of livestock herders could have died. Others suggest even more, perhaps two-thirds of the population.[7]

In the cool wooded hills north of Lewa, amid forests of tangled cedar and olive trees, elders still pass down stories of the plague known as 'the drought of the red marrow', a sign of the sickness seen in the animals' bones. Cattle-herders who lost all their live-stock retreated to the woods to hunt what they could find to sur-vive. They joined older groups who had lived there for generations, foraging food and keeping hives of bees, living in hidden homes in the caves. The forests were known as the *Mukogodo*. 'The people who live in the rocks,' it means.

Colonial forces eyed their chance. 'In some respects it has favoured our enterprise,' wrote Lugard, a hard soldier with orders for imperial expansion, who had already fought from Afghanistan to India, and from South Africa to Sudan. 'Powerful and warlike as the pastoral tribes are, their pride has been humbled and our progress facilitated by this awful visitation. The advent of the white man had else not been so peaceful. The Maasai would undoubtedly have opposed us, and either by force of arms or conciliation (whose results would have been doubtful), we should have had to win our way to the promising highlands.'

In 1895, just four years after the plague, Britain planted the flag, and claimed the land as the 'East Africa Protectorate.' It was an area larger than France or the state of Texas. The disease was devastating, but for the longer-term, it would have a much bigger consequence; it would have a fundamental impact on how outsiders saw the land.

* * *

The animals that had survived, both wild and domestic, built up some resistance to the disease. Numbers slowly returned. But with the herds of cattle knocked so low, there was nothing to eat the grass, which soon reverted to thick scrubland. That provided perfect breeding places for the deadly tsetse fly, a small biting insect that spreads the crippling sleeping sickness disease. Without treatment—and there was none effective then—it was often fatal to both humans and livestock. Herders who took their animals into the bush soon succumbed to terrible fevers.[8]

Areas that were once grasslands where herders and their livestock mingled with antelopes and buffalos, were now left for the wild animals. It not only helped colonial forces seize control without the outward appearance of too much violence, as if the people who surrendered their land had done so somehow willingly. It also gave the impression that the land had been unclaimed by man.

Of course, many of the officers who came to East Africa were all too well aware of what had happened, but since they came to seize massive tracts of land, the image of an unspoiled Eden was a simpler story to tell. The vision of a land untouched by human habitation is, and always was, a myth. It is a vision of Africa created by outsiders—mistakenly by some, wilfully by others.[9]

'There were big tracts of lands used for other purposes than cultivation, and which were equally important to the community,' wrote Jomo Kenyatta, who would become the country's first president in 1964. 'It is of these lands that the early European travellers reported that they had seen huge lands "undeveloped" and "unoccupied". To them it may have seemed so, but... these lands were no more unoccupied than moorlands in England.'[10]

For the travellers and hunters arriving from Europe or America, seeing the endless herds of colossal buffalo with their ferocious horns, or the mighty herds of elephants pacing across the plains, it seemed like a pristine and primordial wilderness that time had forgot. In their countries, the environment and wildlife of their homeland had been hammered, the wild areas fenced in, forests cut down for industrialisation and the land cleared for fields of crops. Those who came saw the wildlife as a bounty without end, to be exploited as they saw fit. For hunters, that meant shooting sprees. For the farmers that followed, wholesale clearances.

'A scene unaltered since the dawn of the world,' wrote Winston Churchill, who in 1907, less than a decade after Britain had seized Kenya, came on holiday from Parliament to shoot animals to stuff as 'trophy' heads for his wall. A *safari*, a Swahili word rooted in the Arabic for 'travel', simply means a journey—and Churchill interpreted that in his own extravagant style. He had a garden bench bolted to the very front of the steam engine as it chugged its way inland, relaxing on the cow catcher, where he sat to fire at antelope as the train rattled past. He also equipped a smaller railway trolley laden with fine wines, food, ice and whisky as a trundling shooting platform to creep up close in comfort to the animals before opening fire. 'So-fari, so-goody,' he said, at the end of each day's journey. Seeing a rhino stunned him. 'I cannot describe to you the impression produced on the mind by the sight of the grim black silhouette of this mighty beast,' he wrote. 'It was like being transported back into the Stone Age.' Hunting did not seem much of a challenge. 'The manner of killing a rhinoceros in the open is crudely simple,' he wrote. 'You walk up as near as possible to him from any side except the windward, and then shoot him in the head or the heart.'

But while Churchill spoke in wonder at the natural world, he sneered in contempt at the people whose land it was. 'Conditions of prehistoric time,' the future prime minister wrote. 'Naked, painted savages, clashing their spears and gibbering in chorus to their tribal chiefs,' he added.[11] It was an attitude that led to large-scale clearances. The Maasai were ordered from their land.

* * *

Colonial authorities seized the land seen as the best for farming for white settlers. Tens of thousands of Maasai—and millions of their cattle and goats—were driven off immense areas in the Rift Valley and Laikipia highlands, northwest of Mount Kenya. It cut the

Maasai's land by as much as two-thirds. They were instead squeezed into restricted 'Native Reserves'. This was much poorer land, and overcrowded. With the herders unable to move on their ancient routes to find fresh grass and let the ranges rest, the land soon became degraded.[12]

By the 1920s, white settlers were coming to Kenya in large numbers. It was the time of pith-helmeted hunters, aristocratic playboys, lavish parties and champagne safaris—at least according to the stories made famous to the rest of the world by the romance of Karen Blixen in her book *Out of Africa*, flying in a biplane over roaming lions roaring down below.

After World War One, British soldiers could apply for a land parcel as a reward for service. Giant plots were handed out through a lottery. Ian's grandfather had Scottish roots, but like many at the end of the nineteenth century, had come to Kenya via South Africa. He had served as a lieutenant fighting German forces in East Africa. He put his name in for a land parcel. He arrived in Lewa with wagons each pulled by sixteen oxen, and set up canvas tents on the hills to carve out a farm, to turn rough bush into fields of wheat.

Soon, the land changed. Where herders once drove their livestock alongside wild animals across the open grasslands, now became a dedicated commercial cattle ranch. Rinderpest was brought under control, and thousands of cows crowded the rangelands.

* * *

Three decades after his grandfather had arrived, Ian was born, the third generation of his family to live on Lewa. It was 1952, the height of the Mau Mau uprising. The Mau Mau were fighters who launched a revolution for land, freedom and self-governance, to claim back the farms from white settlers. It was one of the British Empire's bloodiest insurgencies. Dreadlocked guerrillas attacked settlers from forest hideouts, as the Royal Air Force carpet bombed from above. The Mau Mau would be crushed with the most extreme violence and horrific abuses, with those seen as supporters incarcerated in brutal mass detention camps. Mau Mau forces carried out revenge attacks against fellow Kenyans recruited by Britain. At the time, newspapers focused on the gruesome details of the 32 white settlers killed on their farms, but historians say that colonial forces killed at least 10,000 people across Kenya. Others suggest a toll double that, and potentially many times more. The fallout from the struggle would help pave the way to independence.

A decade later, in 1963, Kenya won its freedom, and British rule ended. Some two-thirds of the 55,000 white settlers left, fearful of the future.[13] They sold the farms, packed up and departed. But thousands also stayed on, gave up their old passports, and swore loyalty to the new flag of Kenya. On Lewa, Ian's family remained. The farm, and Kenya, was the only home they knew.

* * *

Ian, a boy aged eleven at independence, was insulated from the politics of a changing world. There seemed much more important matters to him: escaping into the bush, climbing trees, exploring and, his greatest love of all, the wildlife. He was, by all accounts, never without a cut on his knees or a scrape on his arms from his latest adventure.

At that time, Lewa was a cattle ranch, not bush. The grazing lands were reserved for cattle, and in the most fertile areas near the springs, there were rippling golden fields of maize. Antelopes and zebras wandered across Lewa and lion stalked the cows, but you would rarely, if ever, have seen elephants, or rhino, or giraffe. There were few of the big wild animals left, for they had been scared away. Yet it did not take long to walk to the boundary of the farm and step across the frontier into the community-owned lands—and then the wildlife began.

Climb to the highest hills in Lewa and look north at sunset, as the swallows swoop at speed catching flies, ridges of mountains fade in lines in the distance to the horizon. The peaks stretch on, one after another as far as the eye can see, unfolding on through the apparently endless lands of northern Kenya. Light dances across the plains, with shafts of sun slanting down through the clouds like fingers. There, the elephants moved back and forth from the hills to the open lands with the rains, joining the giraffes, zebras and antelopes. The wide savannahs and thick mountain forests are landscapes on a truly epic scale.

Ian's future appeared mapped out—to follow his father into farming—but the boy had other dreams. When children role play, they imagine what they might become when grown up: soldiers or doctors, explorers or astronauts. For Ian, it was to be a wildlife ranger, the government force who managed the fledgling national parks. They were in charge of all the wild animals across the country. 'The rangers were my heroes,' Ian said. 'They were the toughest men, always out tracking animals. They would spend weeks out in the bush just on the supplies they carried, even in the harshest of lands. That was who I wanted to be.' So Ian crept away from home to the wild world around him every moment that he could, slipping off with homework unfinished.

As was typical of many boys of his background and generation then, he was sent away to boarding school, to cold and wet Ireland. It was a journey taking several days across continents and seas. Far from the home he knew, it taught him independence and self-reliance early on. He studied many things—the most important of which were not from dry textbooks, but those learned from escaping school and camping in the woods of County Kerry, casting fishing flies to sneak a salmon out of the river, and brewing firewater moonshine to drink. He mixed with boys whose background and experiences could not have been more different from his, and he learned to make friends with anyone.

When Ian came back home to the sunshine in Lewa, he was determined to spend every minute that he could out following wild animals. You'd be hard pressed to find a world more different from the strict confines of boarding school. He and his younger brother Will would spend their time with an air-rifle, stalking guinea fowl for the pot. Ian shadowed the government wildlife rangers as much as possible, squeezing into their trucks as they went out on patrol. They'd indulge the boy, and let him ride with them for a while. Yet they were also very careful to protect him too, and he never got as close to the action as he wanted. When there was a rogue lion out killing cattle, or an elephant stampeding into villages, the rangers set off on foot with rifles to stop them. But the boy would be left behind in the trucks. 'I'd listen to their stories, and I wanted to be doing what they were doing,' Ian said, remembering his frustration. 'But I was too young. I couldn't go with them all the time, not when they were doing the really exciting work. That was too dangerous.'

Unfazed, the boy headed out on his own. The problem there, of course, was that escaping to play at being a wildlife ranger was no game. A small boy faced any number of threats—and not just being pounced on by a hungry lion or a leopard. Being trampled or gored by a buffalo was an even bigger danger. So his exasperated parents, seeing his insistence, determination and escape abilities were not going to be easily stopped, had to come up with a workable plan.

* * *

'I was asked to take care of him,' said Kinyanjui, with an explosive laugh. 'To make sure he was safe, because back then, he was only a boy.' Kinyanjui had come to Lewa for a job, herding the cattle belonging to Ian's father. He is six years older, aged nineteen when Ian was a teenager at thirteen. Few knew more than Kinyanjui about the animals in the forests, of their tracks and signs, and how they behave. He was the perfect choice to be a guide.

He came from the Il Ngwesi people, who live in the high-soaring hills a few hours walk to the north of Lewa. They are a Maasai clan, but unlike their brothers who place all their value in their herds of cattle, they traditionally had no cows. They were hunters and gatherers. Il Ngwesi means the 'People of the Wildlife.'

Some elders said they had lost their cattle in battle far in the past, and had fled north to a land empty because it was too harsh for livestock, falling back on their skills of survival. Others were among the herders whose livestock was devastated by rinderpest. Some Maasai, who measured respect and rank by the number of cows, looked down on the way of life of the hunters in scorn. The 'people without cows', they called them instead.

But Kinyanjui was proud that he was an expert tracker, from a people whose lives depended on knowing where the wild animals would be. It is an understanding of nature far older than any history book can recall: a knowledge of a way of living alongside wildlife that has been passed down through the long generations from parents to children through stories, custom and tradition.[14] They used the land and hunted the animals, but they also protected them as a resource, so they would continue to sustain them. They lived off the land, stalking antelope with bows and arrows, or rifles. They collected honey from hives they made out of hollow logs wedged into trees, and they foraged for nuts, roots and berries.

It was a hard life, but the Il Ngwesi gathered what they needed. Some of the community had bought cattle and goats too, but they still relied on the wildlife. The natural world and human life were intertwined as one. Kinyanjui's name is derived from 'a gourd full of milk'. He was born at a time when life was good, the herds were healthy and there was enough to eat.

Kinyanjui arrived at the ranch dressed in the clothes that he knew best: shoes of cow hide tied to his feet, and a wrap made from the skins of gazelles and goats around his shoulders. For a boy wanting to know about the wildlife, there could have been no better teacher. 'As soon as his school closed for the holidays, he'd come home,' Kinyanjui said. 'And every time, I'd be waiting for him. We'd disappear off together.'

The pair would slip off from the ranch, carrying all that they needed on their backs. Rhinos were hiding out in the thorn thickets. Snuffling through the undergrowth were families of warthog, with their whiskers and tails upright like car antennas, trotting across the grasslands, and diving back into their burrows dug into termite mounds when scared. Buffalos stampeded out of the groves of trees. And, even if you could not see them because their tawny fur was the same colour as the rustling yellow-brown grass, lions would be watching.

'Sometimes we'd go deep into the forests,' Kinyanjui said. 'Another time, we'd climb up into the hills. I was guiding him, because I knew where was best. I knew that beneath this hill you can find water, or at another one, that there was a good place in a cave to sleep for a night. In that place, the buffalo like to hide, and there, you might find an elephant.'

* * *

Northern Kenya had been treated as an outpost land for decades. British officers called it the Northern Frontier District. They saw it as little more than a gigantic border buffer zone to mark the edge of empire. Much was classified as low-lying semi-desert, a rough land they could not extract a profit from. In the eyes of central government, a journey of several days away in the colonial-built capital Nairobi, it was a distant land not worth the effort. It is hard to tax people roaming with their herds. They are a proud and independent people who have never had much time for outsiders telling them what to do.

Sir Geoffrey Archer, the British officer sent to lead the first expedition in 1909 to northern Kenya, set up camp on the sandy shores on a bend of the crocodile-infested waters of the Ewaso Nyiro river. When the base eventually became a town, it kept the name of Archer's Post. The slow and snaking water feeds a belt of luminous green grass, with the river banks lined with palm trees rustling in hot, desert winds. 'I had been selected to lead what was a veritable expedition to establish administrative control,' wrote Archer, who arrived with a camel train and 600 porters carrying his kit. 'Until now this region had been a complete "no-man's land", and very inaccessible at that.'[15] For Archer, the people who had lived there for generations didn't count.

Officers declared it a 'Closed District.' It was run almost as a separate entity, cutting people off from the rest of the country. 'A special permit had to be obtained to enter it,' Archer wrote. 'A sort of paper curtain of pass laws,' another officer called it.[16] Central state control was weak, but for the British, it mattered little. Instead, they used it as a cushion, to guard the profitable green farmlands taken by the white settlers in central and southern Kenya. It divided them from the lands beyond: independent Ethiopia to the north, today's South Sudan and Somalia. The 'closed' zone was gigantic. From its start at the town of Isiolo it stretched to Ethiopia, the distance from New York to Montreal, or London to Edinburgh. In the dry season, which was most of the year, the challenge for travellers was carrying enough water. In the rains, road crossings on dry riverbeds could be cut for days by raging torrents.

The policy Archer helped set up in Kenya he would roll out in neighbouring Uganda too. 'There is only one way to treat these Northern Territories, the home of nomadic camel, cattle and sheep owning people, and that is to give them what protection we can under the British flag and, otherwise, *to leave them to their own customs, as far as possible, and under their own chiefs*,' Archer wrote. 'Anything else is certainly uneconomic, and if we attempt to go too fast, there will be trouble in store for us.'[17]

It would set the tone for outside engagement for the years to come. After Archer, only a sparse scattering of British officers were ever posted there. There was no pretence at a 'civilising' mission. They left the people of the north lagging far behind the rest of the country. They were marginalised from the rest of Kenya, and starved of infrastructure in terms of roads, railway, schools and health services.[18] For many years, and still sometimes today, people of the north will say they are travelling south 'to Kenya', as if it were another country. The legacy of misguided rule echoes down the generations.

'My job was to control movement of people,' said Richard Luce, the last British District Officer posted to the town of Isiolo in the early 1960s. Luce was sent to Isiolo straight after leaving Oxford, made second-in-command over a land nearly the size of Ireland. The twenty-four-year-old was given the power as a magistrate to arrest large numbers of people, jail them in the prison dubbed the 'Queen's Hotel', and then deport them out of the area. 'I've never felt so powerful,' Luce said, speaking over tea in the House of Lords, Britain's upper house, where the former government minister and Lord Chamberlain to the Queen now sits.

Lewa was one of the furthest north of any of the colonial farms. Beyond, settlers had been kept out. The land had been left almost as it had always been, with communities like the Il Ngwesi living with the lightest of footprints alongside the wildlife. Many of the traditions and customs remained unchanged, from the Samburu, Turkana and Rendille draped with their colourful beads to the Gabra, Borana and the Somali moving with their herds of camels. Unlike the huge tracts of land to the south on the cool high altitude plateau of Laikipia, where so many British settlers had made farms it was dubbed the 'White Highlands', the land north of Lewa was owned by the people who had always lived there.

The enforced isolation had benefited the wildlife. In the south of Kenya, the land was being sliced in two by roads, broken up by growing towns, and divided by a patchwork of commercial cereal farms. In the north, the wide spaces remained open. 'Giraffe and buffalo would come right up to the house,' Luce remembered. He helped organise camel trains for Wilfred Thesiger, who headed off into the bush for months on end. While Luce stayed closer to town, he told stories of how even just walking outside Isiolo, with his wife Rose and dachshund Nutkin, he had to throw himself into razor thorns as a rhino charged him, escaping only because he had been alerted seconds before by the animal's puffing snorts like a steam train. 'It was such a privilege to live there,' Luce said. 'It was a magical place to be.'

After independence, little changed. Colonialism was over, but the old rules and attitudes were adopted by the new government. They often had as little time for the northern people as Britain did. Many of the 'Closed District' restrictions remained in place.

But those rules didn't worry Kinyanjui. The tracks he took Ian on were those made by elephants. They slipped through the woods unseen. No one was going to demand a permit where they went.

* * *

When Kinyanjui began speaking, his stern frown looked deadly serious. Then he exploded into fits of giggles. His speech is peppered with sudden laughter in utter delight at the memory of every story he tells. It is as if, half a century later, he still found the whole idea of him being put in charge the funniest of notions, because if Ian was a troublemaker out for exploration, then he had met more than his match in Kinyanjui. For while Kinyanjui would take to heart the responsibility entrusted to him of guiding the young boy, protecting him with his life against wild animals, there was a snag in the plan— Kinyanjui was as keen for every adventure as Ian was. Each time, they went always a little further, far beyond the last blue mountain they could see.

'We would go out for five days, then we would come back,' Kinyanjui said. 'Then a few days later, we'd just disappear again. That time we'd go off for ten days, then the next time even for two weeks. We went all around to every area that I knew. Sometimes when we ran out of things to eat, we'd shoot an impala for food. We would be in the bush as much as we could until it was time for him to go back to school.'

Of course, some questioned their friendship. Kenya was independent, but there was deep distrust on both sides. For Kinyanjui, elders of the Il Ngwesi said the young warrior should be proving his courage with daring feats—not spending time with the young white boy. For Ian, there were many among the old white settlers who looked down on Kinyanjui. 'My father had a hell of a stormy relationship with the Il Ngwesi—I remember him burning houses and people fighting,' Ian said. 'A really good friend of mine very nearly speared my dad; it was a real stand-off. But we were a different generation.'

When Ian arrived at his cousin's farm with Kinyanjui as his friend, his uncle said Kinyanjui was nothing but a poacher and cattle rustler. In a rage, he threw him off the ranch. Ian followed Kinyanjui, furious with his uncle. 'Ian is my friend,' Kinyanjui said. 'We did so much together.'

Their grandfathers, and then their fathers, had fought each other over cattle, grazing and land. Yet the history of the past does not have to determine the path of the future. Far from the settlements and roads, among the animals and away from people, they were just two young men who loved exploring the wildlife. As Ian grew into a man, the pair became the greatest of friends—and mischief-makers. Their exploring would take them very far from home. Together, they'd get into a whole heap of trouble.

2

THE BUSH BANDITS
(HOW THE ANIMALS WERE KILLED)

The old photo, hung in a frame above Ian's desk, is faded from years in the sun—but the grins from the two men look the same as today. They are just back from a long adventure in the bush. Ian poses with a cheeky smile, a blue beret stuck jauntily on his head, and a powerful rifle slung nonchalantly on his shoulder. A bandolier wrapped around his waist stuffed with a dozen large calibre bullets strong enough to knock down a buffalo pulls his dark green camouflage jacket in like a belt. His face is still boyish but his legs, in shorts despite the thick scrub he stands in, are those of a man. Kinyanjui stands beside Ian, towering over him. He is dressed in a long brown overcoat, its shoulder epaulettes flapping from the thorns they have burst through, and his rifle rests between his legs. Together, they look like outlaws, a pair of highway bandits on the run.

* * *

'The boy so loved all the wildlife,' said Kinyanjui, remembering the treks with Ian far from Lewa. 'We'd be out walking, and come across the track of a rhino. I knew that these rhinos are really aggressive, and that they could be hiding just in the next bush ahead. They can charge in seconds.' Even when rhinos are snoozing, they have a natural alarm with them; the little red-billed and brown-winged oxpecker birds, who pick ticks off the rhino's hide, and in return, provide a calling alarm when danger approaches.

'But instead of trying to avoid it, Ian would look at the tracks, and say, "if we follow, can we find him?"' said Kinyanjui. 'So we'd track the prints, tracking and tracking, with me in front, and Ian just a footstep behind, until we found the bush where the rhino was. That was the really dangerous time.'

Kinyanjui paused to thank his wife, also in her seventies, who had carried out a large flask of sweet tea to the grassy courtyard outside their neat home. She clearly knew that when Kinyanjui told stories, everyone listening would be there for a while. Kinyanjui poured out the tea, then leaned forward.

'With the rhino just there, Ian would say he still wanted to go on,' Kinyanjui continued, lowering his voice to a whisper, as if the rhino was really just ahead as he spoke. 'Slowly we'd get closer, as quietly as possible. But I'd show him that you don't just go straight up to the bush—because the rhino will know you are there. You have to go around the side, so that your scent doesn't go towards them. You have to be so careful and ready all the time in case they sense you. We'd get so close, and then I'd look as if we should leave, but Ian would want to just stay there. He'd watch the rhino for as long as he could, right by it.' For a guide tasked to watch over a boy, Kinyanjui admitted that tracking up close to a sleeping rhino was risky. But then he burst into laughter again. The rhino were the easy ones to follow, he said. 'Try getting that close to a lion,' he said, between giggles. 'Because we would do the same tracking them.'

* * *

Kinyanjui taught Ian everything he knew about the land and the animals in it. He trained him how to identify what had passed by, through the faintest scratches of spoor in the dust, and to read the signs of the wilderness like a book. They would be up early, for the slanting low light of dawn casts the best shadows on the tracks. Dusk works too—but you wouldn't want to be following a lion trail into the long grass as the sun sets and the land falls dark. They'd stop and watch how the animals move, following alongside the paths they make—not on their tracks, for that covers up the signs.

Kinyanjui showed Ian the honeyguide, a little cheeping bird that leads people to a beehive with a flying dance, hopping from branch to branch—so that it can feast on the scraps left behind after the honey is taken. He could tell him how many hyenas there were from their eerie whooping howls, or how far away the lion was that called in the night with husky, heavy coughs. Then, beside the flickering fire in the rock shelters where they found a place to sleep at night, roasting meat sizzling on the flames, he would talk of the folklore and fables he grew up with. Kinyanjui spoke of how his people saw the world, their position in it, and the environment all around. Kinyanjui taught Ian lessons that lasted his lifetime. Ian shared with Kinyanjui something in return: his absolute passion for the wild. 'I could hear from Ian's heart how much he cared,' Kinyanjui said. 'It was as if he was born loving wildlife.'

For Kinyanjui, the wild animals had been a fact of life he had grown up with. It was not some utopian peace with wildlife. People did as all humans do everywhere; they took what they needed for themselves and their families. Wildlife was a valuable resource to be managed. 'We saw wild animals like antelopes as meat,' he said. For the Maasai, their cattle were too precious to kill for daily food. Cattle were a sign of status, and eaten only for feasts on the most special occasions. Instead, the cattle were milked, and blood to drink was tapped by opening a neck vein with an arrow, which was then sealed carefully with hot wood ash and earth, leaving the cow otherwise unharmed. So antelope filled a vital gap, hunted for food and leather from the skins. Many Maasai call wildlife 'second cattle', a fall-back store of food in times of drought.

Predators like lion were killed to defend the cattle. 'We protected our animals from lions,' Kinyanjui said. 'We hated them when they attacked our cattle.' Yet the lions were valued too. They were much feared, but also respected. The hunts were a rite of passage for warriors to demonstrate courage. The lions played a core role in the culture of the people. 'No one ever thought that all the lions could be killed,' Kinyanjui said. 'If one was speared, there were always more in the bush.' The mane and tail were used as headdresses and spear decorations. They were a dangerous animal that threatened, but against which a boy could prove himself to be a man.

'For me, the animals were just what lived in the bush,' Kinyanjui said. 'They were ordinary. But every time that we would see an elephant, a rhino or anything, Ian would be so happy. And when he saw a buffalo, his legs would actually shake with excitement. He was always asking, is this a male, is that one female? Why does it behave like that? This calf, who does it belong to? I knew all the histories of the animals, so I could answer them. But every time I thought he had finished his question, he would always have one more thing to ask.'

For Kinyanjui, it was normal to live with rhinos and elephants all around. Ian was younger, but he had already travelled to very different lands—places where such extraordinary abundance of wild animals had long been exterminated through hunting or loss of land. He saw it was finite—and in a changing world, increasingly at risk. Nature could not be taken for granted. 'He made me think,' Kinyanjui said. 'I thought, this little boy, why is he always asking all these things? If this boy is so interested—what is so special about the animals?'

Each helped the other to see through new eyes. It is the same, for all of us, wherever we might call home. Our day-to-day reality becomes normal, and we are surprised at the wonder that an outsider can find in it. Friendship opened the door between the two cultures. It left each man with one foot in a different world.

* * *

But trouble was growing. The adventures of the pair took place against a backdrop of hard times. Northern Kenya, after being effectively separated from the rest of the country as an imperial frontier zone, felt like a different land. To the people living there, it was self-governed. To central government in Nairobi, it seemed ungoverned.

Kenya, like so many African nations, was created by colonial force. Dozens of peoples with different languages and cultures were pushed together—or split apart. European nations drew straight-line frontiers on maps to carve up the continent for exploitation between them. For the Somali people, their homeland was sliced up between the country of Somalia and neighbouring nations. In northern Kenya, some Somalis thought they should be joining the nation of Somalia instead. Aggrieved and ignored, politically and economically marginalised, they felt they had little in common with rule in faraway Nairobi—and some took up arms.

One month after Kenya declared self-rule in 1963, it was sucked straight into war. For Kenya, taking its first steps as a sovereign nation, the secessionist Somalis saying that they belonged to another state posed an existential crisis to the very country itself. The separatist guerrillas subverted the young state's authority. So the government called them criminals without a cause. They said the rebels were bandits, or *shifta*.

But the 'bandits' had support. The Shifta War was not just scrappy rebel attacks. The leaders in Somalia's capital, Mogadishu, saw in the instability an opportunity, providing training and weapons.[1]

The young rebel recruits already knew how to shoot a rifle straight to protect their livestock from a lion. Now they were trained as guerrillas to fight a war. They learned insurgent tactics: how to fight as a team, lay landmines, throw grenades, and to use their mobility and knowledge of the land to their advantage to ambush larger forces of regular soldiers. They were lessons that lasted a long time. Hit-and-run raids on police posts became more deadly.

Others saw benefit in chaos. They joined the rebels not because of politics. They signed up to get a gun, and take advantage of the crisis to settle old scores with neighbouring groups by raiding livestock. For some herders it was a chance to smash colonial rules that decreed which groups could graze where. The turmoil was a time to grab back land they saw as rightfully theirs.

Government retaliation was brutal. Heavy-handed army raids carried out collective punishments against the communities the gunmen came from. When cattle were stolen, soldiers just grabbed any livestock they could find—not necessarily the original animals. Then the army issued orders of compulsory 'villagisation.' To separate civilians from the rebels, the government forced tens of thousands of people into settlements. Fixing people in one place made it easier for security forces to control communities, but it threatened the herder's roving way of life. It added to the sense of injustice, and fed a cycle of violence. Attacks led to reprisal raids, and that led to more recruits wanting revenge.[2]

In 1967, a peace deal was agreed between Kenya and Somalia, and the Shifta War was declared over. Or, at least, Somalia's clandestine support for the rebels was at an end—because the bitter legacy of the war continued. Building peace takes more than signing an agreement to end a war, and the impact of conflict and societal breakdown cannot be fixed overnight. Northern Kenya was now awash with AK-47 Kalashnikov assault rifles. It was a Soviet-built gun invented by a Red Army sergeant wounded in battles against the Nazi blitzkrieg, who had seen the need for a rifle that still fired in the roughest of conditions.[3] His design, the AK-47, would become the guerrilla weapon of choice worldwide. 'When guns find themselves in a place, it is very hard to wipe them out,' former shifta fighter Abdub Galgallo told one historian.[4]

The Kenyan government had said the separatists were bandits to deny them political legitimacy. Ironically, once the official war ended, that is what some would become. Raiding and robbing became a way of life. The fighters found cattle raiding an easy alternative, especially now that they were armed and trained to fire rifles. So the violence carried on. The nature of the war altered—and the shifta found a new target: wildlife.

* * *

'The shifta came,' said Losupat Lemacheria. 'They'd shoot a buffalo or a giraffe for us, and everyone would feast. Then, after we ate, they'd ask us where the rhino and the elephant were. They'd pay us to show them where they could kill them.'

Losupat, a Samburu elder, a wiry herder now well into his seventies, sat on a dried goatskin spread out as a blanket. He was resting in the forests, on the slopes of the great green-cloaked mountain of Ol Doinyo Lenkiyeu, part of a long, jagged chain that rises sharply from the surrounding desert plains. Losupat wore a camouflage jacket on top of a bright red wrap around his waist. He also had a thick white bracelet on his wrist, heavy and cracked with age. Unasked, he insisted it was made of plastic, not ivory, and then pulled his sleeve down sharply to cover it. Losupat said he had no interest in the battles of Somali secessionists. Their politics were nothing to do with those in neighbouring Samburu lands. But the money the shifta brought? Well, that was a different matter.

'It was easy to show them where the animals were,' Losupat said. 'We knew the land here, but they were strangers. So we'd guide them.' To start with, the animals seemed endless. The idea that shooting a few animals in the hills could lead to such levels of destruction it would wipe out rhinos and elephants from huge areas was inconceivable.

The foreign big game hunters had shot rhinos, to have a stuffed head on the wall to brag about. But traditionally the people who lived alongside them had seen little point in killing them, apart from in self-defence when the big animals surprised them. The strong-tasting meat was rarely eaten—many regarded it as disgusting, or even taboo—and trying to kill a rhino with a spear was a dangerous challenge few saw much value in taking on. Their tough hide was used for shields and to make sandals, but no one was going to risk death from a rhino to repair a shoe. As for the horn, it was used as a war club, or a more prosaic kitchen pestle to pound grain—or simply discarded.[5]

'In the years after independence, rhinos were common,' Losupat said. 'You could get groups of three or four close by together. Most of the time, you didn't have to worry. You could hear them snort-ing before you got too close.' The rhinos were far easier to avoid than to kill.

'There was no reason to kill them, unless they attacked you,' Losupat said. 'They weren't a big problem; because even if a rhino charged you, you just had to make sure you jumped behind a tree. If it missed you, then it was gone. It wouldn't come back. It was the lions we feared.'

Life was often a daily struggle. People wanted to have better conditions for their families. When they saw the quick cash made by poachers, many Samburu wanted to do more than just act as guides. They could earn more if they shot the animals themselves. The Samburu still carried spears, and some had old rifles. But the young men eyed the shifta's AK-47s enviously. Even a boy could fire off all thirty bullets in its magazine in a matter of seconds, shots zipping the length of five football pitches. They wanted one too. If their neighbours now had such powerful rifles, they feared losing their cattle in livestock raids.

'When the Somalis came asking for tusks, I went straight out and speared an elephant,' Losupat said. 'They still wanted ivory, so I went out again and speared another right away.' It was more ivory than he could lift in one go, far heavier than a man. The shifta took the tusks out through remote tracks to Somalia, and from there by sea to Asia, a well-established smuggling route.[6] 'The Somalis paid us straight away,' he said. 'I bought an AK-47.' In time, Losupat became a regular hunter, shooting at least a dozen elephant. The money earned seemed to Losupat a fortune—enough to buy a herd of some forty cattle—but it was only a fraction of what the gang leaders made.

Losupat refused to say how many rhinos he killed. He speared his first one as a young man in the late 1960s, when it charged him and his livestock. 'It came crashing straight towards me,' he said. 'I only saw it at the last moment. There were only a few steps between the rhino and me. It ran straight into my spear.' He picked up his spear, longer than his lanky body, with a leaf-shaped blade bigger than his hand. The sharp edge was covered in a red leather guard. 'I didn't even have time to take the sheath off,' he said. 'But the blade went through that and into its chest.'

Apart from the one rhino he speared in self-defence, he would not talk about killing others. He seemed ashamed. In the end, every single rhino from the hills here would be hunted down until there were none left. All had been annihilated. 'I know it is wrong now, but we didn't think every rhino would die,' he said. 'If I was a young man now, I would not have done the same. I regret to say that I bought my cows from such killing.'

* * *

Yet it wasn't just the shifta slaughtering the wildlife. They operated largely in the north, but the killing was a free-for-all across the country. There were rich pickings to be made and that attracted businessmen—including at the very top of government. Politically-protected gangs moved trucks packed with ivory across the country right to the port—under police escort. For the politicians, it was easier to blame it all on the nameless gunmen like the shifta, and on a marginalised people like the Somali. It diverted attention while they raked in the cash.

There was still a largescale domestic market. Almost every tourist shop in Nairobi was stuffed with carvings, from small statues to entire tusks. By the 1970s, tourists were coming to Kenya in huge numbers—and everyone wanted to take home souvenirs.[7] But the markets in Asia were growing too. There had, of course, been a long trade in ivory, but large-scale factories had been opened in China, with Hong Kong a key trading centre.[8] Other tusks went to India, to Japan and the Gulf states.

Elephants in northern Kenya fled to find what safety they could. They crammed into the government parks such as Samburu or Meru, or to private ranches on the Laikipia highlands. They were still killed there, but the limited protection was something. But that resulted in intense concentrations in spaces too small for a giant animal who needs space to roam. Overcrowding meant that when drought hit, there were too many for the limited water, the vegetation was stripped bare, and so thousands died of 'natural' causes.

To make matters worse, people used the deaths as a sign that poaching was no problem. They pointed at the huge numbers of elephants squeezed into the small sanctuaries as a sign of booming numbers—glossing over the fact that the elephants were effectively imprisoned. So some argued then for the sweeping cull of entire elephant herds, as was done in other countries, where herds were wiped out using machine guns and helicopters. The skins were sold for leather, and meat for food. Only the orphaned babies would be left alive—and they were shipped to zoos.[9]

Rhino were being hammered just as bad, pushed to the very brink of extinction. From some 20,000 at independence, numbers spiraled down until there were barely 200 left. Rhino horn had long been an ingredient in ancient Chinese medicine—touted as able to bring down fevers, as well as an antidote for poisoning. Patients would have done better to chew their own toenails, for the horns are made of the same material, keratin. They were an expensive false promise of medicine that did nothing for health, but left only the corpses of rhinos rotting on the ground.

At this point, the horn was not sold as a magic cure solving everything from cancer to impotence. That dangerous marketing myth, the main reason for sales today, came later. But large numbers of horns went to Yemen, where a new fashion for rhino-handle daggers had caught on, with businessmen flush with earnings from the oil boom in the Gulf.[10] Extreme greed for an entirely pointless product inspired by human vanity drove an animal to near total obliteration.

The gunmen didn't care if the animals all died. There was even a grim financial rationale. The more they killed, the rarer the elephant and rhino remaining became, and the more valuable the prices of tusks and horn were. The exclusivity was part of the strange appeal for those who desired it. 'Banking on extinction,' economists called it.[11]

The poaching kingpins knew how many animals were dying because their grossly bulging bank accounts grew ever fatter. Yet there was otherwise little sense of the scale of the problem. The wildlife rangers at national parks knew the extent of the bloodshed in the area they patrolled, but as government employees, the warnings didn't go far when officials were part of the trade themselves. It needed someone on the ground to gather reports from across enormous areas, to put together the fragmented pieces and see the whole picture. So those who rang the warning bell included a group that might seem initially unlikely: the professional hunters.

* * *

Tony Dyer was once gored by a buffalo, his body flung high into the air by the curved horns with their sharp tips that look like the iron head of a spear. The wounds had healed, though he had been knocked flat four other times by the great animals too. But the tough farmer bore them no grudges—accepting that, if anything, the buffalos had taught him a lesson he had probably needed. 'I always figure that the smartest thing I ever did was to retire from professional hunting,' he said with a grin. He was also Ian's uncle.

The scars, like the lines on his craggy face, showed the long lifetime he had spent trekking far across the mountains and valleys of northern Kenya. He was of British stock, but his heart was home on the hills of Borana, overlooking Mount Kenya and neighbouring Lewa. He was from a generation that has now almost all passed, who thought nothing of days marching marathons in the severest of terrains, for whom hardship was just an adventure to be enjoyed. Tony, who became a professional hunter at the end of World War Two was deeply scornful of the introduction of cars strong enough to drive far off road in the 1950s. 'The death knell of the proper hunting safari,' he called the vehicles. 'It suddenly became too easy for any good bush driver to go on bouncing around the country.'

Tony was the last president of the East Africa Professional Hunters' Association, formed in 1934 in the historic Norfolk Hotel in Nairobi, a colonial-era institution, where the hard drinking old settlers riding in from the country had tied their horses up outside, placed their pith helmets on the long wooden bar, and swapped tales of exploration and memories of home over champagne. (Hunters said it kept its condition on the steamy sea voyage from Europe through the Red Sea better than wine, and wrapped in a wet cloth hung from a tree, could still achieve a decent chill.) Tony had learned to hunt as a boy, a time when tales of stalking lion by men such as Baron Bror Blixen—the errant husband of Karen Blixen—were not past stories of dusty books, but adventures told in person.

'Times change,' he said, looking around at his small and simple farmhouse. It was a single storey building made of brick and rough-hewn stone. He sat on an old leather folding chair on the veranda, pouring out tea from a battered silver pot. Apart from a television, there seemed little sign it had altered to keep pace with the gadgets of the modern age. 'It is better to shoot photos of animals with a camera these days,' he said.

Yet the big game hunters, rightly or wrongly, also acted like watchmen of the wildlife. They had significant economic interest in protecting them, but also saw themselves as gamekeepers, who, as if in debt to honour the individual animals they killed, were the fiercest defenders of the wider species and their environment.

After the early days of butchery of animals, the hunters had introduced a strict regulation system of licences, and pushed for laws to protect vulnerable game, such as female rhinos and lionesses. Permits authorised each hunter a specific land block for a set time. Each animal killed was carefully recorded, and the details sent to government offices. Wanting a stuffed head on your wall might baffle people today, but for hunters, it meant that they chose to kill the oldest and heaviest males with the biggest horns or manes, animals who had already mated several seasons.[12] So the animals shot were individuals specifically selected.

'Our main concern was to assist in the preservation of the fauna and flora,' said Tony. The Hunters' Association's members had been some of first wardens of national parks in Kenya, Tanzania and Uganda. 'The association was the moving spirit behind the creation of the national parks system of Eastern Africa,' added Tony. 'This was our proudest achievement.'[13]

As the elephant carcasses piled up, the Hunters' Association sounded a warning. As an organisation, they collated reports across an enormous geographic area, remote places where killings might otherwise have gone unnoticed. The picture they built up showed it was not a matter of isolated shootings, but was on a scale and across an area that would drive species to extinction.

It put pressure on Kenya's government to act and so, in 1973, elephant hunting was outlawed. But it didn't stop the carnage; in fact, the rate increased. The problem was that the number of elephants the Hunters' Association members had killed had been only a tiny fraction of the industrial slaughter. So the killings continued.

Export of ivory collected from elephants that had died naturally, or animals which had been killed by wildlife rangers because they were causing problems, could still be sold. With the right connections, or if you paid off officials and bought government permits, the laws were easy to circumvent. It was a loophole exploited on a massive scale. Within less than a decade, from 1970 to 1977, scientists calculated that Kenya lost at least half of its elephants.[14]

Tony directly blamed government officials at the highest of levels. He said they had colluded with the gunmen to amass ivory and horn at a staggering rate. 'To my certain knowledge there are four officials using their positions to obtain income from illicit game trophies,' he told the *New York Times* in 1977, adding that that there was plenty of evidence that several others were also involved. Tony gave the example of the case of a truck packed with ivory stopped by police, that was then released within a day when a government minster turned up in person, and the lorry moved on.[15] The idea that an entire truck could have been full of ivory from elephants that had died of old age was laughable.

Intelligence briefings from the CIA back up reports that the major ivory dealers sat comfortably at the top of government, protected by power from prosecution. 'Ivory smuggling is taking a heavy toll on Kenyan elephant herds, the main tourist attraction,' the CIA report read, estimating that between 10,000 to 25,000 elephants were being killed each year in the country. It noted that the tusk size being exported was getting smaller—suggesting the age of those killed was growing ever younger. It included a report of a shipment made up of tiny tusks taken from over 650 baby elephants—animals that could never have been killed as 'rogue' troublemakers, yet which had all the right paperwork for export. 'Heavy ivory from mature bull elephants is down, leading to speculation that animals over the ages of 30 to 35 are almost extinct,' the CIA added.[16]

The hunters' criticism stirred resentment. They were almost entirely white sons of the old empire. They seemed like a group from a bygone age. It put them on a collision course with those who found big benefit in the butchery—the new leaders of independent Kenya. The government turned the finger of blame back towards them, and said the white hunters were the cause of the carnage. In 1977, just over a decade after Kenya's independence, the government outlawed all hunting. There are few today who would mourn that, but Tony believed the main reason it was banned was 'to keep our prying eyes out' of the lucrative ivory trade.

'Nothing in the affairs of men is constant except for the beginning and the end,' Tony wrote. 'History it is. Never again will hunters roam over Africa, taking out clients on safari as they did in the old days. To be sure, the safari business will continue in parts of Africa for years to come. Visitors will come, fall under the spell of safari, and probably never know how different their experience has been from that of their predecessors.... so farewell to the past; here is to the future.'[17]

The time of the big white hunter was over. The members of the Hunters' Association put away their rifles. Yet the killing of elephants and rhinos not only continued—but actually escalated.

* * *

For Ian, aged twenty-five in 1977, the end of hunting meant an abrupt change of career. After school, he had learned how to fly as a pilot, and had worked for a year in Alaska as a moose hunter. But the sunshine on the golden grasslands of Lewa had called him back. He still dreamed of being a wildlife ranger —but being a professional hunter had proved more lucrative. Kinyanjui had worked alongside him as his partner, guiding guests to shoot game. 'Buffalo were what we loved,' Kinyanjui said. 'It was good money, and we went all over East Africa for them.' The ban would push them into a new direction entirely.

To begin with, Ian went into farming. In 1977, he took on the running of Lewa as a cattle ranch. 'I'd been brought up on the farm, so it was our life,' Ian said. 'We were running the show ourselves, and it was a good place to be.'

Ian had fallen in love and married Jane, born to an English family, growing up on Kenya's Indian Ocean coast. Jane shared Ian's love of wildlife—and his enjoyment of adventure and exploring. They would start a family and build a home, but it was no solid walled farmhouse. With a thatch-roof and open-sided to the wide plains, it was as close as possible to the wildlife that he loved. The pictures still on their wall are not of cattle, but of the animals that were an adversary to the old farmers—leopards, lion, wild dogs and buffalo.

For several years, the farm took up all their time. At its peak, Lewa had some 3,500 cattle on 60 sq miles, 155 km sq, employing around fifty people looking after the herds. They still needed to guard against lion, who under cover of darkness, would creep back in to the ranch to claim back their old land—and the cattle. Normally lion would stalk their prey from downwind, taking their scent away from the unsuspecting animals. But because thorn bushes had been cut down to make thick corrals for the cattle, walls too strong for the lions to break, they worked as a team and came from upwind. The breeze blew their lion scent directly over the herd, terrifying the cows. When the cats rushed forward roaring, the cattle stampeded in panic—and smashed through the protection of the walls. Then the hungry predators could pick and choose their prey.

The ranch was a large, modern and intensive operation and, from the outside, appeared a successful one. But it was a struggle. 'We were working our hearts out, but financially, it was a disaster,' Ian said. 'We were borrowing money from the bank, and we nearly went bust. We swore to ourselves we'd never ever borrow a single shilling from anybody.' Each year, the farm faced a new challenge. Herdsmen armed with AK-47s swept in from the north, raiding the herds and stealing cattle. The grasslands of Lewa had been where they had brought their cattle to graze for generations, and the big herds on the ranch were tempting to take.

But the bigger fundamental problem was the running of the very ranch itself. Lewa had a good spring of water in the swamps at its centre, but like so much of northern Kenya, the hills were dry grassland. Keeping too many cattle stripped the grass bare, and when the rains were poor, there was not enough to keep all the animals going. Wild animals would have moved to find fresh grazing, but the cattle depended on humans. They had nowhere to go. It was just on the crossover cusp of marginal land too dry and hard to intensively farm; possible for a short time, but heavy grazing soon stripped the land of the nutrients built up over generations far faster than they could be replaced. In the long-run, it was heading towards collapse.

'We were born into farming, so that was what we were told the land was supposed to be used for,' Ian said. 'But the way we were farming wasn't good for the land. Every two years we'd have what we'd called a 'drought', but it was simply that we just had too many cattle on too small a piece of land.'

The dreams of the boy remained in the man—and Ian's heart was not in running a struggling farm. 'When you are born a farmer, you are always a farmer,' Ian said. 'But what really mattered to me was the wildlife.'

* * *

All around Lewa, Ian could see the damage the gunmen were causing. The clouds of vultures would show them where the bloated bodies of elephants and rhinos were left. The rotating spiral of birds above the latest victim could be seen from far across the plains. Even when the bodies were gone, eaten and the bones scattered by lion or hyenas, the giant white skulls would be left like headstones at a graveyard. The rot left behind a black stain on the grass. From the air, the strange circles of death dotted the landscape.

'We'd see the impact of poaching first hand,' he said. 'It was carnage. We'd go out and see the bodies of elephants, or the rhino left to rot. The rhinos that were left, that had managed to survive, were scattered in ones and twos hidden in mountains to the north. It was only a matter of time before they would be found and all killed too. Even if they managed to hide, they were not a viable population.'

So, in the early 1980s, he began talking with family and friends about what could be done. 'I knew that unless something drastic was done then black rhino were going to be exterminated in Kenya,' Ian said. 'We were about to lose them all. It was a simple as that.'

Peter Jenkins, one of the most experienced men in the government wildlife department, was deeply worried too. He had put every effort in to protecting rhinos, including leading teams at Meru National Park, south-east of Lewa. Meru was where some of the first Southern White Rhinos introduced in Kenya were brought in the mid 1960s, to bring back rhinos to where they had been killed. 'The countrywide decline of the rhino has reached catastrophic proportions,' Peter said. 'What has occurred clearly demonstrates how a large animal, whose presence was once taken for granted, can suddenly verge on extinction.' He spoke from bitter experience; when Peter's posting at Meru ended in 1978 and he moved on, within months, fifty-six rhinos were killed inside the park. He was also a close friend of Ian, and the pair spoke long about what they could do. 'The species is now so fragmented and dispersed it could undoubtedly disappear to all intents and purposes, even if all poaching was to cease immediately,' Peter wrote in a report in 1983.[18]

But the one thing Ian did have was land. 'Peter suggested we fence off part of Lewa,' Ian said. 'Then we could ask the government for rhino, and provide really intensive protection for them so they would have a safe place to breed.'

The idea began of turning the farm into a secure sanctuary to stop the total annihilation of the species. Single rhinos out in the wilds would be tracked and found, then darted, and moved by truck. Creating a sanctuary was a last line of defence, but if it could work, it offered a chance of saving the species.

It was a huge experiment, and a giant gamble. 'We were going to try something new to Kenya,' Ian said. 'We were pioneers—and nobody knew if it would work.' Many thought he was mad, but Ian realised that if he didn't even give it a crack, then the wildlife he cared so much for and had grown up with would soon be only a memory. Kinyanjui, at least, didn't need much persuading. 'I just said yes,' Kinyanjui said. 'I thought it was a good idea. After all, tracking rhinos is what we'd been doing together for years anyway. If I could help, I would.'

They would go out into the wildest spots, and find the last rhino before the poachers did. Catching the sharp-horned and fleet-footed beasts, however, is somewhat easier said than done.

1. Women meet in front of the sacred mountain of Ololokwe, also called Sabache.
   © David Chancellor

2. Blessing the dead: A Samburu herder places branches onto an elephant skull as a mark of respect. © Peter Martell

3. Lewa is a crucial wildlife corridor to Mt. Kenya, the peak seen on the horizon. © Peter Martell

1. Pastoralists in northern Kenya move with their livestock on ancient routes to the same areas each year to find water and grazing. © Pete McBride

5. An orphaned elephant is looked after at the Reteti community-run sanctuary, before being returned to the wild. © David Chancellor

6. A family 'manyatta' compound. Herders live across the community conservancies, grazing livestock alongside wild animals. © Pete McBride

7. The Samburu are nicknamed by some the 'butterfly people' for their love of colourful fashion. © Pete McBride

8. Boys play with a makeshift football. As cattle raids have diminished, more children are going to school. © Pete McBride

9. Mobile home, Samburu-style, West Gate Conservancy. Pastoralism is a sophisticated system of land management built up through generations. © Pete McBride

10. Ian Craig and Kinyanjui Lesderia, friends since they were both young men. © Jane Craig

11. In 1983, philanthropist Anna Merz provided the seed funds for a rhino sanctuary at Lewa. © Fuzz Dyer

12. Elvis the Rhino, after destroying a bed. © Jane Craig

13. The highway north. Under British colonial rule. the north was declared a 'Closed District', and run as if a separate land. © Pete McBride

14. Northern Kenya was once awash with guns. Here police officers take a wounded comrade – shot in a battle between rival herders in Moyale in 2013 – to a clinic. © Peter Martell

3

THE RHINO GUARDIANS
(HOW A SPECIES WAS SAVED)

There was a crackle of twigs and a snap of a branch. Then the great hulk of a speeding rhino shot out of the scrub like a tank.

'We'd heard reports there was a rhino in the hills,' said Kinyanjui, who took the lead of a team of trackers trying to pin down the position where the animals were hiding. 'So we had gone to find it. First we talked to communities, to the herders who knew the area the best, and asked them, "Where is the rhino?" Then we searched for it ourselves where they thought it could be, for weeks and weeks until we found fresh footmarks and dung.' The tracks, the three-toed hooves of a black rhino, were clear.

The first time that Kinyanjui, Ian and their team-mates set out to capture a rhino to bring to Lewa was in 1984. It was a black rhino, a solitary female hiding out on a rocky hilltop near Shaba National Reserve, northeast of Lewa. Outcrops of jagged peaks reared up, with sharp serrated rock ridges like a crocodile's teeth. It was too dry and too harsh to be much good for cattle. The rhinos were not being killed to feed an expanding human population, or because they were a threat to livestock herders. They were being killed for the two horns on their nose. For rhinos, the horns were tools it had used for defence for millennia, but now human greed put the very existence of the species at risk.

The team of trackers, from the Il Ngwesi and the Samburu people, were experts at finding rhinos—but they knew if they could locate them, then so could the gunmen out for their horn. 'Everyone wanted these animals,' Kinyanjui said. 'We wanted to capture them, and the poachers, they wanted to kill them.' The clock was ticking. All knew that the chances the rhino would survive much longer there were slim. 'The problem is that killing is much easier than capturing,' Kinyanjui said.

* * *

Finding the rhino was just the first step. The capture teams faced a far harder task. They not only had to get the expert vet into place to dart the rhino, but make sure that it went down in a suitable place. 'If you dart it where we see it, then you end up with this huge animal asleep,' Kinyanjui said. 'But you can't just carry it while it dreams. You have to move it before it wakes up. You had to make sure that you darted it where you could get the rhino out on a tractor or a truck.'

It was also usually far too far to dart a rhino and bring it back to Lewa straight away, especially because the rhinos were hiding out in the remotest parts of the hills. Driving out involved a slow journey through a rugged land without roads. Carrying a precious and fragile cargo like a drugged rhino could take a whole day.

So they had to build a holding pen, close to where the animal was captured, where the rhino would rest for a couple of weeks. This allowed it to calm down and recover its strength before its onward journey. That was no small task either. The stockade had to have walls made of the strongest logs. It had to withstand a rhino, first waking disorientated, groggy and with a heavy hangover. Then as time passed, it had to hold a fearful animal that could get pretty angry at its confinement.

After weeks of tracking, Kinyanjui's team had the female rhino in their sights. They called for the capture teams to come, including a government vet. As the trackers crept forward, the rhino took matters into her own hands. All the rhino's companions had already been killed, and she, cunning and careful, had survived by hiding in the densest thickets, and by clambering up into the most inaccessible rocky hills. She had learned not to trust humans.

Unlike many species facing extinction, it was not because of a lack of habitat. Rhinos are tough. They could cope with rough areas with little water, browsing from a wide range of bushes, and could thrive in lands seen as marginal by cattle herders. Even where it moved among livestock, it posed little threat to them. For centuries, herders had tolerated rhinos around their herds. It should have been doing well.[1]

The rhino in Shaba was scared—but also smart. She had made her home the remote mountain top, devoid of water, so dry that few could imagine anything could survive. But she lived alone, peacefully grazing on the spiky cactus-like *sansevieria* plant, chomping through the needle thorns. The liquid in its fleshy leaves was enough for the rhino to survive. Rhinos can go four or five days without water, so she could retreat to hideouts far from people. The water in the plants meant she could stretch out the time needed to drink even longer, sometimes apparently for almost two weeks.

Kinyanjui laid in wait to spot the rhino. In the thirty-six days camped out in the searing heat of the most remote bush, the rhino only came down from her rocky fortress top once. In the cleft of two rocks, inside a small and dark cave, water seeped out into a small pool. Kinyanjui brought a team and laid in wait for her there.

Rhinos look like fearsome creatures: a barrel-shaped animal with a sharp horn longer than your forearm on its snout. Left alone, rhinos are peaceful vegetarians. They gallop only in emergencies. Angered or alarmed, or protecting their calf, they can be very dangerous indeed. Almost the height of a man but with legs like concrete pillars, it would outsprint an elephant and hippo. In fact, rhinos would overtake a sprinter breaking the Olympic 100 metres record.[2] If you haven't had time to scramble high up a strong tree, your best chance is to try to dance a sidestep like a nimble matador, and hope the rhino blunders safely past. 'Dismayingly agile for its bulk,' one safari guide described the rhino. 'It operates on the principle that the best defence is a good offense.'[3]

The rhino was not to know that these humans creeping up on her wanted to offer help. But now that her hideout was clearly found, and the humans were approaching ever closer, she was not going to go down without a fight. The rhino had decided that enough was enough of these bothersome humans bothering her.

* * *

'They had sighted it near a dense tangle of boulders and bush, where the mountain came down to the plain in a series of the rock falls,' said Anna Merz, who was watching the operation to capture the rhino. Anna, a wealthy retired English lawyer passionate about wild animals, who was the key financial backer to set up the sanctuary, had joined in the capture effort on the ground. For her, looking up at the cliffs, the tumbling rock edge looked like it would be hard for a narrow-footed antelope to scale, let alone the heavy bulk of a rhino. But rhinos are nimbler than they might look, and she and the others would be surprised. 'Little did we know then of the abilities of rhinos,' Anna wrote later.[4]

On the ground, the team of around a dozen searched for tracks. Kinyanjui and the trackers, along with Ian, were following the rhino. But once foot patrols had located the rough area of a rhino, airplanes stood the best chance of seeing it first. So from the air, Ian's brother Will flew a small plane trying to spot the rhino, and a helicopter with a vet with a dart gun buzzed above. Even then, it was hard to find, unless it was on the move. Rhinos maximise the shade of the tree by aligning their spines with the shadow of the thick main branch. They become effectively invisible, blending into the undergrowth despite their bulk.

The rhino pushed on deeper into the scrub, hiding from the humans, who had only brought trouble to it in the past. But one of Kinyanjui's trackers spotted the rhino sneaking off the mountain, slipping down a ravine. So in a wide semi-circle, the team moved towards the cliffs. 'Slowly and silently we crept into the tangle, until we came suddenly on an area full of fresh rhino spoor, rank with its scent,' Anna said. 'Ian whispered that I should be ready to leap up a tree, and I nodded.'

She did not have time. 'A black patch of bush moved,' Anna said. 'There was a furious snort.' It burst out like an express train. 'A hand grabbed me and knocked me down behind a tree,' she wrote. 'I missed the ensuing action when the fleeing rhino charged.' Falling backwards, breaking her hand, she was otherwise unhurt as the rhino charged past. Overhead the helicopter hovered—and the vet shot a tranquiliser dart into its galloping rump. The rhino charged on for quarter of an hour, twisting and turning in the thorns, as the team chased her on foot behind. Then she slowed to a halt as the drugs kicked in, standing confused on her feet. Minutes later, she slumped to her knees.

The team caught up to the rhino, peacefully asleep in the sand. 'I was able to get her nose out of the dust and raised across my legs while water was poured over us both,' Anna said. To the surprise of the trackers, she had whipped off her shirt to use as a blindfold to keep the sun out of rhino's eyes. The rhino's temperature and breathing had to be constantly monitored. 'I sat with her great heavy head on my legs and prayed the tractor would come soon,' she added.

Everyone pushed together and rolled the rhino onto an enormous sled covered with grass-stuffed sacks, then trussed her tight with padded ropes. The journey began to take the rhino to the holding pen. It was a slow journey across the bumps taking two hours before they arrived. 'We gently injected the recovery drug into a vein in her ear and then climbed out,' Anna said. 'Still she lay prostrate. We re-entered the pen and sprinkled water over her. Slowly and unsteadily she lurched to her feet, and stood there looking angry, bewildered and magnificent.'

The new Lewa sanctuary had rescued its first rhino. The rhino, named Shaba after the area she was found, would almost certainly have been killed for her horn had she stayed in her hideout. The strewn corpses of the rest of her species were evidence for that. Instead, she had a new home in a huge fenced sanctuary. She would join fellow rhinos, safe and secure. The hope was that they'd then begin to breed and help the species survive.

* * *

At the beginning, Anna Merz was no expert on rhinos—but she knew from experience what happens when destruction meted out to wildlife is not stopped. 'When we went to Kenya in 1968, we saw rhinos everywhere,' said Anna. 'When we went in 1976, we saw corpses everywhere. The massacre was unbelievable. They were being killed at such a horrifying rate that I decided to do something '[5]

Anna had seen the annihilation of animals before. Born in England, she had moved to West Africa in the 1950s, to Ghana, where she'd been horrified at the lorry loads of antelope arriving each morning for the butchers in the markets. 'Many were carried alive with their legs broken, others arrived already smoked and salted,' she said with revulsion. 'Meanwhile in the market, leopard skins were stacked high.' In time, even that trade dried up. 'As the years passed the supply of bush meat in the market dwindled,' she said, describing how when she travelled into areas in Ghana once rich with herds, they were strangely quiet. 'We saw no more animals, not even footprints. The land which had once carried large herds of kob, roan antelope and hartebeest was empty.'

When she came back to East Africa, she realised to her horror that the same destruction was taking place in Kenya. The tourist shops in Nairobi were packed with animal souvenirs: piles of zebra and monkey skins, ivory carvings, coffee-tables made from elephants' feet, lion teeth necklaces and even trinkets made of the horns of the tiny dik-dik antelope. 'The trade in wildlife products was obviously out of control,' she said. 'And this I had seen before.'

Many feared that any conservation efforts were too little, too late. A devastating 98 percent of rhinos in Kenya had been slain. Barely two hundred were left—and because so many were isolated in pockets, there were few viable populations able to breed. Left in peace, they can live up to forty years, but without change and within a handful of years, there would be only a remnant population too small to survive. Biologists estimated a population of at least fifty animals was needed to ensure the rhinos did not suffer from inbreeding. Any less than that, and even with all the protection, the animals would slowly die out.[6]

Anna had met with the Craig family while visiting Kenya in 1982. Ian's family, his parents David and Delia, older sister Susan and younger brother Will, were among the first to take tourists on walking expeditions, out into the wilder corners of the ranch and beyond. They had already seen the need to diversify beyond the struggling business of cattle ranching alone, and were among the pioneers to develop a new kind of safari encouraging people to take photos of animals rather than hunt them. One of the clients to come was Anna. She saw their passion for nature, and heard what had become a Craig family motto: 'Always leave room for the wildlife.'

Anna, walking with them across the plains, listened as the Craigs spoke of their fears for the future of the wildlife. So Anna came up with a proposal. She would provide the funds, if the Craig family provided the land.

* * *

The Craigs agreed to set aside an initial 5,000-acre sanctuary for the rhino, or just over 2,000 hectares. The sanctuary was still a small portion of the rest of the ranch, but this was no zoo enclosure. It was six times the size of New York's Central Park, or more than twice the size of London's Richmond Park with its herds of wild deer. They called the sanctuary after the river that flowed through the bushy hills, the Ngare Sergoi. 'The River of Donkeys,' it means in Maasai. Where the donkeys were once brought to drink, the rhinos would gather too.

'It was very fortunate that at this stage of the operation I had little real concept of what my ideas entailed,' Anna wrote. 'I have always been a dreamer of dreams, but I'm not a very practical person.'

Part of the team to overcome the logistical challenges to make it happen was Francis Dyer, better known as Fuzz. A friendly can-do man with a ready grin able to turn his hand to just about anything, Fuzz grew up next door to Lewa on the neighbouring ranch, called Borana. He was also Ian's cousin. Fuzz had to figure out the way to best build the sanctuary. Then, together with Ian, Kinyanjui and his crew, they had to work out how to trap a massive animal in the wild. It was a team effort that required intense preparation to plan—and then enormous daring to carry out. Technical support and advice came from wildlife vet Dieter Rottcher, a skilled expert with years of experience of working with large wild animals.

'It was a bunch of people with a cool energy, just saying "let's do it"', said Fuzz. 'We learned from each challenge.' Fuzz, who had taken on the task as a young man aged just twenty, played a key role in every aspect of the work. 'It brought together the amazing knowledge of trackers like Kinyanjui with their understanding of the animals, with vets like Dieter Rottcher—who was always professional even when rhinos were charging him on the ground,' Fuzz said. 'I was doing tons of exciting flying watching the action below. It was a lot of fun.'

It was thrilling work. 'The government had given us permission to capture any remaining rhino,' said Ian. 'That in itself was a fantastic exercise; rhino conservation is bloody exciting. You're charging across mountains, and flying aeroplanes, and tracking them on foot. It is all the same elements as hunting—except you're doing something that matters, because it has a future. And the more you got into it, the more it became an absolute passion. These rhino, we absolutely lived for them. They were virtually your family.'

The sanctuary itself had to be fenced off and heavily protected, to keep the rhinos inside safe—otherwise they would have simply been rounding up the rhinos for the poachers. The formidable boundary was wired up so that it rang an alarm if touched. The power came from truck batteries, charged by solar panels, that generated a whopping blast of 5,000 volts.

That security was needed. Kenya's national parks were meant to be protected areas—one giant sanctuary in other words—but they were too large, unfenced and impossible to protect from determined poachers. In many parks, rhinos had been almost wiped out. In mighty Tsavo, numbers of rhino had plunged from some 8,000 to less than 100 within a decade, while around the same time in Amboseli, the famed swamps below the white peak of Kilimanjaro, just eight rhinos were left.[7] The numbers being killed declined—but not because the poachers were stopping. It was because all the obvious animals had already been shot.

By the early 1980s, there were few places seen as safe for rhinos. There was only the government-run national park in Nairobi, relatively secure because it was so close to the city, and the private Solio ranch in Laikipia. Both areas, however, were already full. In that state of emergency, private ranches were considered to be safe places. With the fate of rhino hanging in the balance, the team at Lewa was given government permission to go ahead to collect the rhinos if they could.

* * *

So much was new. The scale and ambition of what the team at Lewa was trying to do had never been tried before. The teams read every research paper they could, but much of the work remained trial and error. Ian wanted to not only capture the remaining wild rhinos at risk of being killed from some of the remotest sites imaginable, but to then bring them together to start a community from scratch where the rhinos would bred. 'The dream was also that we could eventually restock the lands they came from, when the wave of poaching was over,' Ian said. No one wanted to create a zoo. They wanted to return the old intensively farmed cattle ranch back to nature—and make the rhinos feel like they were in the wild.

'Nobody knew if it would work,' Ian said. 'Researchers had done lots of studies, but we still didn't know how much area a rhino needed. Was the area we had too small? We weren't sure how many we could put together, and if there wasn't enough space, if they would fight.'

There were few who had ever tried to catch a rhino in such remote spots. Later, the vets became so skilled with the doses and types of anaesthetic drugs they were able to dart a rhino, calm it down—but still be able to walk it out for a short distance at least. It would be woozy and wobbly, but you could get it to the truck to drive it out. But in the early days, when a rhino was darted, it went down and out. Then you had the mighty problem of how to lift such a sleeping weight far from any road.

Each capture was a massive operation that took major planning. It took anything from six to nine months to carry out: from finding the rhino, to raising the money for the project, building the holding pen, to the actual day of capture itself. Then, once the rhino finally got to Lewa itself, it had to be held in another holding pen for a few weeks, preparing it for release in its new home.

Each time the teams thought there were no more rhino left, someone would arrive at Lewa, dusty and tired, having walked in from far with the message that the tracks of another had been found. Then they would jump into action. 'We paid money to anyone who could come in with rhino dung,' Ian said, noting he and Jane soon became unlikely experts differentiating the close-chopped nibbled grass in the dung of hippo, and the less chewed tougher vegetation left by a rhino. 'So we'd suddenly get reports of a rhino. Then we'd jump in the car and try and head there to try to find it—all across northeastern Kenya. Sometimes we'd scramble and get there and... find it was a hippo. You lived, ate, breathed—everything you did—was about rhinos.'

There were many lessons to learn. Buffalo were encouraged to move into the sanctuary. They lived happily alongside the rhinos, but herds of the sharp-horned and quick-to-anger buffalo were an extra guard against poachers too. Cattle could still use the land too, partly to show that livestock and wildlife can be raised together.

But a handful of rhinos was not going to be enough to ensure there was a chance of breeding. Other rhinos came from parks where they were not safe, or from other rhino sanctuaries where they were full. Those extra rhinos, from Nairobi National Park, and Solio Ranch, helped build a breeding stock. Slowly, the numbers of rhinos at Lewa grew and grew. The initial sanctuary was too small, and within five years, the fenced area was doubled in size. The rhinos benefited from the space that Lewa offered. Fuzz put up a signpost on the entrance to the sanctuary.

'No liability accepted for any accidents,' the sign read. 'Do not leave your car. All rights reserved for rhinos.'

* * *

Close-up, rhinos look invincible. Their thick skin is like armour plating, and their double horns can be sharp like spear points—useful for defence, as well as a tool for digging up roots. But they were nothing against the rapid fire of the AK-47 rifles. Their defence, their strength and thick hide, was no use against a stream of bullets. It made it worse that they also have a relatively small range they move in, meaning that if you want to track them, they were not roaming over endless distances. They are also often solitary, except for mothers with their calves. For the poachers, that made them easy prey. They were shot at close quarters. As they still lay bleeding from the bullets, knives were driven deep into their faces.

They were being exterminated for their horn, but the absurdity was that it was little more than matted hair grown solid. The horns are not like an elephant's tusks. Ivory is like a tooth rooted far into the flesh, and takes time to be hacked out. That means if there are responsive rangers who hear the first gunshot, they might be able to catch the killers before they flee. In contrast, rhino horns are attached to the nose bone by only skin and gristle. It takes a matter of minutes to saw through the flesh, splitting horn from the muscle. They are also far easier to hide and to carry than the heavy tusks of elephants—strong but surprisingly light. When cut, the horn is like a close grained grey-brown wood.[8]

So those that survived in the wild were those that had hidden in the harshest and most remote corners. Unfortunately for the teams from Lewa, the ones they were trying to find were black rhino—the most dangerous of the two species, white and black. Perhaps confusingly, both white and black rhinos are coloured grey—though since their favourite afternoon occupation is bathing in mud, they often just appear dark brown. It is commonly said the name 'white' comes from the old Afrikaner word for 'wide', referring to its square jaw it uses for grazing grass, and the 'black' was named just to differentiate it. The black has a narrower mouth better for browsing on thorny trees and woody bushes. But historians say that is a myth; that when the Boers arrived in South Africa and met rhinos, they named the one species 'black' for danger like a pirate flag as a warning note to indicate its fiery temper, compared to what they saw as its larger but relatively more placid cousin, a gentle giant, named white like a flag of peace.[9]

Learning how to safely catch a rhino on the job was dangerous enough. The fact that they had to capture the far more unpredictable black rhino simply compounded the risk.

* * *

Then a report arrived that rhinos had been spotted in one of the most inaccessible places of all. The mighty cliffs of sacred Sabache soar up from tumbling green forested slopes with a rock face taller than the Empire State Building, an island mountain as if cut off from the land below. There are few places where you can sit on a cliff edge, feet dangling over an abyss with views like an airplane, and actually look down on soaring vultures gliding on the thermals far below. With sheer walls and flat top—it is also called Ololokwe, the 'round-headed' mountain—it resembles Australia's Uluru red rock peak, but it would dwarf that mountain in size. For the Samburu, the mountain is a protected place. Animals are not allowed to be killed on the peak, unless part of a special ceremony. Even then, only their own livestock brought up can be sacrificed, not wild animals. Trees cannot be cut down. If herders are cold and need a fire, they must take only deadwood, or branches that will not kill the tree.

It was, according to reports from herders given to Kinyanjui in 1985, also home to a large holdout population of black rhino. 'We climbed to the top of Sabache to verify the news of rhinos,' said

Kinyanjui, explaining that the north-side of the mountain has less extreme slopes, and that the steep tracks are walkable. 'In the dry season, elephants go up to the forest at the top for water, because it gets the rains from the clouds. But we also found the rhinos.' They too had found their way up through the rocks to the cool tops in the mist.

After more than a week in the jungles on the flat top of Sabache, Kinyanjui had counted seven rhinos. Then as he watched one mother, she gave birth. He trekked back off the mountain, and headed to Lewa excited with the news that eight rhinos had been found. The teams decided to keep a watch until the rhino moved, or someone could think of a plan to take them off. But the mountain's inaccessibility had lulled them into a false belief the high tops offered some form of safety for the rhinos.

'Getting a rhino off Sabache would be very hard,' Kinyanjui said. 'But we thought that, up there, the rhinos would be well hidden and safe.' They were wrong. 'I went back to monitor them,' he said sadly. 'After six months, we found only three. Then three months after that, all the rhinos were gone. The forests were empty. There was no sign of them at all.'

'To speak the truth, it was not only the shiftas that were killing rhino,' Kinyanjui said. 'Even the game wardens were guilty.'

On Sabache, on sacred ground, the rhinos should have been protected. Yet the government game warden had also heard about the rhinos hiding on the mountain, and sent his sergeant up to kill them for him. After the warden took the horns, he refused to hand the promised share of the profits to the sergeant—who promptly shot the officer dead at his desk.

By 1986, there were no more signs of rhinos on Sabache, nor have there ever been since. Of the eight rhinos he counted, Kinyanjui believes only one was rescued. That one fled its mountain hideout down to the plains, and in time, was captured, and taken to Lewa. All the others were killed.

* * *

Within the first year, fifteen black rhinos arrived in Lewa. Seven would be rescued from the wild, with the others coming from parks. As the rhinos grew accustomed to their new home, the work continued to find the last few before the poachers did. Many of the remaining rhinos had already fled as far as they could from humans, but even where the rhinos were around people, few seemed to care about the fate of single animals.

'For years it had just been open season for the rhinos,' Ian said. 'There were traders who paid for the horn, and people used every means possible to kill them. Historically, the policing of wildlife was all about government, a protectionist approach only of arrest. So people just saw the animals as belonging to the state, not to the community.'

But not everyone. For some, the rhinos mattered too. The Lewa capture teams—and the poachers—were not the only ones looking for the rhinos. In the high hills, there were rhino guardians watching out for them too.

After a report of a lone male rhino in the thick forests of the Kikwa Valley, in the soaring mountains northwest of Archer's Post, Ian and Kinayanjui rushed to look for signs. There were definite tracks, pressed deep into the earth. They divided the land up into zones to search.

It was one of the most challenging attempts at rhino capture the team had tried so far. A helicopter and airplane scouted the bush above. A truck crawled deep into the valley, far off any track, struggling up the steep sides and slipping in the mud. The lorry had to be ready to take the rhino in a special cushioned container—if it could be found. It was a huge logistical test, but would also be one of the stranger episodes that the teams faced. To start with, everything went wrong. Days of heavy rain each night obscured the tracks, washing them away by dawn. Everyone struggled in the torrential downpours in their basic camp, soaked and cold.

Then in the midst of the operation, an elderly man emerged from the trees, called Lemageroi Lenanyuki. He watched the men struggle in the lashing rain, the truck sinking into the mud.

Lemageroi, an elder of the Rendille people, was dressed in a tattered jacket and a very old trilby hat. He was a Lais, a much respected leader, a cross between a priest, a herbalist healer and powerful seer. For many Rendille people, god is the great being of *Wakh*—similar to the *Nkai* god of their Samburu and Maasai neighbours—a deity all around, in the sky and the sacred mountains. The Lais can act as a connection between the two worlds, a link to the spirits of the hills and forest, between human and the divine.[10] In the jungles were hidden sacred sites under holy trees—often fig trees with their spreading shade of branches like a church roof—where he performed rituals of cleansing and forgiveness. He guarded such sites fiercely. He was the custodian of the land and the animals within.

'He and others in the hills had been watching the rhino,' Kinyanjui said. 'They had been protecting it, and taking care of it. He said that if we had come to help it, he could show us where the rhino was hiding.'

The Lais said he had guarded the rhino for nearly a decade. When the poachers came to hunt, the Lais had gone to find the rhino, telling him to hide—and the animal moved on to the deepest hideout he knew far up high. When men arrived at the entrance to the valley searching for the rhino, he said was protecting the animals in the forests.

The Somali traders wanting the horn might have dismissed his threats, and scoffed at his claims to talk to the rhino. But the Rendille and Samburu trackers the poachers used as guides did not want to risk a curse. Fear of his powers was a formidable deterrent. One way or another, the spells worked. They were better protection than anything a guard with a gun could have offered. The rhino had stayed safe because the Lais of the Kikwa Valley.

Yet such guardians seemed out of place amidst modern technology, where the teams with crackling radios coordinated helicopters and trucks, scouts and airplanes. His offer to help was declined, but the old man stayed to watch everyone work. After five hopeless days of wet and cold struggle in the rainstorms, people were ready to give up the search. It was at that point that the elder offered to help again. Ian and Kinyanjui accepted.

'He said he knew exactly where the rhino would be,' Kinyanjui said. 'And as he predicted, just a few hours after dawn the next day, we found clear signs of the rhino's tracks.' Within an hour, the helicopter with the government vet had spotted him. He fired the dart, and the rhino was knocked out and snoring peacefully—in a perfect place close to where the rhino could be loaded onto a waiting truck. After days of struggle, another rhino was safely captured.

Then the Lais wanted to be paid. 'He had been looking after the rhino for years, and now we were taking his rhino,' said Kinyanjui.

Deep in the forests, Ian gave him what cash he could gather then, about a teacher's salary for two months. The Lais was disappointed. 'We paid him all that we had,' Kinyanjui said. 'But he wanted more.'

People worried he would place a curse. As everyone packed up to leave, it appeared their worst fears would come true. First the airplane flown by Will Craig lost power and he crash landed. He walked out shaken but unharmed, and an engineer came up from Nairobi to repair the aircraft. When all was fixed, he took off again. But despite working well on the ground, the engine failed on take-off—and this time he wrapped the wing around a tree. Will was stunned but safe, but the wrecked plane had to be sent out on a lorry. The truck then slid off the muddy track and crashed into trees. The driver survived, but the aircraft was a write-off. It was the start of a long list of problems.

Two months later, two rhinos in Lewa fought each other, and rolled off a cliff in the scuffle. Both died. Weeks after that, another rhino slipped off a steep rock face, breaking her leg. Then a short time later, a female rhino, and then afterwards a male, fell sick and died in separate incidents. All the events were apparently unconnected, but it made many uneasy.

On top of that, the rains that year were late. Many, staring up at the cloudless sky, feared they had failed and were not coming at all. The drought was harsh. It left the grasslands thin and dusty, and the animals struggling. Such a run of disasters within less than a year made some look for a reason to explain the terrible luck.

'People were fearing the power of the Lais,' Kinyanjui said. 'So Ian asked to go back to see him.'

It was nearly a year since they had been up in the hills, and there was no way to tell the old Lais that they were coming. Yet when Ian and Kinyanjui arrived in the forested glade, he was sitting under the very same tree where they had last seen him, as if he had never left. 'He didn't say a greeting in surprise,' Kinyanjui said. 'It was as if he had been waiting for us.' The Lais smiled, and raised his trilby. 'You came back then,' he told them. Then he took the remainder of the money he had asked for initially, no more, no less.

'He said that when we got back to Lewa, there would be a sign that, from now, all will be well,' Kinyanjui said. 'There will be something good.'

As the team drove back into Lewa, the air was cool, and the birds were singing. The rains had come in the night they had been away. It had been a dramatic storm. They found deep pools of water on the dirt road. The earth was soaked. The fine dust had become dark mud. The heavens had opened, and the drought was over.

From then on, the rhinos in Lewa flourished. The rhino guardians in the hills had, it seemed, given their blessing.

4

THE GREAT REWILDING
(HOW NATURE WAS RESTORED)

They arrived soon after dawn. The shimmering light was still low and slanting across the plains, so that the great grey shapes were black silhouettes against the slowly lightening sky. For a while, until the colours came with the rays of the sun, it was not quite clear what they were. They were clearly fearful, shrinking back into the bush at the scent of a human, but unless they moved, those in the tangled bush were near invisible. Then, as the light washed down onto the plains, their grey shapes emerged from the gloom. The elephants had come back home to Lewa.

Ian stood on the top of a hill in the heart of Lewa, overlooking the swamp. The sanctuary had been running for more than year. As the rescue teams raced to find the last few rhinos before the gunmen, the creation of the sanctuary had another consequence. News that Lewa was a good place to be spread on the bush telegraph. Protecting rhino meant all species in the whole ecosystem were safe too.

'They came from the north,' Ian said. 'I remember the first elephants coming back in.' The bravest bulls arrived first. Some appeared on their own, others in small groups, exploring the land and seeing where was safe. For many, it was new land. In the past, knowledge was passed down from the great old bulls and matriarchs, the sixty-year-olds with long memories of the ancient routes to find water across the land. But the oldest elephants were also the 'tuskers'—those with ivory so long it nearly scraped the ground—and so were targeted by the gunmen. The oldest were killed first.

The young bulls, full of bravado but also scared, keen to explore but without guidance of where to go, tested the edge of their range.

Single male elephants out looking for adventure and females could march the equivalent of three marathons back-to-back in just a couple of days, and run further if scared by gunmen. Each time, they pushed a little beyond the last time.

'When they reached Lewa, they stopped and rested,' Ian said. 'Then more followed behind them, and they all met up together.' It seemed that when they returned eventually to other elephants in the herd, they had passed on the message that Lewa now was safe. The next time, they brought companions with them. 'I stood on the ridge of a hill, and all around, there were elephants,' Ian said. 'I looked out, counting more than 300 elephants. It was amazing to see.'

* * *

They had come from areas north of Lewa, where the same poachers shooting rhinos were slaughtering elephants too. Most of the national parks and reserves were not safe places. Where they were, they had become overcrowded with elephants seeking shelter. With too many squeezed together, they were ripping down the trees they depended upon. Lewa offered a new safe place. The impact of providing security in one small area had a ripple effect far beyond the wire. The returning elephants could not get through the electric fence of the rhino sanctuary, but the rest of the land was safe because the rhino guards were nearby.

'The poaching outside was going bananas,' Ian said. 'The killing was just mad. So the elephants kept running and running from all over until they were safe, and found that when they got to Lewa, nobody killed them. We'd fenced off the sanctuary for the rhino, and then expanded it later, but it was still a tiny part of Lewa. But with the security guarding the rhino, the elephants soon found that meant they were safe too. So they would stay here.'

For the elephants, it had been multiple generations since they had roamed the hills of Lewa in such numbers. Elephants move following the rains, to find water and fresh growth, as well as to socialise and mate. They had always used Lewa as a corridor, connecting the thick forests on the slopes of Mount Kenya where they felt safe to the open savannah across the north. But after Lewa became an intensive cattle ranch, the big herds of elephants stayed away. They would come through rarely, only occasionally sneaking through scared in the night. They crossed the cattle plains as quickly as they could on their way up to the quiet forests, leaving only their footprints in the dust as a sign for the sharpest-eyed trackers to show that they had even passed through, like grey ghosts in the dark.

An elephant, if left to grow old in peace, can live for almost as long as humans, about seventy years. It is therefore just possible an elderly matriarch might have remembered what the land had once been like before it was a ranch, when she was a calf in the herd. But it did not take long for the elephants to return, and once they had led the way, then they paved the route for all the others to follow.

Big animals like elephants need the space to move. Little islands of sanctuary can shelter animals, but in time, if cut off, they can weaken and struggle. If too small, inbreeding is a risk. But linking isolated populations provided more chance and more choice—plus a happier environment—for mating. It improved genetic diversity, and strengthened the wider species. With Lewa safe again for wildlife, the critical piece of the land jigsaw puzzle was put in place to reconnect the forests and the plains.

* * *

Old home movie recordings, jerky and grainy footage shot in the 1950s, show the transformation of the land. On the flickering film, only the shape of the hills above Lewa are the same. Almost everything else has changed. Lewa, as a farm, is a dry and dusty land. Dozens of herds of cattle, each a hundred strong, move across a dry but forested plain, packed with stubby whistling thorn acacia trees. The herders, with leather shawls on their shoulders and wraps around their waist, drive a long chain of a dozen paired oxen, pulling timber on wooden carts, rumbling over the rough ground.

There are few wild animals seen on the videos. Lions were shot, and poisoned bait laid down for other predators. Hyenas disappeared, and the once plentiful packs of painted wild dogs vanished. Even zebras and antelope were unwelcome and pushed away from cows. Apart from eating grass the cows could graze, it was feared they carried ticks that would harm domestic livestock.

So the return of the elephant was a clear signal of change. The elephants ripped down the thick bushes that had grown up on the cattle ranch. It was not the elephant's intention, of course, but clearing the trees ended up providing more grazing for the cattle, as well as the antelope that came back and bred. Then the black rhino munched through the thorns, allowing more grazing again. That encouraged more antelope, more zebra, and more giraffe—more everything, in fact.

Animals long absent that preferred the open spaces started to appear—like the elegant desert antelope, the oryx. They have delicate black-and-white face markings, horse-like tails and dramatic double horns swept straight back from the forehead. Some say they were an inspiration for medieval tales of unicorns. Then came the most graceful of gazelles, the gentle gerenuk. Giraffe-necked, the name means in Somali. Its neck is so long it looks as if it actually does have a touch of giraffe in its blood. It feeds standing up tall on its long hind legs, balancing like a ballerina on her toes, long eyelashes fluttering as it sashays, reaching up to nibble the choicest of leaves out of stretch of its rivals.

After that came the Grevy's Zebra, the largest of the stripy species. It is identifiable by its striking thin-hooped coat—one reason it had been heavily hunted was for its skin—and rounded ears that look less like a horse, and more borrowed from a teddy bear. They had nearly been driven to extinction, with numbers in the low thousands. The return of antelopes and zebras encouraged the leopards and cheetahs that liked to hunt them. Smaller cats like the little genet, a beautiful spotted long-tailed nocturnal feline, reappeared. The birds came in flocks. Scientists have measured double the number of species—and in far greater densities—on savannah land compared to farms in the same area.[1]

More and more elephants came. 'There were way too many for this tiny piece of ground,' Ian said. 'But they changed the land too. The whole of Lewa had been covered in woody vegetation, but as more elephants became resident, they opened up the grass.'

* * *

As the land returned to life with wild animals again, the rhinos continued to make Lewa their home. The first rhino born inside the sanctuary arrived in 1985, just over a year since the work at Lewa had begun. 'The calf was just visible in the long grass,' Anna Merz said. 'We could just see the long little ears poking above the grass and hear tiny bird-like mews.' But the baby was abandoned by her mother immediately after birth. Three days later, and with no sign of the mother returning, the decision was made to rear the rhino by hand.

'A stable was prepared with warm, dry grass for bedding and the calf was installed,' Anna wrote. She lay next to the baby, who seemed to be freezing to the touch, as if she did not even have the energy left to shiver. 'She took some milk but was very cold and very weak,' she added. 'I wrapped us together in a blanket for the night, but even so it was chilly and uncomfortable—and the mosquitoes were bad. At about midnight I decided it would be a lot warmer and more comfortable if I took her to bed with me.' She called the calf Samia.

The baby rhino recovered—and soon grew stronger, following Anna like a dog across the grasslands. In the early days, the rhino would trail behind its surrogate mother, nervous at the sounds of even birds coming from the thorn-bushes on their daily walks. But then, as it grew in size and strength, it would be the rhino that would stand in front to defend Anna when there was a rustle in the scrub.

After Samia, another rhino was abandoned by his mother. Jane and Ian would take this one into their home. 'A new-born rhino is about Labrador-sized,' said Jane, as she patted her dog snoozing at her feet. 'But heavier, and much more solid.'

In this case, the mother rhino, called Mawingo, was blind—and predators were waiting to pounce. She had already lost one calf, found draped over a branch, heaved up high by a leopard, storing the meat in a tree-larder away from scavengers. 'You couldn't imagine anything more macabre,' Jane said. 'The predators knew Mawingo was blind, and that she obviously couldn't defend her calf.'

So when Mawingo was about to give birth again, the rangers tracked her every move. Once again, Mawingo wandered away. The baby was left alone to fend for himself. 'We couldn't work out if the mother had actually abandoned it, or if she had just lost it, because she was blind,' said Jane. 'So Ian tweaked the baby's tail and it squeaked, and with that Mawingo came thundering back over the horizon, the poor old thing. To start with, it looked like it had worked. We thought we had got them back together—but soon she just wandered off again.'

So another rhino had to be raised by hand. It was easy enough to capture the baby rhino. A towel wrapped around its eyes as a blind-fold and cotton wool in its ears quickly calmed it down, and its cries quietened. Jane had made a special rhino substitute milk, made up in bottles as big as her forearm with giant rubber teats. Cow's milk wouldn't do, because it had far too much fat compared to what a mother rhino produces. So ground porridge oats, tablespoons of glucose, plus a dash of salt, were all whisked into baby formula milk powder. The rhino soon started to suckle. But great care had to be taken not to become too attached to the rhino.

'They are used to being with just one mother, of course, so you have to make sure that they don't imprint on one person alone,' said Jane. 'You need a whole rotation of keepers—but they always have to wear the same jacket when they feed the rhino.' For the young rhino, with good smell but not great sight, scent was key. 'The keepers found that if they hung the coat up on a tree—the rhino would smell it, and still go and sit next to it,' she said. 'It was heart-breaking.'

A visitor on safari to Lewa, keen to help the project, wanted to sponsor the cost of the feeding—rhinos guzzle enormous quantities of expensive formula milk. In exchange, they got to name the rhino: Elvis. But naming the rhino did not make him a pet. No one wanted a domesticated rhino. Everything was done to ensure that it could, in time, live among its own kind. 'The aim was always for them to return to the wild,' Jane said. 'We taught them how to integrate back into the rhino community by always taking them for a walk.' This, however, was very different from an afternoon stroll throwing sticks for the family dog. The orphans were led to the neat piles of dung left by wild rhino, where animals marked their territory by returning to specific spots each time.

'They did their business there, then they scraped it in with their feet, rubbing their smell in, and they took away the scent of others,' Jane said. 'For the rhinos, it was a reflex action—and a very impor-tant part of releasing them back. It was a way of making sure they can understand the community they come from, and of integrating them into society.'

However, the keepers also discovered another trick that helped the orphaned rhinos: giving it a friend to grow up with. 'Rhinos love a companion,' she said. 'A goat or a sheep works well for a time, but they don't last that long—and then it is a disaster when they go.'

When another baby rhino needed a friend, Jane had a different idea. She had just been handed a baby warthog found abandoned, whose mother had been killed. Without its mother's warmth, the warthog had been chilled—so Jane popped the piglet on top of her oven to warm it through, putting it on the lowest heat. 'Warthogs feel the cold terribly,' said Jane. 'Of course, the best thing would have been for another warthog to lie alongside to keep warm, but we didn't have that.' So Digby, as the warthog had been named, was introduced to the rhino, Omni. Soon the unlikely pair would spend their days trotting beside each other through the bush. Few predators would take the risk of a warthog treat when there was a loyal rhino pal puffing just behind. Omni and Digby became best friends. At night, the body warmth and skin-to-skin contact reassured both warthog and rhino. 'Digby would lie right on top the rhino,' said Jane. 'It kept his belly warm. They were constant companions. They really loved each other.'

* * *

Bringing up baby rhinos allowed people to understand the animals like few had done before. They discovered rhinos were not the brutish and primeval creatures some imagined. Far from being angry creatures who knew only force, they learned the giants were shrewd animals with complex social structures and intricate methods of communication. 'Everyone I spoke to in those early years described rhinos not only as short sighted, but also as bad tempered, stupid and solitary,' wrote Anna. She lived in Lewa to carry out unique studies to interpret the snorts, squeaks, huffs and puffs they made. She documented how rhinos have the same range of visible signs to display emotion as other animals. A flicking tail expresses happiness as does a wagging dog, while the rhino's twitching ears fringed with hair would prick up when interested, and lay flat back when fearful like a horse. 'It is no longer possible to regard this animal as anything but highly intelligent,' she wrote. Few researchers had ever spent as much time watching a rhino develop as Anna.

Once back in the wild, the rhinos remembered their old friends—and would come back to visit. At one point, Samia, now fully-grown and living a life in the wild inside the sanctuary and with her own child, wandered back into Anna's house. Fatter than she remembered, she promptly got stuck in the doorway. 'Luckily, she had the sense to stand still,' Anna said. 'I grabbed a gallon of cooking oil, poured it over her and she then backed out.'

Elvis, the other orphaned rhino, was also successfully returned to the bush. For several years, he'd return regularly to where he grew up, wandering right into the home of Ian and Jane. One time, he took it a step further. It started with the warning wails of panicked monkey shrieks—usually the sound alerting each other to a leopard. However, the screams were then followed by a heavy crashing sound of splintering wood. Elvis had got into their bedroom, an open-sided thatch hut built into the hillside, with a wooden decking terrace overlooking a cliff. 'As I put my head around the door, there was Elvis, getting onto our bed,' Jane said. 'Now, our bed was on wheels, so it could be rolled outside onto the deck, beneath the stars at night. And the whole bed was shunting forward—two front feet on the bed, two pushing.' To Jane's horror, Elvis was about to push the bed outside and off the decking—and down the huge drop below.

'Thankfully, the bed collapsed,' Jane said. 'Elvis just lay there, pushing the blankets around him with his horn, trying to get more comfortable. He looked pretty pleased with himself too.'

Since then, Elvis has avoided the house, perhaps learning a lesson of sorts. For a while, he used to visit the offices and lodges down on the plains in Lewa—terrifying the tourists. 'Now he's all grown up, and he hasn't been back to visit for years though we still see him around,' Jane said. 'He's too busy these days with all his own females.'

* * *

Elvis the rhino was not the only orphan raised and released on Lewa. A whole line of orphaned animals passed through Jane's caring hands. 'The first thing you do when you find yourself with a new strange animal, is to understand what it would be doing naturally,' she said. 'But always the ultimate aim is to release them back to the wild.' A love of wildlife meant that almost every possible injured or orphaned animal came to stay.

'Lots of cheetah, all sorts of antelope, plenty of warthog, giraffe, genet cat, and baby elephant too,' Jane said, flipping through a faded photograph album, packed full of pictures of all the animals that had joined the family over the years. She stopped at a picture of curious Goose the Mongoose, a brave snake-chomping cousin of the meer-kat. 'Just never a leopard,' she said. 'That's about the only thing we didn't look after.'

Jane paused at the photo of Elvis on the remnants of the broken bed, with great tree logs shattered like matches, then flicked on to shots of a wide-eyed kudu antelope with beautiful spiralled horns, wandering past a full dining table of the Craig family at Christmas Day looking for a salad scrap nibble. 'There were lion cubs too; they're easy to bring up,' she said matter-of-factly, as if they had been no more of a challenge than rescuing a kitten. 'Their formula is just milk and eggs, plus a little bit of mincemeat.' Photos of a trio of cubs show fluff-balls dotted with dark splodges as if a leopard, for new born lions have spotted fur for camouflage. 'They're just like a cat,' said Jane.

The list of animals rescued and raised was long. Among her favourites was Sticky the bush baby, a squirrel-like primate usually seen only at night, leaping like an aerial kangaroo through the forest canopy. He fell out of an old fencepost being chopped for firewood just after he had been born. He was pink and hairless, initially the length of a finger, so tiny that no one knew what he was. Soon he grew furry ears, and became a fist-sized bundle of energy with a character far greater than his body. 'Sticky could bounce like a jack-in-the-box, and would jump from one side of the room to another,' Jane said. 'He was nocturnal, so he would creep into our bedroom and try and open our eyes. It was the last thing you needed, to be woken up by a little crying bush baby.'

Then there was Corky the crested crane, a stylish long-legged bird, with beautiful grey plumage topped with a golden crown of fluttering feathers. 'Corky absolutely adored Ian,' said Jane. 'It must have been a female.' Corky, who arrived with a broken wing and was unable to fly, took the self-appointed job of lawn defence. She guarded her territory even at night, refusing to go inside any undignified box after sunset for protection from leopards. 'She was beautiful, but such a funny character prancing about,' said Jane. 'At night she would be on the lawn with a hurricane lamp lit, so that the night watchman could keep an eye on her.'

She would guard her garden with her life. Ian and Jane one day found her wounded, with the top of her beak broken off. A vet would have put her down—but they were determined to try to help. There was no internet back then. So after leafing through all their animal and bird books, they resolved there was only one course of action. 'We thought that was going to be the end of Corky, but we couldn't bear it, we had to try something,' Jane said. 'So we found the bit of the broken beak, and got out some super glue.' After injecting her with anaesthetic, they stuck the top of the broken beak back on. 'The real problem was when she came back to,' she said, noting that the vet guidance gleaned from books said the bird should wake in the dark and feel secure. To do that, as the bird wakened, they decided to mimic the soothing purring *'prr-rrp'* sound Corky made in her throat. However, all the rooms of their home were open sided to the bush. 'The only place we could make dark was a small bathroom with blankets over the windows,' she said. 'So we sat there, on the floor of the bathroom, talking to a bird with a superglued beak, making the *prr-rrp* noises Corky liked, to reassure her as she was waking. I remember thinking: if only people who could see the life we live.'

Corky survived, continuing her guard duty. 'She went on happily beating up our guests with a glued beak for many years after,' Jane said. In the end, her stubborn streak meant she eventually met her match, dining out with a leopard. 'One morning, there was just a sad ball of feathers left on the lawn,' Jane said. 'And that was the end of Corky.'

* * *

Most loved of all were those who to many others, might seem the unlikeliest: a pair of spotted hyena cubs. People fear hyenas, terrified of their eerie giggles and whoops, and doubt they could ever be friendly—but that is based more on reputation than reality. While as a species they are closer to cats than dogs, the cubs look like puppies with endearing eyes and upright ears. They are also fiercely intelligent animals. They live in a matriarchal society, where the females are bigger than males—and dominate them. These were not the ugly cowards of *The Lion King*. Everyone who met the cubs would find their opinions changed.

'They were the most loyal, dedicated animal you could ever have,' Jane said. 'They were real characters; you never knew what they were going to do next.' The orphaned hyenas were given a large part of the garden, fenced in to keep them safe at night, where they dug themselves a burrow. Hyena can eat almost anything, so when a cow was killed by a lion, Ian put the head into the enclosure for the cubs. 'We thought it was a super hyena treat they could chew on all night,' Jane said. 'But when we came in the morning, we found they had dragged the head to the very farthest corner as far as possible away from them. They had hidden it with everything they could find—dirt and sticks and leaves. They were clever little things; clearly their instinct was that they didn't want anything that could attract a leopard or a lion.'

Despite a penchant for stealing odd articles from the house—a single shoe, a hat, a child's toy—and taking it back to their burrow, they soon became loved by all who met them. 'We knew we couldn't have half-tame hyenas, so we said they had to be part of the family, like our dogs,' Jane said.

So to get the animals used to humans, they started to sleep near them. Having cubs that whooped at night outside the bedroom was not ideal, however. 'We grew fed up with that,' Jane said. 'Whenever we had guests, we would get them to spend a night on a camp bed in the enclosure with them.' For visitors, there was only one problem. 'They were tiny creatures, about the size of a spaniel,' she said. 'Yet from nearly from the day they were born, they could make an adult hyena call. Guests would wake up in the night sitting bolt upright with hyena laughter beside their bed.'

In the end, they were scared, spooked by a car—and they scampered off into the bush. 'We never saw them again,' said Jane sadly. Still, around the house at night, a pack of hyena regularly come to visit, their howls echoing in the air. Just perhaps the cubs, grown up and with their own family, have come back home to visit.

Raising individual animals was not going to save a species, and the financial cost of rescuing a single orphan could be enormous. Yet not everything can be accounted for by money alone. The lessons those hyenas taught in their brief time had a far longer-lasting impact. Their ancestors—possibly even their mother—had been shot on sight as vermin. Thei species had been poisoned and persecuted to the point of near eradication. Now the hyenas found themselves welcome in the heart of an ex-farmer's home.

* * *

Not all animals returned to Lewa straight away. Some needed a helping hand: encouragement to bring a few back, that would then pave the way for others to follow. Of all the wild animals, lions were among the last to return. Some still prowled through at night, coming in under the cover of darkness to hunt, but they would be gone by dawn. However, prides of resident lions were needed. As prime predators, they were critical for restoring an ecosystem, to return the balance of nature. Antelopes were returning and numbers were growing. Without predators, it wouldn't take long before all the grazing would be gone.

Tourists who came to see them did not expect skittish, nighttime scaredy-cats. They would pay money—but only to see a lion in daylight. What was a safari without a photograph of the roaring king? If tourist revenues were to help pay for the operations of conservation, then lions were needed.

Encouraging lions it was safe to return was not, however, so straightforward. 'There had been generations of lion who had been killed or driven away from Lewa,' Jane said. 'The mothers had passed on warnings to their young, and they had then passed it on to their cubs: Lewa was not a safe place to be.'

Ian made an appeal to the government's wildlife wardens that they were looking for lion. It was not a simple request. Those who had lions on their land and wanted them for tourists to see, didn't want to send them away. Those who had lion they wanted rid of, because they were attacking cattle, would often just shoot them dead. Killing a cow-hunting lion was dangerous, but heavy calibre bullets fired by a marksman could take it down swiftly. With a rifle, the gunmen could always add a follow-up shot if the wounded cat charged the hunter.

Firing an air-powered dart gun with drugs to knock it out was a trickier test. Done right, the lion slowly slumped down and slept. But there were often understandably shaking hands, so that the needle pierced the fur but did not go fully into the muscle. A glancing shot could result in a very angry cat furious at the sudden sharp spike. The drugs had to be given in just the right amount. Too much would put the lion to sleep, but could also be fatal. Too little, and you'd have a drugged out lion with sharp claws taking a swipe.

Eventually, Ian got a phone call. On Laikipia, a lioness hunting cattle had been killed—and her three cubs were left. They were nearly ready to live on their own in the wild—but not quite. 'There was one older sibling that had taken on the role of looking after them,' Jane said. 'But she wasn't winning, she was still young herself, and all the cubs were going downhill.'

The team left to collect four lions. They brought two trucks, each with double wire cages on the back, and enough drugs to knock the three cubs and their older sibling out for the three-hour slow drive to Lewa. 'When we got there, they had a fifth one for us too,' Jane said. 'That one was a much bigger, older female.' The fifth lion was an offer too good to miss—but without a cage, they decided to put it in the pickup truck. Without putting a wild and awake lion on a weighing scale to calculate how heavy it is—and that was not a proposition anyone was making—the anaesthetic needed was always a matter of judgement, experience, and guesswork. 'The older lion was darted too,' she said. 'As long as she was sleeping, all would be fine.'

The only hitch was that these things always take a little bit longer than planned: darting the lions, getting them into cages and loading them onto trucks. The team had begun work long before dawn to make sure the lions were transported on the roads without traffic—and out of the heat of the sun. It was thought best to move the lions in the dark, to make the journey as quick as possible for the benefit of the animals. No one wanted to be stuck in a jam with a roaring big cat.

As they drove into the town of Nanyuki, dawn was breaking. Ian looked in the rear-view mirror to see how the lioness was doing.

Suddenly, something moved. 'The ears twitched,' Jane said. 'And then the whiskers begin to move.' Jane looked back again, hoping that it was but a sleeping lion's dream of chasing zebra. 'Then there was a definite yawn,' Jane said. 'We had a lioness in the back of the pickup truck, and she was beginning to wake up.' The cubs in cages on the trucks were still safely dozing with the drugs in their blood. But the older, bigger and stronger lioness stretched out on the back of the pickup was waking with a hangover. Ian put his foot down to go as fast as he could—but they'd couldn't speed or risk harming the animal.

Nanyuki is a bustling market town, home to safari operators and a huge British army base. It was not a place to have a lion on the loose. They rushed through the early morning streets, looking for a veterinary store selling animal drugs. As Jane looked back, another sleepy cat yawn showed there was no time to be lost. 'Can you imagine?' she said. 'Trying to wake up pretty much every pharmacist in town with a lion in a truck.' With minutes to go, they found a store that sold the anaesthetic needed—dashing inside as the alarmed shopkeeper unlocked his gates—and then sprinting back to the truck. They got the needle in, just as the lion really began to stir. 'Thankfully, we got the lioness back to sleep,' Jane said. 'But if the store had delayed opening by even a little bit...' Her voice tailed off as she contemplated what might have happened.

All five lions made it safe to Lewa, and were taken to rest in the long grass in a quiet valley. It was perfect lion country, but empty of any resident pride who would be rivals. 'We drove the crates to beneath a tree, threw a rope over a branch, and then opened the door of the cage from afar,' Jane said. 'We still had to be jolly careful, making sure that it was pointing in the right direction, and that there was space for them get out. Such releases had gone wrong before and the lion had turned back, to teach all the people who had been rude to it a lesson.'

This time, all went well. The lions, still sleepy, wandered out, meeting the other lions they knew. They also found an old cow, that had been killed and left at the paws of the cubs. 'Breakfast was served,' she said. 'And they all flourished.'

Rangers kept a close eye on the cubs, bringing in meat when they were struggling for the first few weeks. But with few other predators to compete with, they were soon standing strong on their own four paws. What's more, they encouraged others to return. Once the precedent was set, new lion tracks were spotted. 'They were females,' said Jane. 'The new lions had attracted the wild lions from the north to come back. It was the kick-start that was needed.'

For the first time in decades, the spine-tingling sound of a lion's roar rang out again over Lewa.

* * *

The only rhinos native in Kenya are black rhinos, but their more placid cousins, white rhinos, had been introduced in the 1960s in a bid to bolster numbers for tourists. So white rhinos were also brought to Lewa. The white rhinos came up from Natal in South Africa, a massive operation involving boats and trucks. White rhino, square-lipped grazers of grass, preferred the open plains. Their black rhino cousins, browsers of bush, liked the thick woods. So there was little competition between the two—and they thrived.[2] The animals were wild, but key backing both in terms of funding and advice came from the American Association of Zookeepers, especially the Saint Louis Zoo in Missouri and the San Diego Zoo in California. Both had long since shifted from being places where people just marvelled at exotic animals, to being scientific organisations supporting species conservation trying to bring wildlife back from the brink of extinction.

The return of each species had a knock-on effect on the next. It allowed wildlife's natural rhythms to restore the land, reconnecting areas of nature back together. So what began as a fenced off pocket to protect one species on the edge of extinction, would become a large-scale restoration of the land back to the wild on an epic scale. Years later, such a programme would be called 'rewilding': the concept of giving the land back to the wildlife, and bringing the wildlife back to the land. As a term, rewilding was first used in the 1990s.[3] But Lewa was far ahead of the game; it had been rewilding for years before, trialling and testing the model in one of the most dramatic experiments of natural restoration to have been carried out.

* * *

It wasn't always easy. Change brought new problems, and the challenges were enormous. It was a long and hard struggle, where the people involved had to learn on the job. There was no handy reference book. Few had ever undertaken a task on such a scale before.

Yet the return of large and potentially dangerous wild animals was not something welcomed by all. For the community who lived on farmland bordering Lewa, they were seen as a threat. As the elephants returned, they raided crops. Animals that had never met a fence before suddenly found themselves up against barriers to guard homes and farms, and elephants did not like to be contained. Electric fences were put up, but elephants are quick to learn. 'They responded by discovering that ivory does not conduct electricity,' Ian said. 'If their trunk didn't touch the wire, they could use their tusks to destroy electric fences restricting them.'

One particular troublemaker was a frequent visitor to the irresistible lure of lush vegetables in the gardens around people's homes. Gilbert, as he became known, led the charge against the electric fences; so much so that the teams eventually resorted to darting him, and while he was asleep, sawed the tips off his tusks. A tusk is like a tooth—with a large nerve running down its centre. Trimming the tusk meant it was far more sensitive to the electric current. But Gilbert, waking with sore and shortened tusks, was in no mood to give up. He soon returned with three young bulls, who he showed how to break the fence. Gilbert, in his own way, had his own clear message: elephants did not like being stopped. It became obvious that bigger changes and infrastructure would be needed. Cutting tusks might deter the very worst of the fence-breaker elephants, but it was no long-term solution. Many also felt it was wrong to remove an elephant's tusks, because they were tools they needed for defence and to dig.[4]

A fence around farmland would be one step, but barriers alone would not be enough. As Gilbert had shown, build a wall, and the elephants will simply rip it down. Another trial tested beehive fences: a line of well-spaced out hives dangling from a chain, linked to fence posts surrounding crops. It was well known that elephants feared bees, because even when hives were hung in the marula tree whose delicious fruits sent elephants wild—the same bounty as used in Amarula liqueur—the trees were left alone. Researchers tested this by playing elephants recordings of buzzing bees. The elephants fled. Not only that, when they galloped off, the elephants emitted a low frequency 'bee alarm rumble' to warn the rest of the herd to run too. Scientists developed a hanging beehive fence, which meant that when elephants touched the chain, the hives wobbled—and the stinging swarms sped out to defend their honey. The bees helped pollinate the farm crops, improved production, provided honey to harvest—and defended the farm. Some farmers even smeared a grease and chilli paste on wires, something elephants turn their trunks up at. But while the beehive fences were a remarkable success to enclose smallholder farms, they were less suited to the long boundary lines of Lewa or for roving herders.[5]

Ever more sophisticated electric fences were developed—with wire outriggers to stop elephants from reaching poles to snap—but they were never going to be impregnable. It was only to construct a deterrent so that the elephants felt that it was not worth their time. Elephants avoided people if they had the chance. So while no one could tell an elephant what to do, they could be guided to areas to keep conflict with humans to a minimum. Fences were not a complete solution, only one tool for directing them.

To fix a problem, you need to find what is broken. For the elephants, the answer was a lack of safe space. Apart from the rhino sanctuary itself, Lewa was not fenced in. But once they had arrived, the herds did not want to leave, because the land outside was too dangerous for them. They were, in effect, stuck in Lewa.

The elephants of northern Kenya were part of historic herds that had journeyed for generations far into neighbouring Ethiopia, South Sudan, Uganda and Somalia. Frontier posts and human lines on maps meant nothing to them. The elephants left were the suffering stragglers of what had once been a massive interconnected population of thousands of animals, who had moved freely, unrestricted by humans, travelling as the seasons changed. But the elephants could not come and go as they had in the past.

For Ian, it planted the seed of a far bigger vision. The answer was not to enclose more spaces to protect people from elephants. It was the exact opposite. The solution was to open areas up, so that the elephants had the room to move as before, which in turn meant establishing corridors to reconnect the open spaces. There was enough land for all—if it was managed. The huge and apparently insurmountable problem—the elephant in the room—was how to achieve that.

* * *

Inside the fence of the sanctuary, the rhinos were healthy and breeding—but the external threat remained. Without protection, they were easy prey for a poacher, corralled together like sitting ducks. So young warriors from the Maasai and Samburu people who lived in areas neighbouring Lewa were recruited into ranger teams. Many came from the Il Ngwesi people, from Kinyanjui's home area. They were expert trackers who could read the ground to understand what the scuffles of footsteps in the dust might mean, and if it could indicate a threat. They were also the ones who could best spot when a stranger was seen among the community, who might be eyeing the rhinos to kill. It provided the start of a network of security, a web of watchers far more powerful than just a fence.

They were like a special forces unit, or a close protection team guarding royalty. Rangers dug foxholes at watch points where the rhinos liked to spend their time. Every night, the men would be watching, out on patrol, in hidden observation points scanning for movement. A central radio room, with maps covering the walls, coordinated movements of each patrol like a military operation. At times, it seemed not far off a war. 'Every animal was like a golden egg to us,' Ian said. 'And just as well protected.'

But getting the support of those who lived nearby was vital. 'They saw that conservation gives people jobs,' said John Pameri, one of the earliest rangers. 'There is value to protecting these rhinos.' With the money generated from tourist revenues as well as donors, Lewa supported schools and clinics. 'There was investment in the community,' said John. 'The people could see the impact on their lives: the guests who came to visit the rhino also donated money that built a school, or piped water from a well, or improved the healthcare at the clinic. So a herder saw that his children got a decent education, or when they were sick, got help from the clinic.'

Outside the fence of the rhino sanctuary, the arrival of the elephants had opened up grazing areas for cattle too. The herders brought their cattle to the grasslands of Lewa. The return of the wild animals not only changed the environment. It began to also change people's opinions. 'Communities were seeing a better life through conservation,' John said. 'Lewa was a benefit to them, it provided security for their cattle, grazing, education and health.'

* * *

Eventually, in 2013, Lewa would be named a World Heritage Site by the United Nations. The UN list is a roll call of places judged to be of outstanding importance to all of humanity, places of heritage that provide 'irreplaceable sources of life and inspiration.' Lewa is in distinguished company: as well as man-made sites from the Acropolis in Athens to Egypt's Giza pyramids, the natural places of beauty range from Botswana's Okavango Delta, Tanzania's Serengeti, to Ecuador's Galapagos Islands, Australia's Great Barrier Reef, the Alps in Europe, Britain's Lake District, and Canada's Rocky Mountains to the Grand Canyon in the USA.

Lewa was added to the list because it was the critical corridor passage between the Mount Kenya ecosystem and the open range-lands of the north. When the bad droughts hit hard on the hot plains, the cool forests in the highlands were a refuge for the animals. Lewa was the lifeline stepping stone between them. It was a staggering turnaround. The eleventh-hour attempt to rescue rhinos so many had dismissed as impossible had made a far greater impact. It had become a haven not only for rhino, but all wildlife.

Across Kenya, two-thirds of wildlife had been lost since the late 1970s.[6] But Lewa was bucking the trend. Within three decades of starting, over 160 rhinos would live on Lewa, more than the entire rhino population in all of Kenya when the work had begun, and nearly half of the country's total black rhino population. Now those rhinos arc fulfilling the dream of the sanctuary at the very beginning. They are being carefully relocated back into the areas that the poachers had exterminated them from in the 1970s and 1980s.

Success with wildlife would bring in tourists, and the profits would be ploughed back into the conservation efforts. The old cattle ranch had employed some fifty people, and had teetered on the brink of going bust. The returning wildlife brought with it a complete change in the economy, employing over 300 people, and turning over up to three million dollars a year. Lewa became one of the most famous, and most praised safari sites to visit on the continent. It was even listed in the bestselling book *1,000 Things to See Before You Die*.[7] The half a dozen camps and lodges set up on Lewa won award after award. One of them, Sirikoi House, was voted by the readers of *Condé Nast Traveller* as both the 'Number One Luxury Resort in the World' and 'Number One Safari Property in Africa.' Meanwhile, Will Craig took over the running of the original thatch-roof family camp, turning it into the chic Lewa Wilderness lodge, getting his well-heeled guests to don goggles, scarves and sheep-skin jackets before taking them up for a thrilling spin in an open cockpit bi-plane, soaring into the skies as dawn broke to see the elephant herds from above.

Lewa's reputation spread across the world in unexpected ways. It became a global inspiration as to what could be done. Switzerland's Zurich Zoo had for years ploughed back profits from the million and a half visitors each year into conservation projects around the world, and had been a long-time backer of Lewa. Its ethos was education by evoking ecosystems to replicate the animals' natural habitats as closely as possible—with spaces where animals can retreat hidden from visitors. So when zoo keepers opened a flagship 'African savannah' section, including giraffes, white rhinos and zebras mixed in an open air site of bush and trees the size of six big sports fields, they knew what to call it: Lewa. It even included a reproduction dirt airstrip—complete with zebra-striped painted bush plane—and a replica classroom, so that visiting Swiss schoolchildren can learn not only about the animals they see, but also understand how conservation and education can go hand-in-hand. For visitors in Zurich who might never make it to northern Kenya, it offered information and education of the challenges of conservation—and helped raise money to support the real Lewa.

But that is rushing far ahead in the story; the sanctuary was only one step towards that. A reserve like Lewa offered respite. But it didn't offer a solution for the far wider threat facing wildlife. That was a challenge so tough most simply thought it was hopeless to try. Outside Lewa, the killing of animals was as bad as it ever had been. With all the rhino outside the sanctuary dead, the poachers had turned their guns on another animal: elephants. Now they too were hurtling towards extinction.

5

FROM THE BLACK ROCKS
(HOW PEOPLE GOT INVOLVED)

'The first thing we heard was the gunshots,' said Ian, his voice crackling through the headphones, as he banked his two-seater Super Cub airplane down towards the plains of acacia forests and red dust north of Ololokwe, the sacred mountain of Sabache. The tiny airplane, gusts of wind buffeting its wings, skimmed the tops of the trees along the mountain ridge so near you could pick out individual leaves on the branches. 'When the shooting stopped, we were so close, we could hear the elephants crying,' he said. 'We were watching as the poachers shot the whole herd, one by one.'

Ian is a thoughtful and gently-spoken man. When he speaks about wildlife—especially his passion for elephants—he becomes animated. As he flew, peering down deep into the valleys between the rugged hills, the stories tumbled out. Every fold of the landscape held a tale, and he recounted the memories as he passed over the site of each. Of all the sights he had seen in these hills, a life spent trekking across almost every possible corner, one event stood out. It was the horror of that massacre of the family of six elephants, killed right in front of him.

It was in 1989. He had not been alone; Kinyanjui had been with him, hiking in the bush together looking for old bull elephants—when they heard the shots close by. They scrambled up above the tree-line onto a cliff edge called *Soitik Narok*—the 'Black Rocks.' Sitting up there, they had a view far across the plains. They could see the poaching gang clearly through binoculars. There were around half a dozen men, all armed with assault rifles.

As a young man, Ian had been a hunter. Together with Kinyanjui, stalking buffalo had been their great passion. Ever since hunting was banned, and their move into rhino rescue, they had left those days long behind. Still, just sometimes, the dreams of a boy live on in a man, and the stories of stalking animals could give them a thrill. After witnessing the slow slaughter of the elephants, everything would change. The cries of a wounded elephant are terrible, a howl of pain and of torture. It made them sick to their stomachs. From then on, everything Ian and Kinyanjui did was dedicated towards keeping the wildlife alive.

* * *

When elephants are threatened, they call. There are two warning sounds they make. The first is for the family; matriarchs call the herd close together with sub-sonic rumbles. It is a throbbing silent thunder, too deep for humans to hear. Elephants communicate through low-frequency rumbles transmitting over huge distances far beyond the sound even of a gunshot, vibrations also picked up through their sensitive feet.[1] The second sound is intended for us to hear: a terrifying trumpeting shriek to scare.[2]

For defence, they co-ordinate as a family. Mothers form a circle facing outwards, flapping their ears to increase their size. They surround the children behind a massive body, or hide them between their legs. The survival tactics developed over generations no longer worked when the threat they faced were men with automatic rifles.[3]

The gunmen shot the biggest elephants first—those with the largest tusks, and the easiest to hit. Once they were killed, the youngsters were left bereft, wailing and crying, and not wanting to leave their bleeding mothers. They were easy targets for the gunmen to stroll towards and shoot. 'They were firing into the entire group,' Ian said. 'The poachers were thorough. If they saw even a small tusk coming out, they killed.'

Ian and Kinyanjui lay hidden, watching from afar. They crept closer, using the rocks to hide. Ian had a rifle, but there was no way that they could stop the whole gang. 'We watched the poachers chopping the tusks out,' Ian said. 'They were going slowly, just taking their time.' Axing the ivory out from the face took hours. They appeared unconcerned about being caught.

It was before the days of mobile phones, but Ian had a radio that, with the weakest of sputtering signals, he managed to connect to the rangers in the radio room in Lewa. He told them to send a message to the government for help, detailing exactly where the poachers were. As darkness fell, Ian and Kinyanjui stayed put, watching the flickering flames of the cooking fire as the poachers partied in cele-bration at their ivory haul.

The next morning, the sun was already high by the time a pla-toon of soldiers appeared on the horizon. They slowly smashed through the forests in a truck too big for the thin tracks. They had orders to head to the hill Ian had described in detail, but they drove to the wrong outcrop a little further away. Ian and Kinyanjui could only watch in despair. Still, even had the soldiers not got lost, it would not have made a difference. The poachers had heard the truck coming long before and slipped away. They did not carry the heavy ivory to slow them down. That had been buried in the night like a pirate's hoard. The gunmen would come back later to collect it, loading it onto camels, hidden as firewood. None of them were caught, nor the ivory recovered. All the soldiers found were the bloating bodies of the elephants with their mangled faces, stinking in the hot sun.

The officers recorded the details of the animals killed, but that was all they could do. 'The country didn't have any resources for stopping poaching,' Ian said. 'Everything was run down back then, and what there was, was focused on the national parks. There was no energy outside, because they didn't have the money and they didn't have the training. The poaching was chaotic, the rhinos were all gone, and now the elephants were being hammered.'

The shooting of a family herd in the lonely hills of northern Kenya was nothing new. It was the sort of attack that was taking place every day, not only across northern Kenya, nor even the whole of the country, but in almost every African nation where there were elephants left. Yet to sit and witness it before you was something different. The killing changed Ian's life.

'We were there, on the rocks looking out,' Ian said, pointing to the shoulder of the mountain, flying right over the spot he had been hiding, swooping down to nearly skim the rocks. 'We could hear the elephants scream. I watched them get annihilated, but we could do nothing. That is what really hit me. Something had to be done.'

* * *

It should have been perfect country for elephants. The Black Rocks, where Ian and Kinyanjui watched the elephants being killed, lie at the very southern tip of a long chain of forested misty mountains. The highest would not be out of place in the Alps or the Appalachians. The tops soar up from the surrounding desert plains.

Looking down from the high flanks of the mountains into the dusty haze below, the thirsty plains appeared like a rolling, brown sea flecked with green. The peaks catch the clouds and bring the rain down, forming a separate environment from the hot plains around. Botanists call them a 'sky-island'. The highlands create their own mini-weather system, and are therefore home to plants found in few other places. Deep in the woods are dotted huge rare plants called cycads, a palm-tree like bush that would have been familiar to dinosaurs, some 280 million years ago. As if truly stuck on a lost tropical island, the animals who find shelter in the shady forests rarely venture out.

In the worst droughts when the grass crackles to walk through, and the baked red soil splits open so wide feet fall into the fissures, there was always at least a lick of water in a scrape of a rock in the cool forests on top. Even then, herders usually brought their cows up high only in the dry season, when easier grazing fed by streams plunging in waterfalls into the valley below was all gone. So for generations, they had also been a refuge for wildlife.

Some Samburu call the range *Lodikiko*, a name that trips off the tongue like its meaning—the hills that 'keep on rolling onward', like a bouncing ball. Each time you reach breathless to the top of a summit, and you think you must be at the end, another rises ahead. Others call them the Lenkiyeu Hills, after the Samburu name for the great peak of *Ol Doinyo Lenkiyeu*. It means, 'The Mountain of Fat Cows'. The *lenkiyeu* is the layer of fat cattle put on after munching the lush grass of the hills, but it is also the very first part sliced off after an animal is killed. It is like tender bacon, roasted and eaten sizzling. The name is also therefore symbolic of the community, because it brings people together in a ceremony of sharing. Yet the name on most maps is still the Mathews Range, after a long-forgotten British imperial general.[4]

The elephants of the mountains had learned to avoid humans if they could, but they helped the cattle herders too. Elephants and livestock herders relied on each other in a relationship that had developed together. Elephants powered through the forest, making pathways that people then followed. They ripped down the trees and devoured the thickets, munching four times the weight of a man in vegetation each day. When elephants opened up the thick bush, the light got in, and new grass grew. Then, when the elephants moved on for new woodlands, the herders followed in the footsteps with their cattle. The cattle ate the grass but left the bush, so in time the scrub returned and became trees and the shade closed over again. So as the herders moved on for fresh pasture, the elephants came back. It was a delicate balance, advancing and retreating around each other. 'Like phantom dancers in a languid ecological minuet,' one scientist described the relationship poetically. The Maasai put it more pithily. 'Cows grow trees, elephants grow grasslands,' they said.[5]

In these lands, forests were associated with people; tree cover is often thicker around people's homes and where they graze their livestock. It turned the common perception of herders as destroyers of the forest on its head, so that instead, they were the ones encouraging more trees.[6] As much as the elephants tore down trees, they helped healthy forests grow. They pulled down the weak and old, to let new growth begin. The combination of enormous appetites, inefficient digestion and powerful long legs able to wander far was an ideal seed dispersal system. Many seeds had also better chances of germinating once passed through an elephant's gut. Each seed was deposited embedded in giant balls of manure, the perfect fertiliser boost to nourish the first sprouts. If they didn't eat the seeds, they trod the seeds deep into soft earth, with their round footprints providing a tiny rainwater reservoir for the plant too. It benefited the wider environment. Tearing down smaller trees encouraged fewer but bigger trees to grow, which have denser wood that absorb a much greater degree of carbon. The gardeners of the forest, some called them.[7]

* * *

75

'The forests had gone quiet,' said Kosima Leleitiko, a Samburu elder, who had spent his life herding his cattle on the edge of the mountains. 'Once we had seen elephant all around, but it became rare to find their tracks. They had run away from the mountains. There were still a few left, but they were hiding and scared, and only came out in the night.'

Within a few years, the landscape changed too. 'The forest became like a wall,' Leleitiko said, waving his arm towards the jungle, describing how the trees blocked the light below. Herders could hack paths through the thorn bushes up the hills, but what they wanted was for their cattle to have the space to roam. 'It was too thick to get the cows in,' he said. 'It was not good for the grass.' Without elephants the forests were closing over. Leleitiko, an elderly man wrapped in a red checked blanket and smoking a long pipe, his wrist jangling with brass bracelets made from melted bullet casings, had not read the thick piles of scientific papers detailing how elephants are key to ecosystems. Yet he had spent more time in these lands watching elephants than any biologist could ever dream of doing. His research was based on a life spent living among elephants, and he had come to similar conclusions as the scientists. Leleitiko said that the Samburu had always known the role that the elephants have.

'When the elephants are here, the land is strong,' he said. 'When the land is strong, we are safe.' Losing elephants was harming all the grazing species. 'People didn't care what happened to one elephant,' Leleitiko said. 'But we needed the elephants to remain. When the elephants all were killed, then the grazing for our cows disappeared too.' Elephants seemed to be able to sense the clouds long before they were visible to a human's eye, and would return to the hills days before the rain arrived. For the Samburu, the appearance of large elephant herds answered their prayers, a sign to celebrate for they heralded the end of the drought. 'The elephants bring the rains,' said Leleitiko. 'And the water brings the grass.'

Healthy environments evolved to rely on all the species that live there, but some play a critical role. One suggestion for the origin of the word elephant is 'huge arch'. It is a meaning that resonates.[8] Ecologists call them a 'keystone' species—the central block in an arch that holds all the rest safe in place.[9] If removed, the others collapse.

Knock out too many of the bricks, whittle away the foundations of biodiversity, and structures that seemed so solid suddenly tumble.

The impact the elephants had on the land only became apparent after they were gone. Ending the killing of elephants was not just about protecting a species, but about preventing damage to an entire ecosystem. Leleitiko paused between puffs on his pipe. 'Elephants don't stay somewhere if it is not good,' he said. 'A place without animals is not a place to want to be.'

* * *

It was not the first time that elephants had been destroyed on an industrial scale. It is easy to assume the fate of wildlife from the past to today has been one of a simple linear decline, from abundance to loss. The reality is a more complex fluctuation.

For generations, for the communities who lived where elephants roamed, their use of ivory was marginal. It was used as jewellery— but a single tusk provided enough ivory for many bracelets. When elephants were killed, it was often done in self-defence, because a herder surprised an elephant in the bush. Hunting for ivory didn't make much sense; it was easier to take from the skulls of elephants who died naturally. For people like the Samburu, eating elephant was taboo, though some groups did kill elephants for meat.

It was the rest of the world that had a fascination with ivory, a material craftsmen could cut into delicate statues. Ancient Egypt and Greece coveted the tusks, while the Romans and Carthaginians, who also trained elephants for war, ended up eradicating them from northern Africa. The trade continued through the centuries. In Medieval Europe, ivory was used for religious icons. 'They have elephants in plenty and drive a brisk trade in tusks,' Venetian travel-ler Marco Polo wrote of East Africa in the thirteenth century. Some became expert hunters with bows and poison arrows, but the scale of trade was a fraction of the systematic killing that was to come.[10]

When English traveller Verney Lovett Cameron trekked across East Africa in 1873, he described how people thought so little of the tusks of elephants that 'ivory was reported to be used for fencing pig sties and making door posts.' The missionary David Livingstone, around the same time, recounted tales of tusks used in building construction as pillars of homes. Other accounts, including how one chief made the entire outer fence of his stockade out of ivory, might be better treated as tall tales of travellers, though the wildest of stories can carry a grain of truth.[11]

The market for ivory had come from outside. In the nineteenth century, ivory hunters had pushed far deep inland from coast. Slavery and the ivory trade went hand in hand. East Africa became the biggest source of ivory in the world, with the income outdoing that from the foul trafficking in humans. Scottish traveller Joseph Thomson saw the situation change rapidly. When he first travelled through Maasai lands, he wrote how ivory was left like bones 'to rot untouched' where the animal fell. Just a few years later, in 1880, the long slave caravans carrying tusks travelled ever further inland to source ivory. 'To supply the demand for the precious article, the traders have to push further and further each year, and now only the most remote and central parts of Africa yield ivory in any abundance,' he wrote.[12]

Aspiring middle class home-owners in late nineteenth-century Europe wanted a billiard table. It needed at least four large tusks to get enough ivory to carve just one set of snooker balls; that meant two big old bull elephants killed for each table.[13] The other status item was a piano with tusks sliced thinly to make the keys. 'Tinkling the ivories' came at a cost. Advertisers were worried enough at the reports that they pushed the myth of the elephant graveyard, the legend that the animals all went to the same special spot to die, pretending the ivory came from natural deaths. In fact, the 'graveyard' reports likely come from hunters who lit a ring of fire around a herd and burned them to death. Those who tried to escape the inferno were speared. It left behind of piles of bones from scores of elephants clustered together.[14] 'This... destruction of elephants cannot continue long,' Joseph Thomson wrote in 1881. 'An iron band of ruthless destroyers is drawing round it,' he added.[15]

European and American hunters joined in. They wrote florid accounts boasting of their sportsmanship, but they were also out for the money that the ivory brought. Colonial officers subsidised their wages from the profit. English settler Hugh Cholmondeley, Lord Delamere, is reported to have used a Maxim machine gun to kill elephants, raking herds with the chains of bullets. In northern

Kenya's Marsabit forests, he hired gunmen to stake out every water-hole and kill each elephant that came in desperate to drink. In later years he would speak of conservation, but in just a single trip in 1899, Delamere shipped out a gory fortune of over six tonnes of ivory from hundreds of elephants.[16]

By the time former US President Theodore Roosevelt came to kill an elephant in 1909, he had to travel deep into the highland forests of Mount Kenya and the Aberdares to find one. All the elephants and rhinos on the open plains had fled or been killed, he said.

The craze for ivory had been so intense as to 'well-nigh to bring about the mighty beast's utter extermination', Roosevelt said, who came to collect specimens for the Smithsonian in Washington before the animals were all gone. He and his son blasted their way across East Africa. Their tally of killing topped 500 animals—including 17 lions, 11 elephants, 11 rhinos, 29 zebras and nine giraffes. On the forests of Mount Kenya, he killed an old bull elephant. 'I felt proud indeed as I stood by the immense bulk of the slain monster and put my hand on the ivory,' Roosevelt wrote. 'I toasted slices of elephant's heart on a pronged stick before the fire, and found it delicious; for I was hungry, and the night was cold.'[17]

* * *

Explaining the history of tragedy is important, for knowing what happened in the past provides an understanding of the present. It also offers possible lessons for the future.

Outsiders might have forgotten the extent of the killing in past centuries, but the stories were handed down by the communities who lived where the elephants had roamed. They were not simply the faded tales of dusty hunting books. The markets shifted over time: in the 1930s, the elephant tusks might be mounted above the bookcase in a European hunter's home, while from the 1970s on, the ivory went to carving centres in China and Hong Kong, or to supply Japan—where the fashion began for traditional ink stamp seals from dead elephants. Yet people remembered. So when a new wave of killing began, and foreigners now came saying people must protect the wildlife, few listened to the warnings. It seemed like hypocrisy. After all, it was foreigners who had carried out the last round of killing—and on a scale far greater than their community had ever done.

The other point is that the extent of the destruction in the past, perhaps oddly, also offered a message of hope; that elephants had recovered before. For, even as Roosevelt feasted on the elephant's heart, laws were being brought in to stop the killing. Talk of the need to protect wildlife had begun from almost the very start of the killing.

In 1896, a year after London announced its claim to the land of the people of Kenya, the British commissioners in East Africa were sent letters from the foreign secretary in London. 'My attention has recently been called to the excessive destruction, by travellers and others in East Africa, of the larger wild animals generally known as "big game,"' the letter read. 'There is reason to fear that unless some check is imposed upon the indiscriminate slaughter of these animals, they will, in the course of a few years, disappear.'[18]

People were aware of the consequences. In South Africa, the extinction of the quagga, a zebra species, and the bluebuck antelope, provided the chilling example of what would happen without change. So in 1900, laws banned the wholesale trade in hides and ivory, and the killing of the young. The laws slowed the destruction, and over the decades, the animal numbers crept back up. Within a few decades, the population of elephants had nearly fully recovered.

Nearly a century later, when Ian and Kinyanjui watched the herd butchered in 1989, it was a different world. Laws protecting animals had been made—and ignored. But the past held a crucial lesson for those who would otherwise see the situation as hopeless. Elephants had been pushed to the brink of disaster before, and survived. Given a chance, the wildlife could recover.

* * *

By 1989, the numbers of elephants in Kenya had plummeted by nearly 90 percent to an all-time low. Just before independence, in 1956, the population numbered around some 150,000 elephants. By 1979, that had nearly halved, to 85,000. A decade later, in 1989, it had been cut by more than three-quarters. Barely 20,000 elephants survived—some say even fewer, perhaps just 16,000.[19]

Northern Kenya was especially hard hit. As well as internal poaching by Kenyans, gangs crossed over from Somalia, some of them army veterans with the apparent backing of the government in Mogadishu. Somalia's official export records likely represent a fraction of the real total, but they show the scale of the problem. The ivory was all listed as being from 'domestic' herds, but far more tusks were exported in a single year than there were even total elephants left in all Somalia. In one three-year period, tusks from over 10,000 elephants were exported.[20] The source of that ivory could have come from only one place: Kenya.

'It didn't take a genius to figure out that such a high rate of killing couldn't go on indefinitely,' said Richard Leakey, who in 1989 was handed the tough job of heading the Kenyan government's wildlife department. Leakey is an academic with a fierce intellect, who had spent his life in the most remote deserts hunting fossils. Born and brought up in Kenya, he was the son of the famous paleoanthropologists Mary and Louis Leakey, tracing our human origins in the Rift Valley. He too studied the bones of humankind's extinct ancestors, understanding the slow process of change over the many millennia. He took an extremely long view of history—but he was shocked by the speed of the elephants' demise.

'Extinctions are part of the evolutionary process,' Leakey said, peering over his desk. 'However they are also relatively rare events—or, more properly, *should be* rare.' But brushing off dust from fossils over a million years old, and seeing a living species that was flesh and blood die off under his watch, were two very different things. 'I was faced with a very real fact that one of the remaining species of elephants—the African elephant—was facing a serious threat of extinction throughout much of its range during the course of my lifetime,' he added. 'When the elephants disappeared from the habitats, other species would surely disappear too.'

Leakey found a state of utter disorder in the wildlife service. 'Each day of the first three weeks I had been in office, I discovered more problems; seldom did I have immediate solutions,' he wrote later, as he sat in the run-down headquarters. 'At one point, I had written in my diary: "No money, no morale, no vehicles, planes grounded, inadequate senior staff, no fuel, no ideas".'[21]

* * *

Leakey's first challenge was to clean out the corruption. The very people meant to be protecting wildlife were accused of taking part in the killings. 'It was one of the most—if not *the* most—corrupt organisation in the government,' Leakey said. Government-paid rangers not only helped the poachers smuggle the tusks out by taking cash to turn a blind eye, but fired the shots themselves. Elephants were so often killed by gunmen pulling up in a car and shooting them at point blank range from the track that the corpses even had a name: 'roadsiders.' When Leakey demanded to know how poachers could drive unnoticed in a park, he discovered that often when a 'roadsider' was found, the vehicle tracks were those of the rangers, and the empty bullet casings lying in the grass were government-issued ammunition. Leakey went through internal files listing all the 'ranger-poacher' officers believed to be corrupt, and pushed them out.[22]

For the government, stopping the killing made commercial sense. In many areas, elephants were threatened by increases of population, with fences put up when land was turned into farms. People needed land in order to eat—and the elephants were seen as a direct threat. But killing elephants for eating crops, and machine-gunning whole herds in forests where there was still yet space for man and animal, were opposite ends of the scale. 'Our economic fate was tied to our wildlife,' Leakey said. 'Tourism employed more Kenyans than any other industry.'

Next, Leakey targeted the trade; if there was no value in ivory, there would be no reason to kill elephants. To get that message across, he decided to set fire to Kenya's ivory store. Tusks taken from poachers, or from elephants who died naturally, were stored in government vaults. Yet often the ivory piles would vanish, stolen by the officials tasked with guarding it. Leakey piled up a 12-tonne piles of tusks from a thousand elephants, and with the help of a Hollywood special effects advisor who smeared them in flammable glue and fuel, the dramatic pyre burned for two days. Critics who said that the ivory would have raised millions of dollars for conservation projects missed the message, Leakey said. The world had to stop the trade itself or face the end of elephants entirely. The efforts worked: a global ban on ivory sales was agreed three months later. Global ivory prices tumbled by more than three-quarters, pushing ivory towards a critical price point where the risks of poaching would outweigh the reward.[23]

After the ivory burn came the reform of the ranger force. Officers were dying in the battle to stop poaching because they were completely overwhelmed and out-gunned. In one case, Leakey visited the scene of an attack where a young policeman had been killed. He picked up a rifle of an officer; it was a pre-World War One museum piece, date-stamped 1911.

In places where elephant numbers had collapsed, poachers were turning to robbery for an easier income. In Meru National Park, where elephant numbers had dropped from 2,500 to 200, another gang shot dead two French tourists and their safari driver. In Tsavo, an American was killed. The violence put Kenya's crucial foreign exchange earnings from over 500,000 safari visitors a year in jeopardy.[24]

So Leakey pushed for the rangers to be given military-style training and modern fast-firing rifles, with the new force now flying into battle on helicopter gunships. They were given a new name: the Kenya Wildlife Service, or KWS. Slowly, they became a team that the poachers feared. In the midst of the reforms, one journalist asked to film elephants killed by poachers. 'No,' Leakey replied with bravado. 'Because there aren't going to be any more dead elephants. Soon the press will not be asking permission to film dead elephants, but to film dead poachers.'[25]

But Leakey's ambitions outstretched his dreams. The KWS rangers had enough of a job just trying to bring order to the national parks. Outside, in the community lands, the killing went on. In places, it even got worse, because poachers now began to avoid the parks. In the north, where KWS rangers were rarely seen, the lands around became a free-for-all for poachers. Communities there were struggling to protect themselves, let alone care for wild animals.

* * *

'I told Ian that what we had done in Lewa, we should take it into the community,' said Kinyanjui, who now worked as the head of security for Lewa, commanding more than two dozen rangers. 'I knew that I could get the people to protect the elephants, if they could see that they could benefit from them too.'

It seemed an impossible task. Poaching offered an immediate reward. Many in the community had profited from poaching as guides leading the gunmen to where the last elephants hid, or as the shooters themselves. Much more importantly, there was deep distrust of any outsider—especially anyone wanting to be involved in their land.

'I was white, and I had a colonial background,' said Ian. 'In terms of land and history everything about me was bad. But Kinyanjui gave me an entry into that community where I could start building a relationship of trust. Everything here is built on trust—especially where land is involved. Kinyanjui opened doors into the community.' He went with Kinyanjui to a village at the foot of the mountains, to speak to a gathering of elders who were widely respected.

'I told them that I wanted to employ a dozen men from the community,' Ian said. 'I wanted to organise them; to say, here is a radio; stay in your ordinary clothes, stay with your cattle, but if you see tracks of poachers, then call us. We have a relationship with the government, and we can tell them that you have seen a gang of poachers, and they will come in and react. I wanted them to be our eyes and ears on the ground. Their reply? They immediately said no.'

Yet Ian and Kinyanjui were determined not to stand by as the last elephants were killed. Lewa now seemed secure, and the patrols of the sanctuary fence to protect the rhino had become largely routine. There were rangers to spare. They selected the toughest men for the hardest job.

* * *

Nginwa Ledupa was among those asked if he wanted a new role. Kinyanjui knew him well. They were a similar age, and as young men they had served as community warriors together. First recruited as a rhino ranger on Lewa, where he helped locate and capture three black rhinos in the hills, he was now sent to set up observation posts to track the poachers. Their job was to hide and to watch—and relay that information back.

Two-man teams set up hidden bases. Often they trekked out from Lewa, but sometimes they were even dropped at dusk by helicopter, unloading their supplies on a mountain top, and remaining there until their pick-up six weeks later. With funds from Lewa, they were well equipped, scanning the horizon with binoculars during the day, and using the latest technology of a night-sight scope after dusk. The scopes intensified light—so they could spot a poacher's campfire across the plains. In those days, with bandits around, few herders would risk sleeping out in such lands for fear of attack. 'In the dark, we could see the flames from far,' Ngwina said. 'It was the easiest way to see the poachers.'

Staying unseen was a hardship in itself; simply smoking or lighting a cooking fire could alert poaching gangs. At night, they crept out to fill their water canteens from a well, and pick up food from a buried cache. 'If the poachers found us, they would have killed us,' Ngwina said.

That was not the only danger. One night, as rain drizzled down, he pulled a tarpaulin over his body for shelter. 'I woke suddenly because I heard something creeping towards me,' Nginwa said. 'I realised that the groundsheet was being lifted up. I was still lying flat on the ground, and there right next to me, were a lion's jaws coming for me.' It was, in fact, not only one lion—but seven. 'I didn't move,' Nginwa said. 'Its whiskers were right by my face. But my rifle was right alongside me, so I was able to pull the trigger.' As the lion lunged for his neck, Ngwina fired to scare the lion off. The bullet went right through the lion's mouth.

If suspected poachers were spotted, the information was radioed into Lewa. It was long before the days of internet maps, so both Lewa and the rangers on patrol had made a strip of photographs stuck together of the panoramic view from their hideout. Grids were drawn over the top, so that the rangers could explain in which square they saw a fire. It was an easy visual reference so headquarters could plot what the rangers saw on a map. Sometimes, government rangers were called in to make an arrest—but the critical part of the operation was to gather intelligence. By keeping concealed, they built up a picture of the poachers. 'We tracked the poachers everywhere they went,' Nginwa said. 'So we worked out who they were and identified the suspects.' When men were found from the community, then they could be approached.

Often, there was not enough evidence that would stand up in court, especially if they were not caught red-handed. However, the fact that Nginwa and his teams could confront them with exact details and dates of their poaching, where they had moved and what they had killed, meant that they knew they were being watched. That was enough to change some. They were the frontline gunmen taking the risks, not the gang leaders who took the majority of the profit. 'We'd go and talk to them, and explain what we had seen,' Nginwa said. 'If they were willing to stop poaching, we would try and recruit them ourselves—sometimes we'd even ask them to become a ranger and help us.'

The reformed poachers provided key information on the crime networks that took the tusks away. Gradually, poaching decreased. 'If we hadn't done our work, it would have all been over,' he said, slapping his hands together, a crack like a gunshot. 'Every elephant would have been killed.'

* * *

The communities slowly understood that the rangers posed no threat to their land, and some saw the value in the anti-poaching work. The elders, bit by bit, softened their attitude. Nearly a year after Ian and Kinyanjui first approached them and were rejected, the elders called them to return.

'They came back and said, yes, we are ready,' Ian said. 'So we started building a little team of community rangers.' A dozen men were recruited. Each was given a radio, and a solar panel to charge it. 'They were not given guns,' Ian said. 'We started building up knowledge of the country. It created an energy within the community too, because they saw the impact of what we were doing.'

Community pressure was a far more effective way to influence behaviour and stop poaching than any warning from a far-away police officer. Heavy-handed arrests by government rangers risked turning the local poachers into Robin Hood outlaws, romanticising them as robbers who duped a hard-hearted government of its wildlife so that they could feed their families. Instead, the community scouts worked by talking to them to win them over. They helped show them they were being exploited by the organised gangs—that they were destroying the wildlife of their community while the dealers were the ones reaping the rewards.

Still, it was far from straightforward. As the community rangers became organised, Ian went to the Kenya Wildlife Service to ask for support. 'We wanted to formalise it, so we went to the government,' Ian said. It sparked a furious reaction. Leakey was dead set against it. 'He said "no way is a white farmer going to run a security operation in northern Kenya",' Ian said. 'He just refused.'

Quietly, the operations continued. 'We carried on paying the rangers, and they sent us news on their radios,' Ian said. 'For five years, all we did was to work out exactly what was going on.'

* * *

To start with, Ian and Kinyanjui just wanted to stop elephants being wiped out. Their goal was to stem the worst of the bloodshed. Yet, just as the efforts to capture the last of the rhinos had become a catalyst for wider change, so the work to rescue elephants would lead to something far bigger. They wanted to focus efforts away from guarding individual animals of a single species, to instead protecting their entire habitat.

'Guarding elephants wasn't enough,' said Kinyanjui. 'I knew that we could do more. So I told Ian, come with me back to my home in Il Ngwesi. I told him to explain to the people there what we have done in Lewa. If people could see the benefit they could get from wildlife, then all the community would want to take part.' So Il Ngwesi was where they headed next.

6

THE LAND OF GOOD BLESSING
(HOW THE FIRST CONSERVANCY BEGAN)

The ways of life had slowly changed. In the high and cool Mukogodo forests above Il Ngwesi, the last hunters and gatherers now also herded goat and cattle, and lived in tin-roof homes not caves. But they still had their hives of honey hidden in the interwoven juniper and wild olives of the forest. The hives were kept in round and hollowed logs carved from aromatic camphor wood, and hoisted high into the forks of trees, growing long wisps of old man's beard lichen that waved in the breeze. The honey combs dripped dark and thick as treacle, tasting of the acacia's bright blossom from the plains below.

The trees were precious. People protected them, because they were fundamental to their livelihoods. There were sacred sites in the forest, trees with spreading branches so wide they felt like a cathedral. Offerings of honey, blood and milk were poured onto their roots. It was a sign of renewal, because eventually the gifts fed blossoms for the bees and green leaves of growth.

Some looked down on their foraging life as outdated in the modern world. Critics saw a people who, because they had few possessions and lived off the land, were somehow simple, with no control over their environment. The truth was the opposite. They were highly adaptive—and knew and controlled every footstep. When there were not animals to hunt, there were roots and tubers to dig up—or stores of honey in the beehives. It was a means of living sustainably alongside nature that had been tried and tested for the greater part of human history.

It was an egalitarian way of life, but the land was strictly managed and divided. There were no fences, but the boundaries were known, with each area set aside for different groups within the community. The people did not have individual land titles; rather they knew which piece of land was controlled by which person. When someone strayed onto hills where other groups usually hunted, then, like a business card, they dropped pencil sized sticks carved with a unique branding, so that those who found their tracks knew who they were, and that they meant no harm.

The Maasai had learned lessons from the original hunters and gatherers in the forests, a people called the Yiaku. Over the years, they had become assimilated with the Maasai. There were only half a dozen people left who could still speak the vanishing Yiaku language fluently, but the elders still handed down the stories from the past. In their tales, there were lessons.

One story told of how a hungry man went out to gather honey. When he returned, feasting on the sweetness, friends passed by and asked for some to share. But the man refused, keeping the honey for himself alone. He said that he had done the work to get it, and that there was not enough for everyone if he shared. 'To each, their own,' he said in a muffled voice, his mouth stuffed full.

So his friends left to find their own. They opened an enormous hive, harvesting the most delicious honey, and filling their containers to the top. It took them time, so that when they made it back, it was much later. The first man was now hungry, and he asked to share. There was plenty to go around, but the others were still cross. 'To each, their own,' they told the man, in between sticky bites, repeating his words back to him in irony. They shared it with each other around the fire. As he watched the others eat, the man realised that if he had offered the first honeycomb to start with, all would now be eating together.

It is easy to share with others when there is plenty; but one must also share with others what little there is in the lean times too. In a community, all must look after the other. It was a parable that children were told sitting around the fire at night—as they shared chunks of dripping honeycomb. Cooperation matters.[1] The view of their society from outside, however, could be very different.

* * *

'Picture a pasture open to all,' wrote Garrett Hardin in 1965, in one of most cited and best known essays on the environment ever written. 'Each herdsman will try to keep as many cattle as possible on the commons… Ruin is the destination toward which all men rush, each pursuing his own best interest in a society that believes in the freedom of the commons.'[2] Hardin's 'tragedy of the commons' theory has become the cliché to explain the inevitable over exploitation of the land open to all—and a metaphor for natural resources in general. In other words, we, as selfish humans, grab all we can before another takes it. There is one fault in the theory, however. It's wrong; the commons aren't free.

What Hardin described was 'open access' land, not shared land. 'Common property', like the lands of northern Kenya, does not mean anyone can take what they want. Rather, it is pooled by the community who live there, and they have their strictly agreed rules of management. They develop checks and balances against individuals in a system to negotiate use of scarce resources. They may not be laws set down on paper, but if you're doubtful, try walking onto Maasai land and claiming the land as yours. You will not be facing a single angry owner—but the entire community.

Hardin, writing far away as a University of California professor in the wealthy winelands of Santa Barbara, failed to account for crucial community self-regulation. It is not the only provocative theory by Hardin. He has been much praised by white nationalists for his argument of 'lifeboat ethics'; the case against helping the poor, arguing that given finite global resources and exponential population growth, those struggling should be left to die.[3]

Hardin's theory was challenged. Evolution of a species is driven by selfish genes; but evolution of social systems depended on succeeding as a group. 'The central role of trust is essential to think through how people cope with dilemmas,' Elinor Ostrom said, as she won a Nobel Prize in 2009 for economics. Her field studies showed that communities can forge a different future through teamwork without the formal regulation of the state. For it to work, there were fundamental requirements, Ostrom argued. Those included having clearly defined boundaries, so that people identified as part of a specific community, and that they—and non-members—knew the limits of their territory. It also had to have a collective decision-making organisation to decide its own affairs, including to punish those who broke the rules it set down, and to manage relations with outsiders.

'It was long unanimously held among economists that natural resources that were collectively used by their users would be over-exploited and destroyed in the long-term,' the Nobel Foundation said, as Ostrom was awarded the prize. 'Ostrom disproved this idea... She showed that when natural resources are jointly used by their users, in time, rules are established for how these are to be cared for and used in a way that is both economically and ecologically sustainable.'[4]

Such matters are not the stuff of isolated academic debate. There was no question that the land was becoming degraded. The challenges of the rapidly changing world, from heating global temperatures to growing populations, put ever more pressure on the land. Yet if you followed the path of Hardin's thinking, the whole system is rotten; the only choices of action are to protect the land by imposing outside regulations—or push out the people who live there. However, if you ask the people who live on commons land how their system works, then Hardin's ideas appear nonsensical. In that case, their answer was to strengthen the community's management of the land. Traditional systems of self-governance needed a new framework to be effective.

Ian and Kinyanjui wanted to use conservation to make that change.

* * *

Conservation, however, was controversial. For many in northern Kenya, it was just another word for stealing land. The organised conservation they knew had been a coercive ideology about shutting them out with guns and government orders. 'Fortress conservation,' some called it. Many feared the same enclosures were coming to their land.

Those peoples who lived by cattle herding were not opposed to conservation; a duty of care of the land was embedded into their fundamental way of life and culture. The Maasai, for example, used the word *erematare*, or a stewardship and care over common resources. It is a term denoting holistic well-being without direct translation, an interconnected vison of land, livestock, wildlife and people.[5] But it was how that conservation was carried out that mattered.

The Maasai had lost their land before. The stories of how the British got the Maasai to press their thumbs to paper in 1911, and then evicted them at gunpoint, were handed down from the old to the young. The Maasai were moved to crowded 'Native Reserves'. When the land became overgrazed, settlers said that was a sign that traditional herding methods were destructive—and used that to grab more land. At Kenya's independence, the structure of power altered in name, but the status quo remained. Ranches exchanged hands, but new Kenyan owners snapped them up. The grazing lands of the Maasai were gone.[6] The hard consequences of the deal were still felt daily.

Outsiders might see conservation as something benign, about protecting wild animals and the natural world. Conservation, however, is always about land—and land is always political. All too often it is rooted in a long and dark chronicle of loss. A short history explains why many viewed conservation with such alarm.

* * *

Under colonial rule, wildlife was treated as a resource, as a political and economic commodity.[7] Wild animals faced a new threat; after diseases such as rinderpest and then largescale hunting, followed the new demands of an industrialising and interconnected world with rapidly growing populations. From the 1940s onwards, there was a push for intensive agriculture to feed troops in World War Two. 'It was considered to be in the country's interests to destroy everything on four legs, and there were no rules,' wrote Noel Simon, a founder of the conservation body, the East African Wildlife Society.

Staggering expanses of open grazing were cleared of animals and turned into commercial fields of corn. One Scotsman, the aptly named John Hunter, slaughtered a thousand rhinos in thirteen months.[8] 'Amateur hunters sallied forth each morning, their pockets filled with ammunition, and returned in the evening having exhausted it all,' Simon added. 'Horsemen rode down the herds, shooting at anything within range and, after dark, spotlights were again brought into use. The carcasses were far too numerous to move, so were merely left where they fell, and the hyenas, bloated to capacity, were unable to compete with the carrion.'[9]

Kenya's population grew from an estimated 2.5 million people in 1925 to 3.5 million by 1940. By independence in 1963, it totalled over 8 million people. It continued to grow at a breakneck speed, more than quintupling in the half century that followed, becoming one of Africa's most populous nations. The people needed land and food. 'Where a few years before the plains had been white with zebra and Thomson's gazelles, and *kongoni* (hartebeest antelope) had roamed at will, there were now acres of crops rippling in the breeze,' Simon added. 'Progress has used her scythe with devastating effect.'

So talk grew of creating protected areas. For colonial officers, it was new ground. Britain had yet to create national parks of its own. The closest thing had been royal hunting reserves, as told in the tales of the English outlaw and deer poacher Robin Hood in Sherwood Forest. But they could look to more modern examples, in the creation of the USA's first parks, Yellowstone and Yosemite, in the late nineteenth century. There, an outsider's 'ideal' of pristine wilderness was forged by forcing the original inhabitants out. In Kenya, a game reserve was first proposed in 1897, the 'Kenia Game Reserve', across large parts of the south. It was formalised in 1906 as the 'Southern Game Reserve', but remained largely a park on paper, with nothing on the ground.[10]

After World War Two, people were sick of destruction. To trigger a reaction, one of the leading British campaigners calling for national parks, Meryvn Cowie, wrote to a Nairobi newspaper pretending to be a farmer wanting all wild animals killed to allow for more crops. It sparked anger. In the backlash, 'Nairobi National Park' was created in 1946, on the very edge of the capital. The letter writer, Cowie, became its first director.[11]

In Kenya, Nairobi National Park was the first, but several others followed. As the end of empire approached, the colonial authorities rushed to parcel off more land, such as the famous Maasai Mara reserve in 1961. They feared the new leaders would not set aside land for wildlife. Since the land was taken in the name of the Queen, some called the parks dismissively in Swahili, *shamba la bibi*, 'the woman's farm', and the wildlife that roamed on it, *ng'ombe wa serikali*, 'government cattle.'

The fears were unfounded. In fact, there were eventually four times as many parks as there had been at independence, covering nearly a tenth of the country. Where they worked, the parks would become vital reserves protecting wild animals.

The creation of Kenya's national park system by colonial authorities preceded those declared back home in Britain by several years, where the first national park was declared in 1951, in England's Peak District. Britain's National Parks, set up to 'conserve and enhance the natural beauty, wildlife and cultural heritage' of the land, would soon stretch across enormous areas—totaling some nine percent of England, seven percent of Scotland and nearly twenty percent of Wales. Yet much remained in private hands, and the protected zones crucially included the farmers who still worked the land. 'Not ours—but ours to look after,' the park authorities say, who work to 'foster the economic and social well-being of local communities within the national park.'[12]

In Kenya, the concept of protected areas became something different. On maps, the constructed parks were marked as a wilderness for wild animals alone. The herders, once an integral part of the environment who had evolved a way of life alongside the wild animals, were now seen as an invading threat.

Another alien concept was brought in too. All wildlife was declared to be the direct property of the government. In the early days, that meant if you wanted to kill wildlife, you had to buy government hunting permits. Nearly all the professional hunting guides and their wealthy shooting clients were white. The people whose land it was, who had lived alongside the animals for generations, were outlaws if they speared an antelope for the pot. 'Black Poachers, White Hunters,' one writer described the hypocrisy.[13] The double standards enraged people.

Even after Kenya outlawed all hunting in 1977, the same mentality lived on. Herders largely lived outside the tax system, but with mass tourism taking off as long-distance flights became cheaper, the national parks became a key revenue earner for the treasury.[14] Yet the tourism lodges were rarely owned by the people whose land it was, and so critics said those who benefited most from wildlife conservation were those with a stake in tourism.

Those who faced the daily challenge of living alongside lions might get menial jobs in hotels. They watched the wild animals enjoy the water and grazing where they had once taken their camels and cattle to drink. Even the money taken in park fees by the government didn't help wildlife. Much was simply stolen by corrupt officials in the big cities, and little filtered back down through the provisions of government services such as schools or health clinics. One report calculated that, in 1988, just one percent of tourism earnings taken by the government were ploughed back into conservation, park infrastructure or anti-poaching rangers. For many, wildlife was seen only as a cost and a threat. It alienated the people who mattered the most.[15]

When Ian appealed to the elders with a model of conservation hoping to involve the community, he represented everything they had learned not to trust. He was an ex-hunter, and a farmer from a settler family. Ian knew he was not going to persuade people with a simple quick speech. He was pragmatic. He had the patience to sit and listen, and return to answer questions time after time. History lay heavy on his shoulders, but he could not change the past. History, however, is also made up of individual stories of those who carve new routes different from the old. Ian took one key choice that did lie in his hands.

* * *

Ian had long since left cattle ranching behind him, but the heart of a farmer always remains tied to the land. He realised, however, that Lewa would do better out of private hands. The ownership of the ranch was shared between Ian, his younger brother Will and older sister Sue—who all had children of their own. If Lewa was split, that could cut the land the wild animals needed to roam. 'If the core ownership was divided, that was a threat to Lewa,' Ian said. 'We agreed to put Lewa into an organisation to take it beyond us.' After more than seventy years as private land owned by the Craig family, in 1995, the old cattle ranch became a charitable organisation focused on conservation.

The shift in land status was crucial. Bit by bit, swathes of land were sold, bought with funds raised from donors. It was purchased at half its assessed market value, then placed into a non-profit trust. After running costs, its income would be spent funding schools and clinics in the community. Those funds supported the people who faced the risks of living alongside an elephant or a hungry lion.

'Everything was growing,' Ian said. 'It was not just about saving rhinos; we realised that it was more about people, and politics and all the dynamics around conservation, than a single species.' It was named the Lewa Wildlife Conservancy.

It introduced a new word, a *'conservancy'*, that became so important to northern Kenya. The word comes from the Latin *servare*, to save or guard. 'We chose the name "conservancy" because it seemed to encapsulate what we were doing,' said Ian. 'Later, we'd struggle at times, because donors would say 'we don't support conservation of wild animals, our funds are for people.' We'd have to explain that a conservancy means far more than the protection of animals alone, but by then, the word had stuck, it had entered the language. People knew that a conservancy brought people together, it brought security, and it brought organisation. So the term "conservancy" remained.'

* * *

With Lewa now dedicated to conservation, Ian poured efforts into persuading Il Ngwesi to follow a similar path. 'The economy of Lewa had transformed with the shift to conservation,' Ian said. 'So we thought; why couldn't the model work in Il Ngwesi too?' Of course, it would be different from Lewa, because the land was owned by everyone who lived there. But the model could be adjusted. Ian proposed the people create their own version fine-tuned for them, in which all who lived on the land got a say in the running—and a share in the benefits. It would be a *'community conservancy.'*

The plan was not about recreating a wilderness by using force and pushing people off the land. It was the opposite—the much harder, and much more important challenge: of protecting the land on which people live, by finding ways to return to a more peaceful coexistence with nature.

It was true that creating a conservancy in Il Ngwesi would be a huge boost to Lewa. Increasing the land where the wildlife could roam strengthened the health of the animal populations overall. It also would form another ring of security around the rhinos. But Ian had a greater vision that went far beyond Lewa and Il Ngwesi. He wanted to reconnect much larger units of land all across northern Kenya, so that wildlife could move as it had always done in the past. In many places, the migration routes were effectively closed, because wildlife had learned from experience that large areas were too dangerous for them. They stayed hidden in small corners where they felt safe. So while people feared conservation was a ploy to fence off land and then evict them, the intention was the reverse. It was to open the land up, so wildlife was able to pass from one place to another. 'What was missing was the coordination to bring the communities together at scale,' Ian said. 'We wanted to work with them to do that.'

Wider ideas about conservation were changing. The new head of the government's KWS wildlife service, David Western, was a scientist who had spent two decades studying the relationship between herders, elephants and savannah grasslands. He wanted to know what people thought about wildlife, and in 1995 carried out a nationwide survey.

'Kenyans were finally having a say, and the message was blunt,' Western said. '"Either KWS will remove its animals from non-park areas, or we'll destroy them. Make them useful to us, however, and we'll protect them." With over three-quarters of Kenya's wildlife living outside parks, that was no idle threat.' Western pushed KWS to work beyond national parks and into community lands.

'It brought in a complete change of events,' Ian said. 'The government got behind it, and that was the trigger. With that, we could raise the money from donors to kick-start it all.'

Ian's ideas had once been dismissed. Now they fitted neatly in with national plans.

* * *

The core function of national parks is to protect wildlife; the focus of conservancies is people. Conservancies are about protecting the rights of the people who live in the community. While donor support was key as investment to get the conservancies set up and running, conservancies were not a charity. Instead, conservation facilitated a restructuring of the economy using wildlife as a tool for

15. An elephant carcass, with tusks cut out. Kenya's elephants have suffered waves of hunting and poaching. © Ian Craig

16. Kinyanjui Lesderia, who comes from the Il Ngwesi people, meaning the 'People of the Wildlife'. © Peter Martell

17. Ian Craig, a cattle-rancher turned conservationist, is the third generation of his family to live on Lewa. © David Chancellor

18. Ian Craig flies along the Ewaso Nyiro river. © Pete McBride

19. A herder scoops up water from a riverbed in Kalepo Conservancy. © David Chancellor

20. Losupat Lemacheria speared his first rhino in the 1960s, before switching to an AK-47 to kill elephants. He regrets his actions. © Peter Martell

21. Tom Lalampaa, NRT's chief executive officer, grew up in a herding family. He has an MBA and won awards, including from Stanford University. © Pete McBride

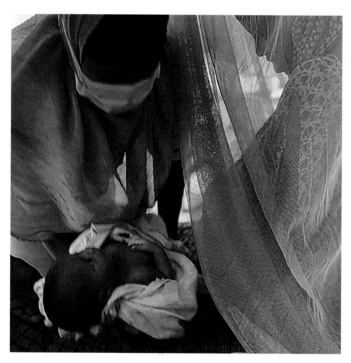

22. A medical officer examines a newborn child at a conservancy-supported clinic in Biliqo Bulesa. © David Chancellor

23. Pauline Longojine, from Sera Conservancy, speaks during a peace meeting. © NRT

24. Josephine Ekiru brings communities together for talks: here she leads a meeting between the Turkana, Somali and Borana, alongside government officials and police officers. © NRT

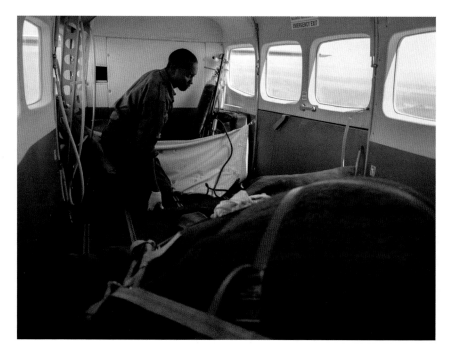

25. Wildlife veterinarian Mathew Mutinda checks the breathing rate of an orphaned baby elephant being flown to get help. © David Chancellor

26. Samburu morans dance on top of the sacred mountain of Ololokwe. © David Chancellor

27. A young black rhino in Sera Conservancy where, just decades before, all the rhinos had been killed. © Pete McBride

28. Rangers take an orphaned elephant after rescuing it from a well to the community-run Reteti sanctuary. © NRT

29. Dancing at a peace meeting organised by a community conservancy. At its simplest, a conservancy is effectively a local council. © Pete McBride

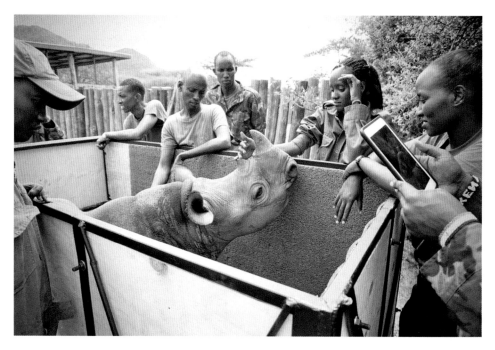

30. Keepers say goodbye to the rhino Lojipu as he begins his return to the wild. © Peter Martell

change. Support the people, and they will look after the wildlife as their own resource. That, at least, is the theory.

The Il Ngwesi community members were split. When the idea was proposed by Ian and Kinyanjui, some thought the plan was a good one. The financial opportunity was a big attraction. 'We liked that the money from tourism would help education,' said Bernadetta Kinyaga, a young mother. 'The profits would go to bursaries for school fees.'

But others were opposed. 'I was leading a group of young men who were totally against the idea,' said Jonathan Kipkorir. 'Ian was a white man, and I went to school and I learned that white men are the ones who had colonised the country. Tourism was not a Maasai way of life; people were worried it would damage our culture.' Several men from Il Ngwesi worked as rangers at Lewa, so they had seen how the land had changed, and what was possible. Yet it was a different matter when conservation was proposed on their own land. 'We were going to be the first to do this in a community,' Jonathan said. 'So we were not able to look elsewhere as to how it all worked.'

Ian sat down with the elders, time after time. But more importantly, he came with Kinyanjui, and he was a man they knew. 'I explained: the land would always remain theirs,' Kinyanjui said. 'No one was coming to take that away.' Kinyanjui pointed out how the Il Ngwesi were a people with a tradition of living off wildlife. The conservancy was a way to do that in the modern age. Still, people were unsure. They needed a proof of concept—so Ian and Kinyanjui organised a trip. First, they travelled with elders to see Lewa, and then secondly, to areas bordering the famous Maasai Mara, where making money from tourism was far more established.

The first time, three elders went. But on their return, people were unconvinced by what they had described. Some said their stories were make-believe tales of old men. So Ian and Kinyanjui organised a bus trip for more than fifty people, including men and women, old and young. They saw how Maasai herded cattle alongside wild animals, and tolerated the losses from lions because the money earned through the visitors who came to see them acted as compensation. On their return, they could now picture how a conservancy might work on their land. Look after elephants as they did their cattle, they reported to those at home, and the wildlife would pay a dividend through tourism.

Yet even the most enthusiastic worried it would not work. So they took Ian to meet a man they knew could hold him to account.

* * *

Francis Ole Kaparo had grown up cattle herding in the Mukogodo reserve. Born under colonial rule, a decade before independence, he would likely have stayed as a cattle-herder—had he not been rounded up by the police. A school had opened, the first in the area, but no one wanted to go. So officers were sent to grab the first forty boys they could. While his friends became *morans*, the Maasai warriors with spears, Francis sat in front of a blackboard with chalk.

'We were taken, more or less under arrest, to the unknown, to that which was called "school,"' Francis said. 'I was the first from my community to go. When I came back from school, I would join my friends herding the cattle. So for nine months of the year I was studying, and then for the three months, I was back. I was a part-time moran.' Of the boys taken to primary school, Francis was the only one to progress to the next level. 'It was the beginning of a lot of firsts,' he said. 'I was the first to go to secondary school, and the first to go to university, and then the first at law school.'

Education set him on a very different path, but Francis did not forget his roots. As a lawyer he worked as an advocate in the high court in Nairobi, but he regularly came north to defend his old friends on charges of cattle rustling. 'I did a lot of pro bono defence,' he said. 'Cattle rustling was not a good thing, but a lot of them were accused of stealing cows when they were actually innocent.'

In time, he would represent his community as a member of parliament. Then he went on to be elected by his peers to become one of Kenya's longest ever serving parliamentary Speakers, leading the National Assembly for 15 years. But beneath his Speaker's robe and horsehair wig, the old herder remained. At one point, when the government cracked down as pastoralists moved their livestock onto private ranches during drought, Francis took the side of the pastoralists. In a furious speech, he threatened to resign from parliament if the government didn't stop harassing herders and start helping them instead.[16] There could hardly have been a more powerful man to oversee the plans.

'I had known those from Il Ngwesi for many years, because we were morans together,' he said. 'The community had told Ian; if you want to sell this idea to us, go and tell it to me.' So Ian, alongside the delegation from Il Ngwesi, arrived at Francis' house. 'We all gathered under the tree at my home, for that is where all Maasai decisions have always been made,' Francis said. 'The elders would not have come such a long distance if they were not suspicious. I was to be a pair of borrowed eyes to watch what these strangers were up to.'

Francis and Kinyanjui were similar in age and knew each other, but Ian was a stranger to him. They explained to Francis their ideas. 'I listened: this was about strengthening the community's control over their land,' Francis said. 'Here was a proposal that could help the people profit from the wildlife through the economic benefit that tourism could bring.'

In the often devious world of Kenyan politics, Francis had learned to judge a person's character and sense the intentions behind the rhetoric. In Ian, he found a man who, like himself, had also stepped between worlds. 'I saw he was a deep thinker, and that he had a real vision seeing far ahead,' Francis said. 'I saw a man of integrity who had the strength to weather the storms—which was needed, because there would be tough times ahead.'

He told the Il Ngwesi elders that, if they went ahead with the project, he would back them. 'Yes, it was a journey to the unknown, and failure was a huge possibility,' he said. 'But we knew we had to do something. We had a very quarrelsome society at that time. Cattle rustling was at its height with many people losing their lives. If it wasn't to be us, who would do it?'

The elders came together to discuss what was needed. Livestock herders rarely have a hierarchical system of organised authority with a single leader. Instead, they make communal decisions in a democratic rule—for the old men at least—by mutual agreement. The problem was that the lack of formal structured rule had become a weakness. Bureaucrats in government offices had little time for long meetings under the shade of trees where all must have their say. They wanted swift answers from one person they could hold to account. The ways of community rule developed over generations needed an update. 'We made sure it was not taking land away,' said elder James Kinyaga. 'We realised we would be stronger than we had been for a long time, because we had a system in place. The young men were fighting, and this could offer a different future.'

Eventually, in 1995, at a meeting of around 500 members of Il Ngwesi, people agreed to the plan. As one community, they set down their joint ownership over the shared rangelands. They designated a collective zone to protect their rights, and guard their most precious resource—the land. It formalised the traditional management rules with the structure of a local committee. They elected a board of a dozen members, with elections set every two years. It provided a mechanism: legally, to give it formal status, and financially, through which it could get support. The 'People of the Wildlife' had chosen a new route.

* * *

In the simplest of terms, what they did sounds straightforward; they created a local council. Formalising age-old but unwritten rules of land management created a clear leadership structure with an elected board. It was a decision-making institution to manage the resources of a fixed area of land. What made it different, however, was that it was not just another layer of wasteful bureaucracy imposed by faraway external forces people did not trust. It was representative government rooted in the most local of levels—and was accountable to them. The conservancy structure gave it legal status, and a system of contact and an address. Bank accounts could be opened, with financial statements and traceable records. That opened doors for international donors to support the work.

A dozen men were recruited as rangers. They made sure community rules were followed, including a ban on the killing of wildlife and the regulating of tree cutting, and helped retrieve cattle when raiders attacked. In time, rangers received government training to become police reservists with the power of arrest, and equipped with rifles.

They also helped manage where the goats grazed. The land was in a poor state. There was growing pressure on the land, with more people, and more livestock. Herders still moved with their animals, but people were increasingly living settled lives. Some areas were grazed harder than others. Never giving grass a rest meant it was nibbled so short that the roots shrivelled and died. When the storms came with roaring rains, rather than the precious water being sucked up by the plants, the floods washed the topsoil away. In its place, woody bush too hard for cattle to eat grew up. Elephants loved that bush, but they had been chased away. The conservancy meant the community could map out blocks of land for cattle grazing zones, rotating where the livestock ate. That gave the grass time to recover.

Three-quarters of Il Ngwesi's 34 sq miles, or 90 km sq, was set aside for conservation, divided into two parts. The first was a relatively small and central core of 2 sq miles, or 5 km sq. That was set aside for wild animals alone, to let them return in peace. The second area surrounding it was a buffer zone of 23 sq miles, or 60 km sq. In that section, herders could bring their livestock only during the dry season. It was a store of grass when grazing elsewhere was gone. It was not an alien idea; prime grazing close to water had often been deliberately left by herders so that, during the dry season, calves and sick animals could stay close to the well.[17]

The wildlife had been badly hit by the poachers. With the rangers in place to provide security, key animals were brought from Lewa. They were enough to establish a starter population that could breed and boost their numbers: buffalo, waterbuck, giraffe and more. Lewa now had enough rhinos that a pair were brought into a small, fenced sanctuary. This meant the conservancy could attract tourists keen to see the 'Big Five' animals—lion, leopard, elephant, buffalo and rhino. They were the animals that hunters once wanted to kill, that had since become a must-see tourist list to shoot with a camera. As for elephants, the herds soon returned when they found they were left in peace on the land, the health of which rebounded. Within five years, scientists counted over twice as many trees and grass species inside Il Ngwesi compared to outside it. 'A conservancy sounds like we are guarding animals,' said James Kinyaga. 'Well, we are—but what we are doing is much more than the protection of animals alone.'

The conservancy needed funds to make change—and one of the first practical steps was to develop a tourist lodge. The community had seen how they worked in the Maasai Mara. Once visitors started coming, then the community would see the financial benefits from wildlife. In 1996, money came from two very different sources: from KWS, and from private donors—including New York fashion designer Liz Claiborne, then the largest women's clothing manufacturer in the US. She and her husband Art had fallen in love with East Africa's wildlife while on safari. 'The survival of these animals was deeply intertwined with that of local people,' they said.

The hotel was a Swiss Family Robinson fantasy, with rope bridges and open-sided rooms. Half a dozen luxury rooms were built in separate thatch-roof huts on stilts circled around a high hilltop. Beds were on wheels, so you could push them out to sleep under the shimmering bowl of stars, and wake to the roar of lions from underneath warm blankets. It was built overlooking a waterhole where the elephants came to drink, with water piped from natural springs high up in the hills to a pool, so that the animals gathered below the breakfast table. It was hidden in the trees, constructed from dead wood found in the forests around. If you walked just a few minutes into the bush, the red-earth adobe walls blended in so well only the sharpest eyes could spot it.

The lodge was owned and operated entirely by the community; 60 percent was used to cover the lodge's operational costs, while the remaining 40 percent of profit was reinvested into community development projects chosen by the board. Setting up the lodge was a challenge. It was very far from mains electric power, so water heating and lights relied on solar panels, while the road to get to it involved crossing rivers alongside herds of elephant. All the employees had, just months before, known only cattle herding. Visitors, however, expected top-end fresh food and silver service staff. One of the first to be recruited to help in the lodge—and become the manager—was the young firebrand leader Kipkorir. 'I changed my mind,' he said. 'I saw the money that it brought into the community. The tourists still came even when the drought was hard and the cattle were suffering.'

Within a year, by 1997, it was winning top international awards for luxury lodges and sustainable tourism development. For visitors, the lodge offered something different: a stay in beautiful scenery with dramatic wildlife—but also a unique connection with the people who lived there. It became a flagship for others thinking about establishing a conservancy to follow. 'It was critical, because it was a test case,' said David Western. 'We could assure other communities: look at Il Ngwesi—it's not going to become a national park; it would remain your land, your tourism operations, your own scouts. It was a small seed of what would in time become a far wider movement for community-based conservation.'

* * *

The news travelled fast. As Il Ngwesi began their conservancy, another group in the forested mountains to the north said they were interested too. It was the area where the community ranger team set up by Kinyanjui and Ian had been operating for five years.

The community set up a conservancy across 325 sq miles, or 850 km sq. They chose the name 'Namunyak.' In Samburu, it means 'the Land of Good Blessing.'

Making lasting improvements in community conservation takes enormous time, and the differences can often be hard to appreciate at first. But Ian had seen how the creation of the lodge at Il Ngwesi had been a rapid and visible sign of investment to people. He was determined to replicate the lodge's success. Setting up a tourism venture in Namunyak, however, was even more of a challenge. In 1997, Ian called on old friend, Piers Bastard, who guided safaris far off the beaten track.

'Ian had got a bit stuck,' Piers said. 'He'd promised people that if they conserved wildlife, firstly they would get security, and secondly that would bring in income for them. So, the problem was: how do you persuade tourists to come?'

Piers had already been instrumental in providing assistance to Il Ngwesi. At the beginning, the community had needed advice on what foreign tourists would expect. Piers, and his wife Hilary, had brought the first guests to Il Ngwesi to get the lodge's operations off the ground. 'Then Ian called bursting with enthusiasm about the most amazing place,' said Piers. 'He insisted that he was going to pick us up and take us.' For Ian, that meant squeezing into his tiny two-seater plane, with Hilary sitting on Piers' lap. As the high peaks reared up, cloaked in forest and mist, Ian bounced down to land on a dry riverbed in Namunyak.

'We were blown away by the beauty of the place,' said Piers. 'But the wildlife had been hammered so hard there was nearly nothing left.' All of the rhinos had been shot, and most of the elephants too. Populations of zebras, large antelopes and giraffes had all been decimated for bush meat. 'Northern Kenya had a bandit problem, it was very inaccessible, and there was poaching,' Piers said. 'But we could see that it was extraordinary wildlife country; there's water, vegetation and mountains. If you just gave it the assistance it needed, it would all come back.'

It was not an obvious business proposition, but Ian had learned in his talks to the elders at Il Ngwesi how he could win people over bit by bit. Piers got the same treatment. 'Taking the first step was hard to do,' said Piers. 'But Ian wouldn't give up. So we went back up by road.' Piers and Hilary drove deep into the bush, setting up a base camp to scout for locations. They saw only the sparse tracks of antelope—yet something about the landscape drew them back. 'We walked and walked,' Piers said. 'And then walked some more.' Piers and Ian had similar outlooks—and a vision for the potential that northern Kenya's beauty offered. Decades after Kenya's independence, the divide between rich and poor remained extreme. Descendants of colonial settlers were all too aware of the privileges that they had inherited, and from where their fortune had come from. 'We were third generation Kenyans,' Piers said. 'It was a chance for us to do something that mattered, and to give back to the communities.'

For the Bastards, they also wanted a place where their top-paying guests could experience the wildlife with a sense of exclusivity, an echo of romantic stories of safari sleeping under canvas. 'High end tourists didn't want to be with dozens of minibuses all around one lion,' Piers said.

A few months later, they flew over the hills in a helicopter, swooping down into a valley called Sarara. 'The meeting place', it means in Samburu. As they curled around the mountain ridges, they saw a wide rock perched high on the hillside. 'We headed straight for it, and landed just beyond,' Piers said. 'We scrambled through the bushes, and came out on this amazing flat rock with a view looking north across the valley. We said, "this is it."'

In late 1997, they set up an initial simple six-tent camp, paying rent to the conservancy for its use. All they saw were the rabbit-sized dik-dik antelope, and a fleeting kudu, with fantastical twisting horns. 'For the first two years, we looked at dik-dik, we counted dik-dik, we examined dik-dik droppings,' Piers said. 'But the guests loved it. They understood that what we were doing was trying to make a change. They saw that their visit itself was part of the solution by providing income for community, and so was contributing to saving wildlife.'

Visitors were offered something different. They would not encounter the same dense concentrations of animals one could see in the famous parks. But walking on foot led by a guide from the community was an experience far more valuable. It gave an insight into how they lived off the land, and coexisted alongside wildlife. For those coming from cities divorced from the natural world, it offered an extraordinary lesson with a much more powerful legacy.

Eventually, the tents were replaced with luxury cottages built from natural materials from the forest, and then, deeper into the valley, a tree-house camp from a *Lord of the Rings* elven dream. Piers, a successful businessman, handed over ownership of the infrastructure to the community, with each tourist paying the conservancy a fee for their time.

Just as had happened in Lewa, the wildlife returned. Animals found the valley was safe, and after decades away, they came back to make it their home. 'It took us a couple of years to start seeing elephant,' Piers said. 'We'd see their tracks when they had passed through, then slowly some bulls became resident. After that, word spread pretty quickly, and a lot more bulls started to come. Then it was three or four years before females would pass through, and five years before they became resident too.'

Yet as security improved in Namunyak, and the income to the conservancy started to improve lives, it put the situation outside in stark contrast. To the east, in the hot thorn forests of Sera, was a very troubled land indeed.

7

THE BATTLE OF THE BARREN RIVER
(HOW TO STOP A WAR)

The gunmen came in the quietest hours of the night. The camels had ceased complaining and the cows stopped lowing, and all had settled down inside their thorn fence enclosures. The three families, in homesteads of clustered huts, were deeply asleep too. There were about fifty people in total, ranging from elderly grandparents to the littlest of babies.

So no one saw the gunmen slip silently around their homes in the darkness. Even the usually watchful dogs didn't bark. The raiders had chosen a thin new moon, when the sky was at its darkest. It meant that even had a guard been awake, he would have had a hard time spotting them as they sneaked up in the shadows along the dry riverbed. The men fanned out, each group coming from a different direction, and lining up to shoot. They had strict orders; no one pulled a trigger until all were in position. Then their leader fired his signal shot.

Muzzle flashes from over a hundred men firing battle rifles followed, lighting up the gloom with terrifying thunder. They were not firing at the enclosures of camel, cattle and goats. They didn't want to kill the animals. After all, they were what they had come to steal. Instead, the bandits aimed their guns towards the round huts where the children were screaming. The thin walls of the huts were only plastic sheeting and cloth stretched over a frame of saplings. They offered no protection against the bullets slicing through. Moments later, the men moved in, firing as they ran towards the livestock pens, ripping open the gates and letting the animals go.

When the families staggered out, husbands grabbing their guns to shoot, their children wailing in the arms of their mothers, the zipping bullets kept flying.

The raiders worked quickly, rounding up the animals and driving them off. Others kept on firing into the houses at the dazed people. When the livestock were gone, the last gunmen pulled back too, melting away into the darkness. The mothers were weeping, but after the frightening echo of the gunshots, even that seemed quiet in comparison. Seven people had been murdered. One of them was a toddler.

* * *

That attack was in 2000. Today, half an hour's walk outside Sere Lepi, a trading centre with a small clinic and clusters of brick houses, it is an unremarkable stretch of land. A couple of new tin-roof homes have been built, but there is no sign to mark the killings. It had been a terrible attack, but such raids were common. They were rarely marked, apart from the piled stones of the graves of the dead, and they soon merge back into the ground as just one more mound of rocks in the dust. Low, scrubby acacia trees moved softly in a sauna-heat wind. But the memories remain.

'The bullets even flew into town,' said Lenadokie Leterewa, a wiry man slender as a spear but strong as iron, wearing a thick beaded bracelet of orange and black on his wrist, marking him as a Samburu. 'They stole almost all the animals. It was everything the people had.'

Lenadokie had been woken at his nearby home by the gunshots. Like most cattle herders, he had his own gun. The AK-47 was the usual weapon of choice, but Lenadokie favoured an M16 assault rifle, the sort US soldiers had first used in Vietnam. He grabbed that and ran towards the shooting. He had sprinted with others as fast as he could, thorns ripping at the flowing wraps of cloth they wore around their waists. By the time they reached the site of the attack and helped the survivors, the gunmen had already gone back into the bush.

From the early 1990s, the violence of cattle and camel raids had escalated out of control. In the new conservancies of Il Ngwesi and

Namunyak, security was improving, with the rangers providing a force to quell battles. But to the east, an area divided between several different ethnic groups, the violence had grown ever more deadly. Systems of traditional authority had been badly shaken, undermined by the sudden lethal power the deluge of cheap automatic weapons had given the young men. Violence had escalated into horrifying levels of warfare. For the hungry and angry, the power of the gun seemed to offer a quick fix solution—except that everyone had the same idea. Northern Kenya slid in a slow descent towards chaos.

Desperate families had therefore moved together closer towards town. In Samburu, the town of Sere Lepi means 'the barren river.' The land here is harsh. Even when there is rain and the river fills with a flash flood, the water rapidly drains away into the sand, so that deep wells yield little water. Where the families had set up home was not a good place to stay for long. People came in close to town for the security they thought it offered. Living together gave them a sense of safety. There was a police post in town, and they thought that being near that would protect them. They were wrong.

'I'd seen such attacks before,' Lenadokie said. 'But never as close to town as this. They fired towards the police station to stop them coming. People were shocked that even here it was not safe.'

* * *

Cattle rustling sounds almost quaint. It had been a traditional activity to restock animals after drought, or to enable young men to get enough cows to pay the bride price to marry, but it rarely involved death. In the old days, young ladies used to stand in a circle and sing about the daring of the men who shouldered their spears to carry out cattle raids. The women would leap up, bouncing rolls of beads around their necks, encouraging the warriors to attack again. 'We proved we were men by stealing cows and camels,' Lenadokie said. 'When I was a young man, I was the best at it. The women sang about me.'

Yet times had changed. These were no longer battles about impressing a girl with stories of derring-do. The days of raids with spears had passed, and the time had come when cattle clashes involved automatic rifles. Three cows would get you an AK-47, and five cows would buy a more powerful G3 rifle, the type used by Kenya's police and army. Six would buy an M16, the gun that Lenadokie liked. You could soon pay off the gun's price-tag with a cattle raid. The guns were illegal, but all too easy to find. Police had shut down one gun shop so big it was dubbed an 'arms supermarket', but the trade continued in pop-up sales out of the back of trucks.[1]

The rifles were specifically designed for efficient mass killing on the battlefield of modern war. They rattled off an entire magazine in a mere matter of seconds. It meant that what in the past would have remained a short skirmish with spears, or the killing with the odd shot from a slow loading rifle, could now all too soon spiral into a battle far more deadly. Dozens could be killed in the clashes, and each death required a response from the grieving community. When one group were attacked, they set out in anger to avenge their loss. But often they did not know exactly who had carried out the killings. They focused their retribution not on the specific individuals responsible, but on the communities that they came from—and so a new village would be dragged into the fight through blood.

* * *

Such battles are often dismissed by outsiders—foreign correspondents included—as 'tribal' clashes, as if no further explanation is necessary. People pointed to the long histories that described it as a wild land full of fighting since time immemorial. Yet blaming 'tribalism' suggests it is an age-old, fundamentally unsolvable, war. It is not only simplistic, but dangerous too. When battles are said to be rooted in the very identity of a people, then there can seem to be little hope for any solution—nor incentive for anyone to try to find one. It meant the government could largely ignore the clashes. After all, for officials, if violence was the normal state of affairs, it was simpler not to have to bother to do much to stop it.

The image that the term 'tribe' conjures up—of an unchanged society frozen in time and untouched by the outside world—was far from reality. Traditions were at the core of the identity of the communities, but they were as much moulded and manipulated by current politics and policies, money and modern technology, as were those living in the crowded high-rise heart of the city.

The truth was, of course, that when people gather guns to protect themselves, it is not because they are inherently violent. It is because the institutions of government have failed. When you can't trust a security force to protect you, you have to look to your own. In need, we fall back on those we can trust and know best. People must rely on those closest to them; first their family and neighbours, then a wider community based on language, life and shared culture.

Those who live around Sere Lepi come mainly from the Samburu people, and earn their living herding livestock. So did their neighbours: the Rendille people to the north, and to the east, the Borana and the Somali. The different groups led similar lives and faced the same daily challenges. Everybody had also stolen cows from each other: the Samburu from the Borana, the Borana from the Rendille, the Rendille from the Somali. The Somali hit back just as hard. Now they had become ferocious enemies. The violence was on a scale that, if the gunmen had had a political agenda, they'd have been labelled rebels and the conflict called a guerrilla war.

Yet the young men were not fighting because their neighbours were unacceptably different. When the two sides met, they often found that beneath their flowing wraps, beads or feather headdresses, their proud identifying cultural symbols, they had far more in common than they had differences. They were not fighting because of ideology or religion. Indeed, most were remarkably tolerant of different beliefs; some were Christian, others Muslim, and many merged those faiths with ancient gods and spirits.

Instead, they fought because they were young men who had been side-lined from economic and political opportunities. They saw no future. They fought because they were angry and frustrated. In that tit-for-tat succession of revenge, people soon forgot what started the violence in the first place. Security and opportunities were needed to offer them a different path.

* * *

Camels and goats are important, but most beloved of all are cows. They are a sign of wealth, and a source of pride. They are their entire fortune, and a status symbol. Losing animals is like someone stealing from a bank account: 'live-stock', literally, stocks and shares that are alive. 'Cattle are everything to us,' said Lenadokie, whose name is rooted in the Samburu word for brown-headed cow, a reflection of the importance of the animals to society. 'If you lose your animals, what have you got left to live on? Who are the Samburu? We are the land, the cattle—because if they go, we are nothing.' He quoted a proverb. 'He who is not treading on cow dung is not alive,' he said. Because the communities were so dependent on their animals, the shocks of drought were felt much more immediately. There was no buffer between the fate of the livestock and the people. In drought, when all were struggling and rushed to sell what animals they had, market prices collapsed.

The heating world had made those problems worse, with the rains more erratic, and the storms heavier but shorter. The lands were growing drier, and the vital showers seemed ever more unpredictable. Growing populations meant more livestock, adding pressure to the grazing lands. Cattle need water, at the barest minimum, every two days—and water in these arid lands is a precious resource. In the hot months, when the wells dried up, tempers were high and patience was worn thin with hunger. Simple arguments over who should water their animals first could soon turn violent.

* * *

It was the job of the police to stop the battles, but no one relied on them. Few wanted to risk their lives for what, in the eyes of many leaders in Nairobi, was just a faraway place of trouble. Kenya's police officers are usually sent to serve away from their homes. It is intended to make the officers impartial, but the lack of local experience and languages also hampered efforts. Officers focused on the day-to-day tasks around their isolated stations. Many already felt that being sent to the north was a punishment posting. They waited to serve out their time before they could transfer to a safer part of the country. Officers were few, and a solitary man could do little against the gunmen anyway.

It didn't help that the police were chronically underfunded, often ill equipped and paid late. With little oversight, corruption was rife. When an emergency call came, the cash for fuel for the police truck was often missing. There were always honest and hard-working individuals in the police who did their best, but the institution as a whole struggled to cope.

THE BATTLE OF THE BARREN RIVER

The government recruited volunteer policemen from the local area who could defend their community. On paper, their role was to protect communities where the regular police were not present. But checks and balances were few. Many were not paid even a basic wage—and handing out guns but not a salary is a shortcut to trouble. Once guns were distributed, they were hard to recall. Some reservists were the very bandits they were meant to arrest.[2]

When things escalated, politicians demanded action, and the army was sent in to quell violence. But they came in with all guns blazing, including, at times, firing from helicopter gunships. They could put a stop to fighting as the bandits fled to the hills, but in the long run, it only made the situation worse. Herders reported that when some officers came to recover stolen livestock, they couldn't tell one cow from another. Instead, they rounded up animals from across the wider community that the raiders had come from. Sometimes, what was confiscated exceeded what was originally taken—and the officers made a profit selling the surplus.[3] For many, the police were seen as part of the problem. Communities feared the security forces almost as much as their rivals.

* * *

As Lenadokie ran towards the shooting, he already knew where the attackers had come from. Often raiders planned their attack for the cold hour just before dawn. It meant that they could carry out the raid and make their escape as the sun came up. But since these raiders had come from far, they had launched their attack in the middle of the night. They knew the raid was to be a big one, and they wanted to get far away before the police could organise themselves and give chase. It gave the raiders the head-start they needed to get home with their plunder.

It was still dark when Lenadokie reached the site of the massacre. The attackers had gone, but the tracks were clear. This time, it was gunmen from the Borana who had carried out the raid, coming from three days hard walk through the dry bush to the east. The Borana men had banded together into a raiding group to avenge an attack on their villages by the Samburu weeks before. Lenadokie and his comrades didn't hesitate to begin pursuit.

'We started the chase straight away,' he said. 'We knew they were headed east.' He pointed towards the dry bushlands running to the horizon. A shimmering heat rose up from scorching rocks. 'They had taken so many animals, it was easy to follow their tracks,' he said. 'So we ran after them to get the animals back.'

By dawn, the men were already far into the bush. 'We ran all day,' said Lenadokie. 'When the police ran out of water they gave up, and said they had gone far enough. But still we kept going.' The Samburu group slowly narrowed the gap. The Borana were slower, since they had to also keep their stolen livestock moving—hundreds of cows, camels and goats. Then the Borana split forces, meaning that the Samburu had to work out which tracks to follow. They were worried that a herder could hang back to ambush them, firing safe from a rocky outcrop to hold them up while their friends escaped.

But the Samburu teams had an advantage. Sere Lepi sits on the edge of Namunyak conservancy. Rangers from there joined the chase. Their support was welcomed, but most importantly, they had radios. With those, they could communicate with their base, and coordinate with each other. They had another tool that gave them an edge too. Crucially, they could also talk with an airplane tracking from above.

The rangers in Namunyak had called up Lewa, informing the teams there of the attack. At first light, Ian Craig clambered into his little airplane, firing up the engine at dawn and taking off north-east towards the route the raiders were taking. Ian is a police reservist himself. The Super Cub, with a 150-horsepower engine in a metal frame covered in fabric, could swoop down low over the bush to spot from close up. It was about as close as it got to being a bird.

Low flying was risky, although old pilots said that the plane's cloth fuselage meant there was a better chance the bullets sailed on through rather than splintering metal sheets into deadly shrapnel. They weren't joking. Ian's plane, painted bright yellow and with a black lightning bolt along its length, had been shot at several times over the years. When shots were fired, puffs of gun smoke some- times showed where the attacker was hiding. Ian just had to hope the bullets didn't hit the engine, or himself.

Ian acted as the eyes in the air, radioing what he could see back down to the rangers on the ground. It meant the men on foot could keep on the chase. They were no longer blindly charging into the bush, but had advance warning if an ambush had been laid for them. 'At times, we also wanted to rest,' Lenadokie said. 'But then the rangers would tell us that they were just ahead, that we had almost caught up with them. It kept us going. If we hadn't known we were so close, we would have stopped too, and then they would have escaped.' Eventually, the Borana were too tired to continue. 'When they crossed a dry river, they hid on the far bank,' Lendakokie said. 'They waited to kill us.'

The men had run more than a marathon in blazing heat across the roughest of rocky terrains without water. It had also been a race in what was, in effect, a war zone where they were at risk of being shot at any time. Yet only then did they begin the battle to get the animals back. Lying down on the sloping hills either side of a thin riverbed, the men opened fire.

'We fought for two hours,' he said. 'Firing at each other from the trees on each side.' Bullets pinged off rocks. Both sides were pinned down, with each side hiding out of sight. Exhausted, hungry, intensely thirsty, the Borana let most of the animals go. It was their way to get a safe route out. They knew the Samburu would rush to collect them. As the Samburu went to round up the animals, the Borana escaped. 'We got many of the animals back,' Lenadokie said. 'But no one was celebrating, because of all the people killed.'

* * *

What stuck in Lenadokie's mind was the advantage that the organisation of the rangers from Namunyak had made. It was no sophisticated military operation, just a dozen men with radios to coordinate, and the tiny spotter plane piloted by Ian, circling overhead, observing from the skies. But it had made every difference. The Borana had learned a lesson that cattle raids were now not without risk. 'The rangers helped us carry on,' Lenadokie said. 'Without that support, we would never have got the animals back.'

The attack made Ian think too. As long as the fighting and feuds continued, nothing could be done. Without security, conservation and wildlife protection efforts were pointless. Ian had seen how the recruitment of small teams of community rangers in Il Ngwesi and

Namunyak had been the catalyst for a whole raft of improvements. Peace was the fundamental pre-requisite for a broad range of connected changes. Violence had stopped everything, from economic growth, to education and wider development—conditions that only made the likelihood of more conflict worse. The cycle had to be broken.

So Ian and Kinyanjui went to the elders in Sere Lepi, and asked what could be done. What had shocked them most was that the attack on the town had been a complete surprise. So they suggested sending a team of scouts who could act as an early warning system, to alert the community of an impending raid. In 2001, a test team of six men were chosen by the elders. With funding from Lewa and support from Ian, and linked up to the trained rangers at Namunyak, the tiny force set out. They were told to trek east towards the borders with the Borana, lands usually seen as too dangerous for herders to go with livestock. These were not wildlife rangers concentrating on protecting animals. The team was focused on a bigger, more fundamental challenge—securing peace.

Lenadokie was not in the initial force selected, but he wanted to participate. He came to the six men, and asked to work with them as a volunteer. 'If we didn't get people's cattle back, then we would only see more raids,' he said. 'If that didn't stop, we'd never have peace. Without that, things were just going to get worse. It would become hell.'

Sending six men to end a war seemed like planting just one seed in the hope of returning a forest. Yet everything has to have a beginning. Their work had a symbolic impact greater than what the men could do alone, for it was a plan that showed people did not have to surrender to the terrible status quo. It was a tiny step, and the likely chance of success was slim, but it offered a chance of change. It offered hope.

* * *

The new rangers were cattle herders used to bush life, but conditions nearly broke them. To begin with, they patrolled out east from Sere Lepi, carrying on their backs everything they needed for a two-week mission. Temperatures are blistering, and riverbeds are almost always dry. Where there is water, it is often too salty for humans to drink. Back then, there was no airstrip to land a plane big enough to carry the supplies they needed. 'We carried everything,' Lenadokie said. 'One big rucksack packed full of food.' The rations were simple: bags of maize flour they cooked into a solid cake, and tins of solid cooking fat, the best weight to energy ratio the men could get. The bush was thick, and progress was slow.

At that time, the men had the support of the community, but they were not formal rangers. They looked like the other men they were watching out for: livestock herders with an AK-47 slung over their shoulder and a tartan blanket wrapped around their back, serving as a sleeping bag and tent. Their job was to monitor movements in the bush, and watch for raiders coming to attack. 'I saw the value in what they did,' Lenadokie said. 'It was providing security for the people.'

Two days' trek east of Sere Lepi, the small force made a secret base for the operations. Lenadokie pointed to a high crag, towering over the rolling bush. There was also water nearby. Lontopi—the 'place of the spring' in Samburu—offers an observation point across the plains. Before dawn, so that their hideout would remain a secret from any passing herdsmen, they would scramble high to the top of Lontopi. From there, they radioed back reports on what they had seen.

But the men could not live on the bleak top in the baking sun. Instead, on its western flank, they found a giant rock outcrop the size of a house, and at its base, a tumbled boulder. In the narrow crack between, the men made a basic shelter inside the cramped cave. The rocks offered shade, and hid the flames of their cooking fires at night from anyone else out in the bush.

'We were based here for a year,' Lenadokie said, crouching down and picking up a fistful of the sand inside the cave, watching it trickle back to the earth though his fingers. 'We slept here and cooked here. This was our home.'

After several months working as a volunteer, Lenadokie met Ian for the first time. A rendezvous point was agreed with the rangers: a wide riverbed known as Fifty Wells. The soft dust swirls like a desert there in the dry season, but herders have dug scores of deep holes, sometimes several times deeper than a man. They are the Samburu's famous 'singing wells'. Herders climb down, scooping up the precious liquid in leather sacks, then hand them up in a chain to each other while singing. It was half a day's walk from the rangers' hideout, and far enough away to keep the ranger base a secret from anyone watching Ian's buzzing plane land.

Lenadokie was nervous at first, hanging back in the bushes when the rest of the rangers went to greet Ian as he scrambled out. In fact, he added more thoughtfully, he was downright suspicious. 'I didn't know what to think of him,' Lenadokie said. 'I wanted to know: what business was it of this man?' His biggest worry was that his prized possession, his M16 rifle, was an illegal firearm. 'I was frightened he'd just take my gun from me,' Lenadokie said. But encouraged by his comrades, he came out to meet Ian. The two men faced each other. He was even more hesitant when Ian asked to see his M16, believing his fears had been justified. 'He looked at me, and then handed me his rifle,' Lenadokie said. 'If he could give me his gun, then it was OK for me to give him mine.' The swap was just temporary, for as long as Ian was on the ground. But the exchange of weapons was a symbolic sign of good will. The first steps of trust were built.

'Everyone wanted the fighting to end, but we just didn't know what do,' Lenadokie said. 'One side would raid the other, then they would take revenge. Then here was this white man wanting to try something different. I didn't know him, and in the beginning, I didn't trust him. But he wasn't an enemy either. He was not Samburu, and not Borana, so he could be a person that could go between them. I thought, what else is there? At least give it a try; if it worked, then it was worth it.' When asked why he would take a chance on the suggestion of an outsider from his people, Lenadokie looked puzzled. 'Do you think we all did this because of one white man?' he asked. 'Of course not. We did it because it was the only way to get peace. Ian supported us, and for that I am grateful, but the risks we took were for our community, not for him.' With his comrades vouching for his determination and commitment, Lenadokie was asked to become a full member of the ranger patrol. 'I joined, because I thought, this was the only way for change,' he said. 'I wanted to help.' Yet one huge challenge remained.

* * *

Armed men could support ceasefires, but they couldn't create peace on their own; the rangers would end up only watching the violence rage around them. The key problem was that creating a ranger team from one group meant that it could easily be seen as supporting one side against the other. There was only one way to remain neutral, and that was to include members from both sides.

To end conflict requires that each side sit down and talk, but the lack of trust remained dire. There was no effective government structure for such talks. Any discussion had to rest on local leaders alone. The communities had always had ways to resolve differences by coming together, sitting under the shade of the traditional meeting place of a tree. There they could hammer out community penalties for stealing animals, injuring or killing a person, and how to calm the most hot-headed of the young men. Yet after years of violence, even trusting that the meeting was not an ambush was a big step to take. Anger was too high.

Ian, flying between the elders, took on the role of messenger. He carried notes between the rivals, the Samburu and Borana, to encourage all sides to come together. He pestered each side to meet face-to-face. In 2002, two years after the attack at Sere Lepi, the elders agreed. They settled on a site called Kom, under a wide-spreading tree at the base of a low and rocky hill. It is a desolate spot with intense heat and little water. It also had a dark reputation as a battleground where much blood had been spilled in the past. But the dry riverbed there acted as the border between the Borana and the Samburu. It was no man's land, where all would gather.

Ian was not alone. 'I asked someone I knew that people would listen to for help,' he said. He brought in the man who had supported the formation of the first community conservancy, Francis Ole Kaparo, a Maasai. 'Ian came and fetched me in his plane,' Francis said. It was very different from the luxury life of Kenya's lawmakers. Ian brought a sleeping bag, a bag of rice and a goat to roast for the Speaker of Parliament. 'We stayed on the dry riverbed for two nights talking to everyone,' said Francis, who mediated the meeting. 'We slept out under the stars.' It was far from the official duties of parliament or government, but Francis supported the meeting, because he saw no other route ahead. 'Northern Kenya was a forgotten place,' he said. 'At this point, the government was absent. You'd have been amazed at the statements that the ministers and bureaucrats were making about it. They didn't know that part of the country—and they didn't care either. Every attempt to make peace before had failed.'

But not the meeting at Kom. It was the first, fragile, step towards reconciliation. 'They all agreed they wanted the fighting to stop,' said Lenadokie, who sat and listened to the meeting. 'Then they shook hands.' The leaders were pragmatic. Words meant nothing if they were not followed by action on the ground. They therefore agreed the Borana would also send men to join the force, a dozen from each side. It was a means of sharing information between the rivals.

'Now we included men from both sides,' said Lenadokie. 'No one had a problem with each other as individuals. We had the same mission.'

* * *

The ranger team was the crucible where the rivals united. There was distrust at first, but in cooking and sharing food, and relying on each other for defence, they grew close. 'In town, we'd meet a Borana at a market, but we wouldn't spend time with them,' said Lenadokie. 'When we were out with our animals, we'd only seen each other from across a gun.' Conditions were hard, but the shared hardship made the men close. 'The Borana became my friends,' he said. 'No, more than that. They became brothers.'

Sitting out for days in the dry woodlands, they found that the similarities they shared were far more than the differences that divided them. They bonded over what might seem an unlikely thing: a little sparrow-sized bird called the honeyguide. The bird, with brown wings, white belly and pink beak, wouldn't turn heads to look at. But its scientific name, *Indicator indicator*, describes its remarkable skill—communicating directly with humans to guide them to the hives of wild honey hidden inside the trunks of trees. For the hungry rangers, out in the bush for weeks on end, the little bird showed them where to find something sweet.[4] Both the Samburu and the Borana have their own way of calling the bird: the Samburu with a whistle, and the Borana, calling through a clenched fist, or using a snail shell or palm nut.

To the bird, there was no difference between the Samburu or Borana call. It answered them either way—leading them with whistles onwards, fluttering from tree to tree, to show the humans where to go. When the humans had smoked out the bees and taken a part of the comb for their fill, they left scraps for the bird. If the honeyguide does not get its reward, the legends say, the next time it will lead people into the jaws of a lion. 'We lived alongside each other, and found the Borana are just the same as us,' Lenadokie said. 'We were not different after all.'

* * *

For six months, they acted as a border guard force, alerting each community to threats. But just as the team was beginning to work effectively together, disaster happened. The Samburu launched a revenge attack. A small army of a hundred men headed to raid the camels of the Borana. The rangers radioed reports to send warning of the attack, letting the Borana know what was coming, but the six men had no hope of stopping a force on that scale. It would have been suicide. 'Back then, we did not have the same support we have today,' Lenadokie said. 'We had orders not to engage in a group that size.' The Samburu force attacked, and were repulsed because the Borana had been forewarned—but the action of the rangers in stepping aside left people furious. They said the rangers were supportive of the Samburu.

Trust was fragile. Where violence had hardened into hatred, anger was quick to erupt. Local politicians ordered the Borana rangers to quit, and the team disbanded. The brief time of relative calm ended, and raiding resumed again with full force. For a while, they went home and laid low. But one by one, the team got back in contact. 'We had not given up,' said Lenadokie. 'We believed in what we were doing; and the men in the team had become friends. We had lived together, and fought together, side-by-side. The members of the team had no problem with each other. So to go back to Samburu fighting Borana made no sense. We were only a few men, but we had seen how things could be different.' He still wanted to try.

'I called them individually,' Lenadokie said. 'I asked them if they still wanted to continue the work.' Almost all said yes. 'We said the same: there would be no peace without change,' he said. 'Breaking up the team just put us back to the situation where we were before, and that only ended in more fighting.' So the team quietly met again, coming together in the bush to discuss what to do. 'If we had given up, after so much work, things would not be like they are today,' he said. 'They would be terrible—many more people would have died.'

So they decided to reform the team. With the support of rangers in Lewa, they agreed to continue. The area around Kom was too difficult, so they became a roving team, setting up observation points on the tops of hills, hiding out for weeks at a time. 'This time, it was a complete secret,' he said. 'Nobody could know where we were. We'd move at night, and we would sleep anywhere.' When they saw cattle raiders gathering, they'd alert the police, so people were prepared. When they saw signs of poachers, they would call Lewa to tell the government's wildlife rangers, or those from Namunyak conservancy, to thwart the gangs. The skeleton team came together to continue their purpose, with a common bond rooted in helping their community and a drive for peace.

'We were always on the move,' Lenadokie said. 'Anywhere there was trouble, we'd go.'

8

THE MOTHERS OF THE MORANS
(HOW THE CONSERVANCIES CAME TOGETHER)

While men fought, women worked. Pauline Longojine didn't have time to sit around being bitter and angry, or wanting revenge. A mother of five from the hot and dry plains around the town of Archer's Post, Pauline is a no-nonsense and direct-talking woman. What she really cared about was her community. In the early 2000s, her family were struggling. The violence of the past years had left the area in ruins.

'The times were really hard,' Pauline said. 'And everything was changing—in a bad direction. We had to do what we could, because the future did not look good. The young men saw the only thing they could do was to steal more cows.'

The cattle raids and revenge attacks rarely came close to the town, but the surrounding lands were dangerous. They were the same battlegrounds between the Borana and the Samburu, the conflict the elders had tried to resolve with the peace talks at Kom in 2002. So people moved ever nearer to the growing town of Archer's Post. They built their homesteads in family compounds, flat-roofed huts with mud and dung plastered walls. In the past, four or five families might live alongside each other, so that a settlement rarely stretched to more than a dozen buildings. A head-high fence circled each cluster of huts with thorn brush to pen the livestock in at night—and keep the lions out. Traditionally, people moved their herds every few weeks to find the best pasture. They shifted before the land became overworked. That had limited the impact on the land.

Being close to town had benefits. It meant children could more easily go to school, and be near a clinic and shops. In the past, the need for water would have kept people on the move, but deep boreholes now brought up water from far below. While animals could drink without people taking them into riskier parts, cattle became grouped in one area, which also meant that people were concentrated around resources in a way they had not been before.

The livestock ate the grass down to the bare earth. When the drought came, the grass was so weak the animals tore the roots out as they ate. When the heavy rains came, the topsoil was bare. There was nothing to protect it, so it was washed away by the storms into the Ewaso Nyiro river—literally, the 'brown water'. The torrents were murky with the best of the soil. The area of cracked earth grew larger. Trees were hacked down for firewood, for people needed something to cook on, and to build their homes. Some turned to making charcoal, chopping down swathes of woodland to burn in slow bonfires sealed under earth, which they sold by the side of the road. It stripped the land even faster.

Archer's Post still has the feel of an outpost to it. The slow rumble of buses and trucks on the highway north to Ethiopia cuts through the town. It is enough to keep one street of tin-roof shops and hustlers busy selling snacks and goods. On the weekly Saturday market, people come into town from surrounding areas, draped in colourful rolls of beads, bringing in animals to sell, and to buy or trade for salt, sugar, soap or medicine.

The young men, stuck in town, had few ways to show off their bravado. Some who could afford it bought a motorbike, cruising the streets carrying people and goods, the long red-painted hair of a young warrior flying behind at speed. They decorated their rides with flashing lights and dazzling colours. It was a poor substitute, however. Frustrated and hungry, they went out to raid cattle to earn respect, for adventure—and the livestock needed to give them status. Stealing animals was often the only way to earn the cattle for the bride payments for marriage.

If it wasn't cattle raiding, it was hunting—sometimes for food, and other times for cash. It had once been a land full of wildlife: just to the south lay the trio of connected government reserves, Samburu, Shaba and Buffalo Springs. Scenes for *Out of Africa* were shot in Shaba, and it was also the setting for *Born Free*, the story of the wild lions raised by Joy and George Adamson. Since then, the wildlife had been decimated. What little was left hid in the thickest bush. If their animals had been stolen, people needed to eat. A zebra or giraffe provided a rare feast of meat. Wildlife was a cost without a benefit. It was either dangerous like a lion and perceived as a threat, or harmless like an antelope, but perceived as eating grass the cattle could otherwise graze. In conflict, basic survival was all that mattered. No one was going to be worried about protecting wildlife when the land around was effectively one step short of a war zone.

The bigger and more valuable targets were elephants. In the spaces left by the gaps in security, there were also bloody profits to be made. For the ivory dealers, often powerful men in Nairobi, the chaos benefited them; the violence meant there were plenty of people living hand-to-mouth to kill the elephants for them. The man who pulled the trigger made enough to stave off starvation for his family for a while. But food is eaten and children grow, and he would soon be back hunting another elephant. As long as power remained concentrated in the hands of those who found profit in the disorder, breaking the cycle of revenge appeared an impossible job.

There seemed little alternative ahead. The peace talks between Samburu and Borana had stalled, and the joint ranger patrols—the men who worked alongside Lenadokie—had stopped their work in the area. 'I thought: How can we make peace?' Pauline said. 'I wanted to bring people together to talk.'

* * *

Power in society lay in the consensus rule of the old men, rather than a single chief. For groups like the Samburu, age groups are strictly defined. Boys become men only after a long ceremony, held with all teenagers of the same age, culminating in circumcision rituals. That group then graduate as morans, the warriors tasked with guarding the community—and the most colourfully dressed of all its members. A few years later, when a new batch of young men become warriors, the oldest morans shave their warrior dreadlocks and become the first rung of the elders, the men at the top with power.

In the past, respect for authority was earned through that slow progression in society, but those structures had been shaken. The young men had found a shortcut to power through the frightening authority of the gun. There were other changes too; the population was rapidly increasing, meaning a bulge of the numbers of young men far outweighed older generations. Sometimes, the young men listened, but experience comes with age—and when the old men told the warriors to put down the guns, they were ignored.

When the moran prepared to go out on a cattle raid, they would often keep their attacks secret. 'The elders are powerful, but when they tell the young men what to do, the moran can just ignore them,' Pauline said.

Yet as traditional power structures shifted, it also allowed a courageous woman to make a difference. Pauline saw that while the young morans might defy their father, even the most fearsome of warriors had a mother they couldn't ignore. 'Morans may act like little gods, but they are really just tall children,' she said. 'They can also open up and talk to someone like me. The young men can tell their mothers: "We are going to go on a raid and steal cows." They would never tell that to their fathers, but even morans find that when your mother tells you over cooking, "this or that is wrong," well, then they listen. Men can be frightened to talk of such things to other men in public, but they all know how to talk to their mother.'

Pauline believed that women had the chance to change the stalemate of conflict. It seemed unlikely; women were side-lined. They were tasked with the hardest jobs—collecting firewood and carrying water from wells, cooking and looking after the children. It left little time for anything else, but Pauline was determined. Her parents had been leaders; her father had been a powerful elder, but more importantly, her mother had also been influential in the community too. Pauline, the youngest of seven children, had gone to school. Her education had opened her mind to different ways of doing things and alternative solutions.

Looking for paid work, Pauline had begun helping with different charities delivering aid in the area, providing water, education and health services. That work took her into different communities outside the Samburu, to families from the Borana, Turkana and Rendille. It connected her to a network of mothers. It started at the market, meeting women from otherwise rival groups, and they shared their common concerns. She said she would work to persuade the men of her community that they should talk to their enemies and resolve their differences. Pauline encouraged the other mothers to do the same with their families.

Eventually, there would be bigger meetings—first of the women, but then, of all the community. She would find a goat or two—or even an expensive cow—to feed the crowd. Sharing a meal built bridges between enemies. Even the angriest men could be persuaded to attend if there was the chance of roast meat. Sometimes, finding the goats meant sacrificing one of her own flock. Once lured by the feast, it provided the forum for people to meet. 'In the past, people did not see a woman as being a leader,' she said. 'Yet women can bring people together—and making peace is about talking. That is what a leader does.'

If the men could sit and share roast meat, they could talk out their differences and stop another round of senseless battle. 'The young men saw that this mother was going into her own pocket to buy a cow to make peace, and they respected that,' she said. 'Peace is costly, and sometimes to begin with the men reject it, but if you get people to talk, then you have the chance of stopping the fight.' But Pauline was not the only woman trying to bring the warriors to heel.

* * *

Helen Halake was also driven by a similar desire to stop the battles. Helen comes from the Borana people of Jaldessa. They live far to the north, on the edge of the black rocks and yellow sands of the Chalbi Desert. As a mother, Helen, feared the future for her sons was one of war. Just as Pauline had organised meetings, so did Helen. Her solution was to go walking. With a few friends, she embarked on a trek across the battle lines into communities who could have been hostile. But no one feared a band of marching mothers, and so they were welcomed.

'Sometimes people just need a reason to talk, to find that the people they fear are no different from yourself,' Helen said. 'They discover they have the same problems; and rather than fight over them, they can work together to find a solution.' As she walked, she talked to everyone she met. 'For two weeks I walked, all through Rendille, Gabbra and Borana territory,' she said. 'They would offer us tea, and we shared food. Then we sang songs of peace, and we all danced.'

In the past, communities had always moved. Whole families packed up their homes onto the backs of camels. The long thin wooden ribs of the disassembled huts stood up like masts above the animals, swaying as they moved, like literal ships of the desert. But as ways of life became more settled, it was often only the men who moved their herds. That meant women from different communities did not come into contact with each other in the same manner.

Helen's walk rebuilt links across divides that had grown wide with violence. Those on the other side were no longer seen as the faceless enemy, but mothers who struggled with the same problems. Each community now could call the other, rather than resort straight away to battle. 'The women built a friendship,' she said. 'And women are important for peace—because they have a lot of influence over the men that fight.'

The pain of conflict pushed another woman into action too. Habiba Tadicha comes from the drylands of Biliqo Bulesa, the Borana lands bordering Pauline's home area. As a child, she watched her father and uncles head off to fight their Samburu neighbours, and then her brothers go too. 'The young men felt like they had nothing,' she said. 'I saw them fighting, and I knew we had to offer them something to support themselves and their families. I believe that when you have something to lose, you are more likely to see the value of peace.'

Habiba trained as a community nurse, wanting to help the people around her. 'I hated seeing what the fighting did to our community,' she said. 'The men were killed in the raids for camels and cows. Children were made into orphans. Wives became widows. Everything was stalled; we could not do any business—and the schools were empty. No teachers wanted to come to a troubled place, so our children had no one to give them an education.' Women in Borana society did not traditionally take roles of leaders, but their people had been hit badly by the conflict—and she was determined it should not continue. 'Women and children suffer the most due to war, so why should we not speak?' she said. When people like Pauline called to organise peace meetings, Habiba would help rally the Borana to join.

Change was painfully slow. Yet the talking showed that cooperation could bring better results than fighting. Step by step, people came to consider what could be done to build a lasting peace. To do that, all conversations circled back to the same fundamental issue— the land.

* * *

The names people call themselves are not just labels, but tell a story too. For the Samburu, that name is in fact what their Maasai cousins call them. Poetically, it means the 'butterfly people' on account of their colourful dress. More prosaically, some say it comes from the name for a leather satchel, a *sampurr*, which folklore said was all their ancestors carried when they had fled defeat in a battle. But the Samburu have a different name for themselves: the *Loikop*. It means 'the survivors', or 'the fierce ones'. Yet some have yet another interpretation—perhaps the most telling of all: 'the people of the land.' The land is the very definition of who the people are. Lose it, and the community collapses.

So when debate began about turning the lands northeast of Archer's Post into a conservancy, Pauline wanted to get involved. People had seen what making a conservancy in nearby Il Ngwesi and Namunyak had meant. At this point, it was bandit land; no one saw the creation of a conservancy to be about guarding an elephant or possible tourism. The conservation she cared about was the protection of her people. 'If it helped wild animals, that was good—but that was not the main reason,' Pauline said. 'We wanted a conservancy for security.'

The idea of demarcating the land for the community was not something new. From the 1970s, the government in Nairobi had pushed a community land ownership scheme. It mapped out specific communal areas for grazing as a 'group ranch.' It was partly done to encourage a more sedentary life, so people could pay tax, and children go to school. Yet while the land was formally registered, beyond approximate lines on a map gathering dust in a government office, there was nothing to implement it. It was up to the community to protect their boundaries, and the men with guns on the ground cared nothing for what a faraway government official might say.

Cynics said the government's mapping of community boundaries was to make it easier to demarcate other areas for use, from the expansion of the government parks and reserves around Samburu to a gigantic area for the military. A large zone had already been sectioned off for Kenya's army as a range for artillery and jets. The British used it too. The hot plains were a giant live-firing training ground.

So while protected areas were not something unheard of, this time the community wanted to make sure they were fully in control. Elders from two group ranches met together. The land they controlled was enormous. At nearly 200 sq miles, or 500 km sq, it was larger than all three nearby government wildlife reserves of Samburu, Buffalo Springs and Shaba combined. Herders called the land Sera—or 'stripes'—for the distinctive banded rocks on outcrops there. They agreed to create one protected area that straddled their grazing lands. Sera Wildlife Conservancy was formed in 2002.

Yet while the first focus was on security, there was also a growing sense that without wildlife, something was missing. The herders looked at where the wildlife remained and saw it was a far healthier environment. Scientists have measured how diversity creates ecological stability; during drought, the environments still rich in species were better able to cope—and recovered more swiftly—than those areas where the wild animals had been killed or had fled.[1] The herders had long known what the scientists were only just discovering; that the wild animals were not just the consequences of a healthy environment, but helped create it in the first place.

'We had to face reality with practical steps,' said Pauline. 'The reality is we have cattle, and the reality is we also share the same landscape with wildlife. Traditionally, of course, we coexisted with wildlife. Somehow we still have to coexist today, even if now there are more people, and more livestock.'

* * *

The gap between declaring an area protected and the hard sweat needed to make it an effective reality was huge. For the first few years, it was a job enough working out exactly what being a conservancy meant on the ground, and what the people it belonged to wanted to see done. 'We had to explain to people: this is not about taking land away from them,' said Pauline. 'In fact, it was the opposite. It was about making sure they protected the land.'

Building up even the most infrastructure was a huge task. Rangers had to physically set up basic bases in the bush, but they also had to be properly trained too. Simply creating rangers by handing out rifles would result in more problems than already existed. Restoring security was a long process, not something that could be done overnight. Slowly, the impact was felt, and helped win over critics. In lands far from any phone network, the rangers had radios that became a literal lifeline for the sick to call for help—with the patrol vehicles doubling up as ambulances to get them to the clinic. 'There were herders who feared the rangers and what the conservancy meant,' said Pauline. 'But when they brought their child to the health centre, they were won over.'

With security slowly improving, herders felt safer taking their livestock further into the rangelands, to find new grass. The conservancy board mapped out grazing zones, rotating them to help the land rest. It also helped fix the exact boundaries of the community's land. Since rivers often formed the border between different communities, they had also become a flashpoint between rival herders, who dug wells into the dry beds to water their cattle. By allocating specific wells to each group, it kept enemies apart. It stopped arguments from even starting.

The conservancy structure guarded the ancient ways of self-rule and living on the land with a structure for operating in modern times. The leaders still debated under the shade of a tree, but restoring authority was not just harking back to a time that was past. They now had the structures in place to work with other organisations. Where government institutions worked, they complemented those efforts. Where they did not, conservancy members could fill the gap.

* * *

The numbers of communities wanting to protect their land in a conservancy grew. From the start in 1995, a dozen followed within a decade. Some of the first were Maasai neighbours of Il Ngwesi, in the dry grazing lands of Lekurriki and Naibunga, and the cool cedar forests of the Ngare Ndare, the wooded hills above Lewa. Word spread among the Samburu surrounding Namunyak too, with the creation of the Kalama conservancy, and then West Gate. The Rendille people, seeing what the Samburu next door were doing, created the enormous Melako conservancy in 2004, across more than 400 sq miles, or 1,000 km sq.

In time, the three women who had done so much to encourage peace would be elected to head the conservancies set up in their home lands; Pauline as chair of Sera, Habiba as chair of Biliqo Bulesa, and Helen, as vice-chair of Jaldesa. For women to be chosen by the community for such a position would have been unthinkable just a few years before. Now leadership wasn't limited to the old men alone. The structure of the conservancy meant all could contribute.

* * *

With the growth in the number of conservancies, it became clear there was a need to coordinate the efforts, to establish an umbrella structure to support the work being done.

'The conservancies had made big changes,' said Francis Ole Kaparo. 'But we saw there was a need to create a much bigger legal organisation to support the efforts.' Many were distrustful. Some of the herders saw it as a new way to demarcate an area that would lead to government control of people and resources. On the other side, government officials feared it was the opposite. Since conservancies were effectively local government structures, they worried they were undermining the power of the state, and, with the training of rangers, the job of the police and army too.

'Troublemakers had an easy way to disparage it; they said we were making a militia, or that it was a crude attempt to steal the land. That story was easy to sell—but it was wrong,' Francis said. 'Everything we did, we always involved the government—the police and Kenya Wildlife Service to train the rangers, and the local administration. People said, "Why don't you just let these things stay the way they are?" But the situation was too terrible in those days to sit back and do nothing.'

The problem was also that there were those who did not want to see a change. There was big money in beef to feed urban populations growing at rapid rates. For some, the violence could be lucrative. Ruthless and determined businessmen saw opportunity in chaos. So-called cattle barons—often based in towns—created huge herds. They recruited herders to be their foot soldiers in a large-scale commercial criminal network, driving their animals onto community lands to grab the grazing, fight off their rivals with guns, and seize their cattle in huge numbers. The US Embassy in Nairobi was worried enough to cable Washington that Kenya's illegal cattle trade risked the 'same fate as Sierra Leone's diamonds or Liberia's timber' where resources fuelled conflict.[2]

Some politicians also saw change as a threat to their control. Since the conservancies were offering the chance to improve security and stem the fighting, and create structures for governance that emerged from the grassroots, they feared it could undermine their power. Kenyan politics is a cut-throat world, and for some devious leaders, power was based on uncertainty. Stirring the pot of old enmities with a fresh taste of violence was an easy way for a leader to make his relevance felt.

Politicians on the electoral stump rarely offered practical plans for the promises of what they would change once in charge. Instead, they appealed to their narrow power base who would elect them as one of their own, to protect the group from the enemy outside. It was a message that resonated in lands where the local community meant more than a national identity and sense of a greater country-wide society. At election time, politicians could mobilise the same cattle raiders to target communities seen as opposition supporters. No one was going to vote if they had fled the area. For the warriors, they either got a direct fee, or promises of being given a free hand to raid an enemy community.[3] It was poisonous politics. It hardly mattered that the promises of the politicians proved, time and time again, to be empty. People were just told that the conflict would degenerate even further without the powerful man to protect them. That fear brought people into line.

Francis had a key strength: he straddled two worlds. His day job was at the highest level of government, but his roots were in the livestock herding rangelands.

'I was the Speaker of the National Assembly, heading one arm of government, and there we were being accused of things that were anti-government,' Francis said. 'But as Speaker, and as a long-time member of parliament—I was not known for being anti-government. That meant the people listened when I explained what the conservancies were doing. I explained it was a partnership between government and people, and that it was making change for the better.' The appeal worked, but he knew what to say to officials in Nairobi that would really make a difference.

'I told them: if you don't take care of communities living with wildlife, the wildlife will not be there—and you will soon say goodbye to the tourists, and with them, goodbye to the dollars, pounds, euros and yen that they bring,' Francis said. 'The mind of officialdom wants money, but they don't care where the money comes from.'

He pushed the core principle: that communities must benefit from wildlife, not just bear the costs. In 2004, the elected leaders of nine conservancies met, and agreed they would work together. Each would remain independent, but the leaders would gather twice a year, meeting under an open-sided thatched roof hall. 'The Council of Elders', it was called. It was a formidable and powerful gathering that brought together representatives of a vast area of land.

The decisions made by the Council of Elders still had to be validated by people at home. Each leader came from communities who would bring them down to size if they claimed power as an individual. The chairs of each conservancy could stand for no more than two terms, before a new leader took the post. The Rendille and Samburu people have a saying: 'there is no small council.' In other words, all decisions must be agreed on by all.

The council created a place to hold negotiations. Neighbours who were once arch-rivals now had a meeting structure to help resolve conflict with debate, not more violence. Each could also learn from the other, and share ideas about how their conservancy was developing. With a wider network, the communities did not stand alone.

Francis was elected as the group's first chairman, and Ian voted in as the executive officer. 'We knew it was a good idea, but we were also mindful it was a Herculean task,' Francis said. 'It created the skeleton of what would later be a huge organisation.'

Beyond a few pockets that the community would decide should be set aside as fenced reserves for the most threatened wild animals—tiny in comparison to the total size—all was open to grazing for the livestock on which most depended for income.

As for a name, the conservancies covered such diverse lands and so many different peoples it was hard to find something shared with all. Yet all had one thing in common: the areas encompassed open country of wild grass and bush—or rangelands. They chose the name, the 'Northern Rangelands Trust.'

9

JOSEPHINE AND THE GUNMEN
(HOW THE MESSAGE SPREAD)

'My people have a saying: the land without wildlife is a cursed land,' Josephine Ekiru said. 'And so the places with wildlife are blessed.' Josephine comes from Nakuprat-Goto. It is a hot land of sandy plains, a day's walk through the acacia forests northeast of Isiolo, where graceful oryx antelope hide and giraffe wander. 'We use wildlife as a sign,' she said. 'When people move with their herds looking for water, one of the first things they consider is if wildlife is around. If there is, then they will decide to stay there, because they can see it is a good place.'

In the mid 2000s, Josephine's homelands were a harsh place to come from. She was born into a Turkana herding family, one of seven children. 'Life was hard growing up,' she said. 'There were very few nights that we slept at peace knowing all was well. The wild animals were killed for meat, or elephants for ivory. Our cattle were stolen—and we survived mostly on antelope meat and wild fruits. If we weren't thinking about where our next meal would come from, we were worried about attacks.' Both the Turkana and Borana competed for the same grazing. 'All we knew was fighting,' Josephine said. 'We had forgotten about living with wildlife.'

As a schoolgirl, Josephine's father married her off to an older man. 'I cried when I saw girls my age going to school—while I was at home with my husband,' she said. She had two children, before getting divorced—but she was determined to find a different future for her family. 'I wanted to somehow make peace,' she said. 'I wanted things to change.'

Josephine had seen the differences that had come from setting up conservancies: the security that came with ranger teams, the organisation from the structure of the elected board, the bursaries that enabled parents to send their children to school. Josephine's children were still little, and she was in her twenties, but she was not put off by critics who dismissed her as too young. All she had was her courage and her power of persuasion. 'I wanted our people to make a conservancy too,' Josephine said. 'But the men did not want to listen to me.'

Researchers, including from the UN Environment Programme, compared poaching levels in dozens of sites across Africa with environmental, economic, social, and political factors. After poring over reams of data, they found two key variables that influenced rates more than expected. One is corruption, as measured by the assessment rankings of the watchdog Transparency International. The other was poverty, as measured by infant mortality rates. High levels of corruption and poverty correlated strongly with high levels of poaching. In fact, poverty and corruption correlated more strongly with poaching levels than the capability of law enforcement.

It shouldn't be surprising: the fate of wildlife rests on those who live alongside them. In extreme poverty, people will do what they can to survive. But if people have a better option, they'll gladly take it. Security helped reduce poaching, but law enforcement alone cannot do the job. It is only part of a bigger picture. You cannot just recruit more police officers or rangers alone; there are other things that need to be addressed—alleviating poverty and reducing corruption. Conservation efforts are doomed if they do not tackle the needs of the community. The fate of wildlife is inextricably connected to the well-being of the people who live in the same lands. Protecting wildlife is about people. It is about human rights. It is about justice.[1]

* * *

'It began when a woman came talking of protecting wildlife by protecting the land,' said Erupe Lobuin. 'I didn't want to hear her. I wanted to kill her.' Erupe, a slender man in a dapper, green-spotted shirt, was for many years known by a simple nickname: The Bandit. Talk of conservation enraged Erupe. He had been one of the fiercest opponents of the neighbouring Shaba National Reserve. Officers there ordered herders out, to keep the grass for the elephants, buffalo and giraffe that foreign tourists paid to see. The government reserve had been declared when he was a boy, but for Erupe, time did not right a wrong. In his eyes, the land was stolen.

'We had lost land that was ours from when time began, good land for grazing of cows with fresh springs of water,' he said. 'It was taken away and made into a government reserve. If anyone had come to ask us, of course we would have said no. But we were just told not to go there anymore.' He was quiet for a moment, but his fury was clear. 'I just took my animals back into their park,' he said. 'And when the rangers came to stop me, I fought them.'

Since the wildlife was valued by the rangers, when Erupe came across animals, he killed them in revenge. Both of Erupe's hands were twisted, burned badly by tumbling into a fire as a boy, but he had earned a deadly reputation. He was a crack shot balancing the rifle on one arm, both as a cattle raider, and as an elephant hunter. Police feared him with good reason.

'The rangers came to threaten us because many elephants were being killed here, and said we had to protect them,' Erupe said. 'I told them: 'I am not a fool; why would I use my energy to guard the elephants, when it is you who get all the benefits?' They didn't feel the pain of having elephants on their land, but getting nothing back in return. I told them that this thing called conservation was not fruitful. What was in it for me?'

He had no interest in seeing the land he lived on become a wildlife conservation area. Carcasses of elephants he had killed lay scattered across Nakuprat-Goto. When researchers came to count them, Erupe was frightened their reports would bring the rangers and they would push people off the land completely. Erupe shadowed the researchers to check what they were doing.

'When people came talking about a community conservancy, I was completely against them. I thought it was another game reserve,' he said. 'We feared that. We told them; you are not taking another piece of our land.'

* * *

Josephine was not deterred. She knew many women were weary of war, of losing husbands and sons in conflict. She also had several elders in the community on her side. They too saw that a conservancy could bring order—stopping the violence from cattle raiding, the fights between Turkana and Borana, and the men killed in poaching battles.

Josephine tried to talk to everyone she met, to win them over to what she believed. So she agreed to meet half a dozen men she knew were killing elephants, who said they would at least listen to her appeal. When she arrived in a clearing in the bush to meet, they had not come to chat. They were diehard poachers who boasted of killing dozens of elephants. Now they were going to kill Josephine too.

'They pointed guns at my head, and made me kneel in the dust,' Josephine said. 'They told me: "We are going to kill you today."' She pleaded to be allowed to speak before she died. 'I knew them, and faced the same problems they had,' she said. 'I told them: even if you kill me today, you will not live in peace. You will be killed in the end too. This has to stop.'

Josephine was clear: neither killing elephant for ivory nor raiding cattle had a happy end. 'Our community will be losing on both sides, losing our resources and losing you men,' she said. 'I gave them examples of their friends who had lost their lives. What is the point in women bearing children if you are just going to go out and die? I told them, you are being used by the dealers. You are taking the risks, but they are making the money. They are the ones building the big houses, but you have no freedom and are living in the bush—and for what? And one of them said eventually: "Aah, just leave her, don't kill her."' The men let her go, as long as she swore to silence. But her message that there could be another way to live slowly sunk in.

Antony Maziwa was one of the men who had threatened to kill Josephine. 'I had lost most of my cattle in raids, and then the rest in droughts,' said Antony. 'I saw the wild animals as a way to survive. I didn't know how else to make money.' Eventually, he contacted Josephine asking for help. 'I was jobless, I had nothing,' he said. 'But I was living in the bush fearful of arrest all the time.' This time he promised not to spring an ambush when they met. He and his gang agreed to meet under an amnesty, and talk to police and government rangers. Josephine was the go-between for the two sides. They were wary. Antony and his gang said they knew where Josephine's children were—and that they would kill them if it was a trap to arrest them. The stakes could not have been higher. But the meeting passed off peacefully, and the gunmen agreed to stop hunting animals—if the rangers agreed to stop hunting them. The gang came in from the bush, and started to live by herding alone.

* * *

The dreams of Ian and Kinyanjui took on a life of their own. The ideas of using conservation to make change for the community began to spread. The seed planted by each conservancy blossomed and then scattered to neighbours all around. The success of each area provided momentum for others to follow.

In Nakuprat-Goto, the community was exhausted by the violence. Among the many requests for help, one was to the nearby Namunyak and West Gate conservancies. They asked how they had made changes for the better. The two conservancies, both members of NRT, said they would show them. Among the group chosen to go was the arch-critic Erupe. A close friend had been killed in a raid, and he no longer wanted to be on the run from the police.

One of the leaders in Namunyak was Titus Letaapo, a man who understood Erupe's worries. Like Erupe, Titus had been one of the strongest critics of the Namunyak conservancy. He had assembled young men to protest with the traditional warning call, the spiral horn of a kudu. 'I was one of the angriest, and I would blow the kudu horn to warn people that the land was being sold,' Titus said. 'But then when it became a conservancy, I saw that the land was not taken.' Titus, who later sat on the board of the conservancy, addressed the fears of Erupe. 'People in Nairobi don't take the time to come and understand what we face, and we have a small influence in national politics,' Titus said. 'But if we take it into our own hands, then we can do something. We must make decisions not just for today, but for the future. Otherwise we are just sitting with our cows.'

Erupe was won over. 'I saw that this thing called conservation was not about protecting the animals from the people, but about helping the people live with them,' he said. The conservancies were beginning to tackle the most important thing to a cattle keeper too—work to rehabilitate degraded grasslands. Invasive plant species were cut, and the brush laid down on the ground to dam the gullies. It slowed the erosion by letting the grass return. It was hard work, and took time for change, but the structure of the conservancy helped marshal the herders together to coordinate efforts.

Rotating grazing zones for the wet and dry seasons gave areas a chance to grow back. Planned grazing resulted in better grass, more wildlife and, crucially, healthier cattle. One study found by rotating grazing, within five years, wildlife populations could increase by half. During the dry season when grass was poor, cattle traditionally lost weight. However, researchers found it was lost at a far faster rate in unplanned grazing. The difference of weight loss between planned and unplanned areas could be as great as 70 percent, they measured. In some planned zones, cattle could even gain weight.[2] Erupe saw the health of the cattle. 'It showed that things could be different,' Erupe said. 'I saw what conservation could do. It made me change my mind.'

But it was not the only thing Erupe had a different opinion about. The visit had included both Borana and Turkana people. They all came from the same area, but were long-time rivals. Distrust ran deep. Even when eating a meal, they stayed separate. 'We feared them so much that we could not sleep in the same place,' Erupe said. 'We thought they would kill us, and they thought the same about me. When we walked, no one wanted to be at the front, because then you couldn't see what the men behind you were doing.'

Yet those who are old enemies at home can sometimes find things in common when away in a strange land. When their convoy of vehicles was crossing a river, one of the cars got bogged down in the mud. A flash flood from rain in the hills roared down, and the water was rising fast. Faced with a common threat, all helped together. They linked arms in a chain to get everyone to safety.

'We said: What if we had not helped each other? What if all were lost? We realised we all wanted similar things,' Erupe said. 'So when we came home, we all came back together as one. The people were shocked when they saw that.'

Boundaries of community land ownership are usually based on the territory claimed by a single group—and that can spark problems along borders. But in Nakuprat-Goto, where so many fights had been fought over rival claims to grazing, the two groups decided what worked best for them was a single unit. After much debate, the Turkana and Borana communities established a jointly protected area across both their lands, a total of 280 sq miles, or 725 km sq, calling it the Nakuprat-Goto Conservancy. Setting up a joint council helped defuse long-running anger. They formed a single ranger team.

Creating a conservancy was only the first and most basic of steps. Community conservation, when successful, could help build better relationships between people and wildlife, but it was not a silver bullet. There was plenty to go wrong—and it often did. There were still quarrels and arguments, people taking too much, and people giving too little. But the community, through its members on the conservancy board, had a way to resolve the local disputes under a process that belonged to the people.

Josephine was elected as the chair of the conservancy, defying the critics who said a woman could not take such a position over warriors. After serving her term, she began work as a 'peace coordinator' for NRT. She brings warring rivals together, spending hour after hour mediating peace meetings. She has even organised sporting events, from athletic tournaments to marathons, with spear-throwing, running and jumping events. 'When the warriors spend time with each other in sport, the myths about other communities are shattered,' she said. 'They make friendships.'

Among Antony and his poaching gang, several of the men trained to be rangers and now work for the conservancy protecting wildlife. As for Erupe, long retired from his bandit days, he was elected to the conservancy's board of elders.

'We do not want the conflict that comes from the stealing of cows,' Erupe said, as he cut up a goat roasted whole on an open fire, sharing hunks with the crowd. They had gathered for a ceremony to hand back two dozen cows, stolen two weeks earlier from the neighbouring Meru community. 'We want to give thanks to the rangers who got the cows back and ended this in peace.' A local policeman and a Meru herder, who would take the cattle back to their owners, were handed sizzling liver and choice cuts as guests of honour. 'A thief doesn't have a future,' Erupe said. 'What they take brings only pain.'

* * *

After the first nine conservancies came together in 2004 to form the Northern Rangelands Trust, work began to encourage other communities to follow. NRT provided technical advice to guide a community through the steps, as well as help to raise funding. There was a sudden explosion of interest. Each new conservancy transformed the security, politics and the economy in that area—and there was a ripple effect to bordering lands. The number of communities joining NRT grew rapidly.

Each conservancy was established with the same basic principles in common, and adapted them in a manner best suited to that community. In NRT's eyes, the more communities that wanted to establish conservancies, the better. In management-speak, it created 'synergy'. It benefited each community, but the combined impact of all the conservancies together produced a greater result than each individual area alone. In linking patchworks of people-protected lands, it provided the gigantic scale needed to enact major change across immense landscapes.

'Community conservation is most effective when it grows organically,' said Matt Rice, who became NRT's first chief operations officer. The NRT team was keen to capitalise on the momentum. 'We were purposely ambitious in trying to create a critical mass of conservancies as a strong foundation for securing serious donors,' said Matt. Within a decade of NRT's creation, the number of conservancies joining tripled to more than thirty, involving communities from over a dozen ethnic groups. In land area, NRT community conservancies stretched over 15,500 sq miles, or 40,000 km sq. They spread to roughly a tenth of all of Kenya, equivalent to the land protected as government-run parks and reserves. This was a conservation effort no longer focused on protecting individual animals in pockets of parks. It was about whole species and entire ecosystems.

For some conservancies, the value of protecting wild animals was easy to see. Communities like Kalama and West Gate, where vistas of dotted umbrella-shaped plains adjoin the government reserve of Samburu, multiplied the safe zone that wildlife could roam in. The tourist potential was obvious. The structure of a conservancy provided an ideal base to develop lodges with the community to bring in income. In such lands, it was therefore relatively straightforward to raise funds from donors.

But the structure of NRT meant that it could stretch its support to areas that, at first sight, had apparently less potential for wildlife. They were among the most marginalised of lands, with some of the poorest people. Conservation work in the past had ignored them. But developing conservation on a large scale meant that every part of the landscape could be included. Areas such as the drylands of Nakuprat-Goto did not have the same intense concentrations of wild animals as other places—but they were just as crucial. They were critical corridors for animals to move along. Elephants passed through in large numbers following the rains. Protect such lands, and the landscape was connected for wild animals. That meant the environment as a whole could flourish. It was like a jigsaw: all pieces are needed to complete it. Lose one piece, and the overall picture cannot be completed. Lose too many, and the puzzle makes no sense at all.

By showing the benefit to the wider ecosystem, donors from a traditional conservation background—those who might otherwise have only put money into the most famous parks—could be won over to help areas that until then had been ignored.

But the people-focused approach also opened up other sources of support. The conservancy offered an existing structure through which donors could channel funds. The governance structure of the conservancy enabled a raft of changes—supporting education including encouraging girls to go to school, providing clean water, improving health and supporting economic growth. They were all on the UN's 'sustainable development goals', the seventeen-point blueprint for a 'more sustainable future', to tackle poverty, inequality, climate change and environmental degradation. For those donors, that the conservancy also benefited wildlife was simply a fortunate bonus. It was a win-win situation on both sides: for those who cared about wild animals, and those who wanted to better people's lives.

In the early days, major support for NRT came from Lewa, who were on hand to provide logistical backing and practical know-how. Lewa also had a useful list of backers they persuaded to provide the seed funds to get the community conservancies up and running. 'Lewa was a key catalyst for NRT,' said Matt. 'Lewa was well resourced and could act as a facilitator, convener and supporter—helping conservancies to get through the tough issues or insecurity.'

* * *

The challenges of supporting rural development across enormous landscapes was something Matt knew well. He brought with him to NRT the knowledge of a decade working in the south-western African country of Namibia, where he had played an integral part in the early years of a conservation movement there. For Matt, who has spent his life working in conservation, the lessons of Namibia were crucial. The conservancy movements in Namibia and Kenya would develop independently, but in parallel. They would become two of Africa's most successful community conservation programmes conducted at scale, covering immense areas of each country.

In Namibia, Matt had worked with the pioneering conservationist Garth Owen-Smith. 'It seemed to me logical that the people best placed to conserve the wildlife were the local people who lived with it,' wrote Garth, who had first sat down to listen to communities in the 1980s. At that time, Namibia was fighting for independence from apartheid South Africa, and in the middle of a liberation war to overthrow white minority rule, Garth's efforts to strengthen people's land rights were revolutionary. 'He was regarded as lunatic fringe by most white conservationists,' said Margaret Jacobsohn, Garth's partner. 'People were into fortress conservation and the communities were seen as the problem—and then we came along and said "no, they're the solution."'

Garth initially developed a small community project, where a tour operator paid the community for each night that tourists stayed. In return, people became 'community game guards', appointed by local leaders. For the first time in decades, the communities on the ground felt like wild animals had direct value. Poaching rates slumped. It would be the start of something far wider.[3] After Namibia won independence in 1990, the new government supported the work. 'We were able to change government policy,' Garth said. 'Local people were given both the rights over the use of wildlife—but also the responsibility to manage it sustainably. What you own, you look after.'

There is no simple one-size-fits-all conservation model, and what works in one area doesn't necessarily work in another. Yet there are core principles that are common and can be applied to each situation. 'These are not complex or earth-shattering things,' Matt said. 'It's about governance. It's about enabling the community to manage its own resources sustainably. It's about a community being able to police itself—whether that is community game guards in Namibia, or rangers in northern Kenya.'

A conservancy provided structure, as a platform on which the community could work. It was not, however, on its own, going to do anything unless people took action. So what was critical was making sure that the conservancy became an organisation that could enact the lasting change required.

* * *

The elders of Leparua, a conservancy near Isiolo, had been shouting at each other for several minutes, each trying to solve a riddle they'd been given. The group were taking part in a training session to understand what being on the board of a conservancy meant in practice. Many of the room were grey-haired men, a mix of Maasai, Turkana, Somali and Borana people. There were jokes, but people were also serious—and no one could find a solution.

The riddle was this. An elderly man has passed away, and has left orders for his seventeen camels to be shared between his three sons. The first-born gets a half, the second gets a third, and the third-born son gets a ninth. How do you divide them?

Since none of the portions resulted in a whole animal, some said that the camels should be killed, and the meat quite literally shared out between the sons. Others said the camels should be sold at market, and the money split.

Then Fatooma Mohammed, an elder of the conservancy, offered her idea: borrow a camel. 'Add the extra camel to make the herd 18,' Fatooma said. 'Half of 18 is nine, a third of 18 is six, a ninth of 18 is two. So that makes 9 + 6 + 2 = 17. Then you can give the borrowed animal back.' The rest of the room was quiet as they pondered the solution, and did the sums themselves. Then they broke into applause.

Each conservancy is led by a democratically elected board, and run by a team recruited from the community. Often, that includes a balance of the different peoples in the area—in practical terms, sometimes mixing old enemies who had once fought each other. Most have no formal education. So NRT provides regular training, bringing in a team of experts, running dozens of courses helping the board members face the demands of the conservancy. Hundreds of the leaders have taken part. 'It provides the principles of leading and managing a team, and support for everything from financial management to fundraising,' said Heiz Wadegu, who helped run the meetings. At times, trainers divided the board into three teams, handed them a pile of children's building blocks, and gave them a challenge: to build the tallest tower they could in ten minutes. Piles of bricks soon reached up high from the floor nearly to the ceiling—and then the bricks tumbled down with a crash. As the teams raced each other to rebuild before the timer ended, with shouts of different ideas of how to structure the tower, people's competitive streaks kicked in. The men who had dominated debate found they turned to the young for help. Other wizened herders, who felt shy to talk because they'd had no formal education, displayed an impressive skill in architectural design.

Amid the laughter, the practical activities challenged their thinking, and that brought the teams together. The board included those who might otherwise have never worked together—men and women, old and young, those with education and those who had never been to school. For some of the elders, the world of donor proposals, emails, budgets and government offices was something they feared. Their authority was sometimes dismissed by the young people with formal education. But while the young who had gone to the city for their schooling and returned with exam certificates could navigate that bureaucracy, they were unsure of the decisions to be taken over the land, where authority still rested in the old ways of control. Each complemented the other's skills and experience, and the training helped them see the value in working as one. When conservancies faced debate over controversial topics, such as the mapping of grazing zones for herders, or drawing up formal boundaries using satellite mapping with neighbouring communities, the training on negotiation would be indispensable.

'A well-governed conservancy provides the institutional framework for conflict resolution, to ensure effective security, grazing and the putting in place of other programmes,' said Allan Ward, who works with Heiz, developing a programme so that those who cannot read can take part. 'But while the lessons are important, the key thing is to bring the board together as a team, expanding the confidence of the members.'

Such meetings were not just talking. Proud of his new skills—and emboldened with confidence—one elder from Shurr had gone into his local government offices. He did not back down, and demanded action. He raised enough funds to renovate schools and improve education throughout the conservancy.

* * *

For Tom Lalampaa, the conservancies gave him education—and he returned the gift. He knew as well as anyone what a herding family needed. 'Conservation is as much about development as it is protection,' said Tom, who became the first manager of the conservancy on his homeland of West Gate. 'Here in northern Kenya, we're helping give historically marginalised communities the tools they need to forge a sustainable future alongside nature.'

Tom, one of seventeen children in his typical Samburu herding family, was all set for a life looking after goats. But when government officers in the 1980s pressured parents to send at least some of their children to school, his father called Tom and his brother. 'My father told my older brother and I that one of us had to go to get an education, and one had to stay to herd the goats,' Tom said. 'My brother refused to go to school.' Because, back then, the conservancy had not begun and there was no local school, Tom was sent away to a boarding school. It put him on a very different course. When he returned in the holidays, dropped off by bus on the side of the main road, it would sometimes take a couple of days to find where his family had moved with their herds. 'I wasn't worried,' Tom said. 'We'd start walking and track them down in the end.'

Education was critical to changing so many people's lives. Tom would go on to study in Nairobi, earning a Masters in project planning and then an MBA—supported by bursaries from the community raised through the conservancy. 'The local community from the villages where I come from supported me to go through university education,' Tom said. When he had finished his studies, he returned home and was employed as West Gate manager, overseeing day-to-day operations. Later he moved to support the wider conservancy movement, and began working directly for NRT. He won a prestigious award from Stanford University for environmental global sustainability, and the Tusk Conservation Award from HRH Prince William, the Duke of Cambridge. Eventually, he became the head of NRT, as its chief executive officer.

'With NRT, we're working to transform people's lives, build peace and conserve natural resources; we provide oversight to all the community institutions, and we build their skills to strengthen them,' said Tom. 'But the idea has always been that the Northern Rangelands Trust will not be around forever—because our ultimate aim is that local communities will be strong enough to lead the process themselves.'

***

Critics said the conservancy model relied too much on outside donors. It is the constant struggle of any development project to ensure that, as quickly as possible, it would be able to stand strong if funding stopped. Each conservancy needed donor funding to get off the ground, and the funders came from all over. Some were private individuals, philanthropists keen to see their money make a visible change. Larger chunks came from foreign governments—from the US and European Union, as well as Britain, Denmark, France, Germany, Sweden and more. But support was increasingly coming from local Kenyan government too, as the regional administrations began backing conservancies. The aim was, from the very start, for a conservancy to achieve self-sufficiency, but donor money was needed to reach that.

'The conservancy model is bringing peace, it really is,' Ian said. 'And there is a hell of a lot to be said for living in peace.'

When societies slid too far into conflict, enormous sums could be spent just stemming the violence, let alone improving society. For donors, funding programmes that supported a community to improve lives—through education, health services, infrastructure, and alternative sources of income—was a much more preferable option. Nation- and society-building, as in the cases of the countries bordering northern Kenya such as Somalia and South Sudan, where millions had fled from as refugees, were eye-wateringly expensive endeavours fraught with failure. Those without hope are easy targets for further violence, radicalisation and extremism. International donors had their own agenda too. In an interconnected world, these were no longer far flung places that could be forgotten. 'The West can't afford to live with totally unstable places—and this model is definitely a stabiliser in that space,' Ian said.

Donors also saw the value in safeguarding ecosystems that went far beyond any motivation to shelter wild animals just to have a spectacular sight for tourists, but to protect the grasslands as giant carbon sinks. NRT's structure provided an easy platform for financing that allowed for the rollout of a giant grasslands soil carbon project across the vast landscape, with funders buying carbon credits. The money was used to support the conservancies to improve pastures, and so boost the removal of millions of tonnes of carbon from the atmosphere—with the extra revenue raised spent on social development projects chosen by the community.

* * *

Conservancies continued to expand, sometimes at breakneck speed. The number of conservancies mushroomed across northern Kenya under the NRT umbrella, with each inspiring others to follow. Community conservancies began in the south of the country, including on land around the world-famous Maasai Mara, and around Amboseli, in the shadow of Kilimanjaro. Within a few years, more than 150 conservancies would be formed across Kenya, on land home to more than five million people.

'Conservancies contribute directly to the conservation of wildlife, and is Kenya's best hope for securing the majority of wildlife found outside state protected areas,' said Dickson Ole Kaelo, who headed the overall body, the Kenya Wildlife Conservancies' Association. NRT was a core member. Dickson understood well the hard balance communities had in juggling demands on the land between livestock and wildlife. He grew up around the Maasai Mara, employed first as a government livestock officer, and later working in newly founded conservancies.

Each conservancy under the national association was different. In northern Kenya, the land is largely owned collectively. Elsewhere, land is owned individually—but the same idea could be applied. Around the Maasai Mara, conservancies were made up of hundreds of private landowners, who pooled their smallholder plots into one, meaning the land remained unfenced to give space for wildlife to move. The way the conservancies operated were two faces of the same coin, because the core principle remained: that conservation can only succeed with the deep involvement of the communities who own the land where the wildlife lives. 'A conservancy is a complex undertaking,' Dickson said. 'It involves balancing many differing interests—the needs of livestock, wildlife, tourism, and other land uses.'

If wildlife conservation was to work, it had to earn its keep—by generating benefits comparable to other land uses. Wildlife tourism, seen by some as a golden ticket for pastoralists to generate and control their own revenues, is hard work in a difficult market. It often fails—and when it did, critics argued conservancies only paid lip service to the community.

But it could be several years before people in a conservancy really began to see positive changes, and there were plenty of people who grew discouraged. At times NRT grew so fast, the funding needed to kickstart visible changes was delayed. In the far north, in the arid Turkana region, half a dozen new conservancies that NRT helped establish turned against the idea soon after they began. Opponents used the fact that donor money there came from a foreign oil exploration firm to claim the community organisation was somehow bought by outside forces. The oil firm was accused of 'green washing'—of supporting communities only to burnish environmental credentials—and the communities ended the conservancies shortly before any meaningful activity had begun.

A successful conservancy put the power over the land back in the hands of the community, but that was opposed by those who had previously profited from that chaos, and who saw their power now reduced. Where access to grazing and water had before been vague, now a community challenged those who came to take it without permission—and that could be a trigger point for conflict. The new system altered land and power dynamics.[4] NRT owned no land, but it was accused of buying up areas. The allegations were not true, but the confusion sparked some protests. Others feared that because creating a conservancy brings in donors, the community could, without care, become dependent on that external aid. If it was taken away, the people would then suffer. Other critics argued conservation was a cover for a 'green grab'—the mass appropriation of land for environmental ends—by powerful elites.[5]

One report from a Californian thinktank criticised the 'militarisation' of what it dubbed a 'neo-colonial approach to conservation'. The report claimed that the communities who had voted to create a conservancy and democratically elect their own boards had, in fact, done so because leaders had been 'co-opted', alleging 'tactics that include the use of fear and intimidation to silence dissent.' In a stiff rebuttal, NRT pointed out that 'community conservancies are owned and governed by communities themselves, and not by NRT', stating that claiming the NRT did so was not only untrue, but also 'undermines the enfranchisement of communities to form conservancies under the laws of Kenya.'[6]

The conservancies brought change, and for some, that set NRT up as the 'enemy.'

* * *

'Conservation interests must necessarily be treated with caution, because they are the new face of imperialism and disenfranchisement,' said Mordecai Ogada, an ecologist and one of the most vocal critics of NRT, who co-wrote *The Big Conservation Lie*, a polemical takedown of conservation efforts across Kenya.[7] Mordecai, a fierce opponent of the fence and guns of 'fortress conservation', is scornful of those who say wild animals must be protected from the people who have lived alongside them since time immemorial.

'Wildlife survived for millennia in Kenya's rangelands together with people who never earned anything from it, consumptively or otherwise,' he said. He sees in conservation an insidious way to steal land from the people who live there. 'Conservation should be something we do so that we have biodiversity, clean rivers, healthy grass-lands, and beautiful forests: if we have that, then tourists come to see it,' he added. 'But if we set aside landscapes because we want tourism, then that is wrong. Once we put tourism at the forefront, local livelihoods will always suffer. I value wildlife, but Africa is the only place in the world where the indigenous people are put behind wildlife in value.'

In Mordecai's view, and many others', the legacy of injustice of conservation under a white colonial past—of land seized, and of the creation of national parks forcing people out—is actively being con-tinued today. He despairs of the white saviour rhetoric used to raise donor funding, where the people who live with wildlife are por-trayed as the problem.

'The image of white men (they are mostly male characters) tak-ing to the wild, devoting their lives to saving wild animals, and engaging in sensually captivating adventures has forever been used to drive the point home that as the planet experiences immense destruction of species, habitats, and ecosystems, it is only white people who really care,' Mordecai wrote in his book. 'Usually, black people are featured either as cargo men, props, victims, or as hindrances to the conservation enterprise,' he added. 'In most instances, black Africans are portrayed as people who need to be sensitised, so that they can either accept or learn to love the animals that live in their midst.' Erudite and angry, Mordecai calls much of the work 'CON-servation', arguing land is being stolen from the people under the pretence of protecting wild animals. 'We are obsessed with the so-called charismatic species at the expense of looking after their habitats and the human communities,' he adds.

Others, such as Hassan Roba, who grew up in a livestock-herding family from the Borana people of Moyale, says that the age-old way of life of the pastoralist animal herders was uniquely suited to the dry open rangelands—and that any change, however well inten-tioned, heralds trouble. 'Just let them be,' Roba said, an academic who worked for several years at the Centre for Indigenous Knowledge at the National Museums of Kenya. 'There is no other alternative land use that is more viable than pastoralism, for the bulk of the rangeland cannot be used for anything else. You cannot irri-gate the desert, or plough the rangelands and turn them into crops—but you can put goats there, and within two months they graze and get fat, and then you have protein.' Roba works for the Christensen Fund, a San Francisco-based group aiming to advance the rights of indigenous peoples as 'stewards of biocultural diversity.' The very heart of community conservancies is aimed to support pastoralism, not to take away land for conservation, but Roba worries that it will change the delicate balance. 'External intervention, both developmental and conservation, is changing the dynamics,' he said. 'The real danger facing pastoralism is what we are doing to it; take land away for conservation, take land away for roads, or even creating more water points so that there will be livestock everywhere—remove what the herders need to support themselves—and we will kill it, and we will regret it when it stops.'

Yet the people working to implement community conservancies on their home lands say what they are trying to achieve is exactly what Mordecai and Hassan say should be done: to strengthen the rights of the people to manage and control their own resources.

* * *

For Dickson, from the Kenya Wildlife Conservancies Association, the community conservancies were about putting power back into the hands of the people. 'Because conservancies evolved ahead of policy and without a structured guideline, many Kenyans misunderstand them,' Dickson said. 'Some see conservancies as a way of acquiring land, others think they are new parks for wildlife that exclude people, and some perceive them as being owned by very rich people. Fundamentally, the conservancy as a concept is a democratic institution, a system to negotiate use of scarce resources among multiple users and a mechanism for securing peace in volatile landscapes.'

His message was clear: community conservation is possible, but it is also almost always a challenge. 'Be careful in raising the community's expectations,' Dickson said. 'It's important to promise less, and achieve more, because any promise you don't achieve can destroy the achievements you've made.'

It is a lesson that even apparently the most secure places ignored at their peril. On Lewa, those greedy for rhino horns had never stopped circling, probing the weakness of the security. They looked for any opportunity to strike.

10

THE RHINO IN THE SCHOOL
(HOW THE BEST SECURITY IS THE COMMUNITY)

In a dark café booth, with curtains drawn against the blazing sun outside on the bustling streets of Isiolo, Malele Abdi kept his wrap-around mirror sunglasses on. Wearing a sharp-cut blue checked suit, fake-gold watch jangling from his wrist, and pointed leather boots, it was clear the businessman had come far from his youth as a herder. 'Dealers offer money for rhino horns,' Malele said. 'And people always want money. They just have to decide if it is enough cash to be worth it.' As he spoke, he took rapid sips from a frothy *camelcino*, a camel-milk cappuccino, his head scanning each new customer coming into the café. His fingers drummed nervously on the tabletop.

Malele knew the poaching networks well—and it was a danger-ous world. A father-of-four in his forties, Malele grew up in Leparua, a land of rocky hills that runs north from the border of Lewa to the very edge of Isiolo town, an area home to at least half a dozen ethnic groups. Many lived in tin-roof villages swallowed up into the outskirts of rapidly growing Isiolo. The area included harsh urban poverty, with neither the space of rural life, nor many of the most basic services of a town. On their doorstep, however, were the rangelands where they herded their livestock—and that led directly to Lewa. They controlled a strategic access route—and for the poaching gangs, that was crucial.

For the people of Leparua, opportunities were few. For the rhino horn dealers, middlemen who came looking for those to supply them with goods, it was an easy place to exploit. The dealers did not need to work out how to get in close enough to kill a rhino.

Their target was to work out which local could do that for them. 'They would say, "help us get a horn, and we'll help you,"' Malele said. 'They'd promise us enough money to change our lives.' They hired men from Leparua to guide them to the gates of Lewa, and once the rhino was killed, to get the horn back out to Isiolo. Once in the maze of backstreets, the dealers had their network ready to get it fast away.

The dealers are not men to mess with. They profit from whatever they can, including drugs and weapons. Rhino horn was, to them, just another commodity to trade—as valuable in weight as gold. Those who try to track the gangs say that across East Africa there are only a handful of networks, with a few big and dangerous chiefs at the top. Some are linked directly to Asian criminal syndicates.[1] They have more than enough cash to ensure political protection and steer clear of justice, paying off those who look too closely at their business. Beneath them, there are the middlemen who source the tusks and horns. Often, they are local businessmen with apparently legitimate companies. That existing commercial infrastructure helps them move the illegal goods and launder money easily—and have the cash to pay off the police. To find someone to pull the actual trigger to kill the rhino was not difficult either—there were plenty of sharpshooters as guns for hire. The hardest part of the network to find was someone to give them the intelligence on the ground, and to guide the gunmen in and show them exactly where the rhinos were.

So they recruited local men like Malele. They looked for the weakest link to exploit—the men with debts to pay off, trouble at home, those that liked fancy clothes or one too many drinks, or wanted a new motorbike to impress. The dealers made the community complicit too, buying their silence with a potent mix of intimidation and money. It was like bank robbers planning a heist, and buying off the security guards not to press the alarm, telling them the money in the vaults wasn't theirs anyway. In this case, of course, the guards were those who lived nearby. Some were willing, but those reluctant buckled with threats. 'They said, "you are either with us, or against us,"' Malele said. 'I had to join.'

Poachers had eyed the rhinos inside Lewa ever since Ian and Kinyanjui had rescued the last of them from across northern Kenya.

In the late 2000s, the dealers made a move. The demand for horn abroad had risen, but that was not the critical difference. The horns could always find willing buyers in Asia who paid extortionate amounts in the sad and false belief it was a magical cure-all. What had shifted was the confidence the poachers had that they could win over the community.

So the gang leaders looked for someone on the inside, to breach the final and most important ring of security. In 2009, they found a man who knew both Lewa and the rhino better than almost anyone.

* * *

Crawling on his belly through the knee-high yellow grass, his rifle cradled between his arms, John Keleshi crept towards a black rhino. Dressed in a green jacket and with a floppy bush hat shading his face, he blended into the landscape. The rhino was at peace, apparently unworried by any threat, grazing on the shrubs where the plains of Lewa met the thicker forest that runs towards Mount Kenya. Normally, the only disturbance the animals had were the safari trucks of the tourists, who drove nearby to watch them. The animals, however, had grown up with that. Most of the time they seemed to simply ignore them.

Dusk was falling. Keleshi was invisible except for a slight rustle of grass when he moved, as if it was blown by the wind. He had first begun working for Lewa two decades before, and had risen through the ranks of the rangers, to become a rhino monitor. He had earned a reputation as a skilled tracker, dedicated to the rhinos he was paid to protect, follow and watch. He was thin and wiry, his ear ripped from an old fight, and he wore his Maasai sword, a blade as long as his forearm, strapped in a red rawhide scabbard on his belt. This time, he came not to protect   but to kill.

Behind Keleshi, two men followed, sliding through the bush close behind. They had sneaked in through the fence, through a weak spot hidden from view that Keleshi had shown them. For a while, they rested, until the sun had dipped far beneath the western hills. There was a full moon, so the rhino was still in clear sight of the three men. The moon was strong enough to cast a shadow from the rhino's great bulk. They were close enough to throw a rock and hit it.

Keleshi raised his ranger's rifle, scanning first the valley ahead of him, then squinted down the sights. The men behind him lifted their AK-47 rifles. Then Keleshi pulled the trigger, and the two men followed suit, raking the rhino with automatic gunfire.

There were screams of pain from the terrified rhino. The three men ran the short distance to the body. Blood gushed out, but the gasping rhino was still alive when they drove their long daggers hard into the rhino's face, circling the edge of the two horns, and popping them off in a matter of minutes. The horns were wrapped in a sack to stop blood dripping behind them. The rhino was still groaning as the men left. They were sprinting, but they were not too panicked. Keleshi had a radio listening to the ranger frequency, and knew they were still scrambling to respond.

They headed for the closest point of the fence. Once across, they had almost a whole night of darkness to escape. A motorbike was waiting. The horns were stuffed into a rucksack, and the bike roared off. The driver was from Leparua, and knew every twist of the thin tracks, zooming away at high speed. He headed through Leparua to Isiolo, and handed the bag to the dealer. Then it was moved on quickly, stuffed into the boot of a car heading south to Nairobi. From there, it was passed through the smuggling network. Eventually, along with other horns, it would be put onto an airplane and taken, via Ethiopia, onwards to Asia.

As for the gunmen, they split in different directions. Keleshi headed home. It was still early evening, and he needed to be seen in the village for his alibi. Several fellow rangers lived nearby his house.

By the time the response teams reached the rhino, it was still bleeding and just alive, though there was nothing that could be done to save its life. There was deep sadness. The rangers had guarded the rhino since it was a calf, and knew every aspect of its character. 'When we heard the gunshots so close by to ranger posts, we thought it was people stealing cows,' said Edward Ndiritu, a senior ranger in Lewa. 'We did not think poachers could ever come to Lewa.' They brought dogs to follow the tracks, and followed the footprints to the forest, and then to the tracks of the motorbike, but from there they were lost.

As for Keleshi, he was turning up at work once again. He had scrubbed his green uniform clean of any flecks of rhino blood, and

31. Villagers in the Sarara Valley in Namunyak dance to celebrate the morans' transition from warriors to junior elders. © David Chancellor

32. Rangers of a 'Nine' team, elite units constantly on the move, carry out training. © Peter Martell

33. A Samburu moran, or warrior. © David Chancellor

34. Morans traditionally protect the community's livestock. © David Chancellor

35. Beisa Oryx in Nakuprat-Gotu Conservancy, home to around a tenth of Kenya's population of the endangered desert antelope. Some say their dramatic double horns helped fuel medieval tales of unicorns. © Ian Craig

36. Swarms of locusts over northern Kenya, with their recent growth encouraged by changing weather patterns. © David Chancellor

37. Members of the community-run Reteti elephant sanctuary lead the young animals for a walk, with the hills of Namunyak behind. © David Chancellor

38. Mary and the orphaned Long'uro (meaning 'cut' in Samburu, after his trunk was attacked by a hyena when stuck in a well) at Reteti. © David Chancellor

39. Community members visit Reteti, which is changing the way that people relate to elephants. © Pete McBride

40. Lobik Lesasuyian and his camels, which he takes to graze in the forests where elephants also live. © Peter Martell

41. An elephant wearing a tracking collar. Mapping how the elephants move helps measure the health of the wider ecosystem. © Pete McBride

42. Zoologist David Daballen, head of field operations for Save the Elephants, holds up a tracking elephant collar. © Peter Martell

43. A hirola, the most endangered antelope in the world, is fitted with a tracking collar in Ishaqbini. © David Chancellor

polished his boots. He put on his Lewa green beret, complete with its brass cap badge—depicting a rhino's face. Then, putting on a glum face as if shocked by the killing too, he went to join the patrols looking for clues. In effect, he was searching for himself. He led his colleagues in circles. A terrible wave of rhino massacres had begun.

* * *

Nearly three decades on since the Lewa sanctuary had opened in 1983, the rhinos were flourishing, with more than fifty new births. Six white rhinos, brought in from South Africa, now lived alongside the descendants of the black rhinos that had been rescued from across northern Kenya. There were more than a hundred rhinos on the sanctuary.

After the Craig family turned the land into a conservancy in 1995, wildlife now roamed across the entirety of the old ranch. The initial fenced sanctuary inside Lewa had been doubled in size, and then, eventually a new fence was placed along the perimeter. Wild animals now had space to roam across 100 sq miles, or 250 sq km, with Lewa open to the high forests of the Ngare Ndare reserve, a community conservancy with centuries-old olive and cedar trees. An electric wire fence stretched along the boundary for 88 miles, or 142 km, but the fence was still open to the north, south and east. There were three gaps left for migrating animals to cross. Rhino were stopped from leaving by piles of loose rocks along the gaps, that they found hard to navigate with their stumpy legs. It was a wildlife fence first, and a security barrier second.

The animals seemed secure. No rhino had been killed since Lewa had been set up as a sanctuary. The idea someone could come onto the land to kill a rhino had seemed almost unthinkable. Tourism was booming, with thousands of visitors each year staying at half a dozen camps and lodges within Lewa. There was even an annual marathon, a unique endurance event running alongside lion and elephant, raising money for community projects. Yet something had gone fundamentally wrong.

* * *

The first rhino killing shocked people, but for months afterwards, all was quiet. It looked like the attack had been a one-off. Yet the message had got out; it showed people that killing a rhino on Lewa could be done. A year later, another rhino was shot dead. Then another followed, and another. The floodgates had opened. 'When people saw that it was possible, it was like a tide,' said Edward, who as a senior commander, made desperate attempts to overhaul security. The problem was that despite new rules, more patrols, more guards and more guns, the poachers still found a way inside.

It hit Lewa hard. Its founding principles had been to keep rhinos safe. If it could not do that, the conservancy would struggle to survive. Finding a solution to stopping the poaching meant understanding why the sudden surge had begun. That came down to two key questions: what had kept the rhinos safe for so long before, and what had altered so that the gunmen now felt bold enough to attack? The answer was the same—and it lay at the very heart of the model of community conservation.

* * *

'For decades it had been open season on rhino,' said Ian. 'Traders offered money for the horns, and people used every means possible to kill them; a rifle if they had one, or a spear or even poison arrows. Communities didn't care, because the rhinos didn't matter to them.' For years, those who lived next door to rhinos saw no tangible benefit from them. Rhinos were a nuisance at best, and a danger at worst. They feared their children would be trampled or gored when they took their cattle through the bush.

Years of work on Lewa meant that attitudes had slowly shifted. They had drawn visitors from afar to visit the wildlife, and through that, money went into the community. The rhinos in the sanctuary had made a visible change. 'The rhinos enabled us to raise money to invest in schools, clinics, and wells,' said Ian. 'So suddenly communities were seeing a better life through conservation. The rhinos gave Lewa the strength to paint a new canvas for conservation, one in which communities were equal partners.'

There were jobs too. People who lived directly around Lewa were employed as rangers. Most of their work was outside Lewa's boundaries. 'One big way we helped the community was to chase the cattle when raiders took them in a stock theft,' said Edward, who led long and often dangerous hunts for stolen cows. 'If you brought back a herder's cows, then they would be Lewa's biggest ever supporters—and they would help us in the future.' Sending the rangers out was the best advertisement that they could give. 'If you've got clean, smart, well-equipped men out working beyond the conservancy, it lets the community know that the rangers are on their side, and are there to help,' said Edward. 'It also shows that we're serious people not to mess with. You won't get that message out if they are just dug in, sitting at an observation post inside the fence.'

Lewa had also developed an intelligence network. Individuals worked to monitor threats to the wildlife from outside: a stranger seen asking questions, a man known to have links to poachers appearing in town flush with cash, even drunken gossip in a bar could help. But by far the best intelligence about potential poaching came from the communities themselves. 'Helping the community brings out those wanting to help for free,' said Edward. 'That's the most reliable information you can ever get.' When something seemed odd, local villagers passed the information on. Many people had family ties to a ranger, so they were known and trusted.

'Lewa went for years and years without having a single rhino poached, and that was because of the investment in the community and the investment in security,' Ian said. 'Those two things ensured that the rhino in Lewa were protected.'

Conservation is not about fences, but about people's relationship with wildlife and nature.

But the work of years can be all too quickly undone. It would be the most bitter lesson for Lewa to learn.

* * *

Lewa had also changed. No longer a private ranch, the land was held in a non-profit trust. Part of the income was ploughed back into the running of the conservancy and wildlife conservation, and the rest was put into community development programmes. In practical terms, that meant Lewa was no longer the same family-run organisation. A new management board ran operations; from the rangers and other staff, to the support given to neighbouring communities, to the needs of the wild animals. Lewa was a member of the Northern Rangelands Trust, and had acted as the catalyst for change in supporting many areas. Its operations were separate from the rest of the work in the rest of NRT, because of the history of the land ownership structure. Yet it worked on the same fundamental principle. Communities would not protect the wildlife if they didn't see it as being in their economic and cultural benefit.

Yet Lewa increasingly took a different route. One of the first shifts brought in was that everything had to pay for itself. It would shake Lewa to its core. 'The new management was focused on budgets,' said Edward, who watched with concern as the emphasis shifted from people to profit. 'The philosophy became that this was a commercial enterprise. But conservation is not a direct profit-making business. Some years there are losses too.' Business and conservation can work together; but when the pursuit of profit alone becomes the sole motivation, and the importance of the community it is based upon is pushed into second place, problems begin. Lewa would learn the hard way what had been understood by those working in the conservancies to the north. Involve communities, and conservation worked. Alienate them, and everything fell apart.

Security was a huge cost, so that was cut back to the minimum. The rangers were told to sit tight and guard their observation posts, just scanning the horizon. 'We became reactive, not proactive,' Edward said. 'We were told to wait for trouble, not to go looking for it. But waiting for an attack was never going to protect the rhinos. If a poacher gets inside, then you're too late. You've lost a rhino. You can follow up afterwards and perhaps you catch them, but the animal is still dead.'

Operations to track cattle outside the conservancy borders, or actively look for signs of poachers, were curtailed. The new management could not see the direct benefit in chasing cows; Lewa's mission was to protect rhino. 'When we were going to deploy teams to chase stolen cattle, we would be asked, how will we get that money back?' said Edward. 'So we had to stop.'

It didn't take long before the change was noticed. 'We were not helping the community in the same way, and so people were not on our side,' Edward said. 'If they heard of a poacher planning an attack, before they would give us that information. Now people said: "If Lewa does not care about us, why should we care about Lewa's rhinos?"'

The breaking-point was about grass. Lewa was now dedicated to wildlife, but protecting the land for wildlife did not come at the expense of cattle herders. Those who lived around Lewa could bring their cows onto the grazing grass. The system was carefully managed, to make sure the land was not over-grazed or the wild animals disturbed, but it had always been free. Then grazing fees were introduced.

'We were told that everything had to cover its costs,' said Edward. 'If the community wanted access to grass, then they had to bring money to pay for it.'

In terms of Lewa's operational budget, the grazing money gathered was a pittance. The levy was put in place for a principle: the idea that people value something only if they paid for it. Get a handout for free, the theory went, and it would be exploited and taken for granted. But the businesses management vision of big cities does not apply to something as fundamental as grazing. The grass came from the land and for herders was not a commercial commodity to be sold.

When the dry season came, and people needed grazing, the wealthier herders could afford the payment. So their cows got fat, and they got wealthier. But the poorer herders were shut out. 'We divided the community,' said Edward. 'And people got angry.' People began to stop seeing Lewa as a partner, and the rhinos inside were no longer seen as the wildlife that brought benefits, but as simply an animal with a walking fortune on its nose. Still, Edward, who had joined Lewa as an eighteen-year-old, never imagined someone from within the conservancy would take action against it.

'People said, it is Lewa that is dividing us and treating us badly,' said Keleshi, the old ranger, sitting on the hill outside his small farm, on the edge of a village overlooking Lewa. 'Something changed in my heart. It became dark and wrong. I had seen the rhinos as helping us. Now they were the way to get money. So I said, let's go and kill Lewa's rhino.'

* * *

Everyone, it is said, has their price. Yet while there are cases where poachers are the poorest in society tempted to kill an animal as a one-off way to change their life, Keleshi was not such a man. He was not wealthy, but he had a regular salary as good as anyone in his village, a career with prospects, and respect and authority from his position as ranger. He was driven by greed, not desperation.

When Keleshi had started work as a ranger on Lewa in 1987, he was a young Maasai warrior from Il Ngwesi, his arms wrapped in beads, and his long-locked hair smeared in the traditional red paste. For the first few years, including when he was tasked with guarding the rhinos as they were brought outside the fenced sanctuary into the wider Lewa area, he stayed in his warrior's dress. It was easier in the early days; without uniforms, the young men saw the job as just like guarding their livestock. It also helped people see the work at Lewa as not something strange, but similar to herding.

'I cared for the rhino; as monitors we followed them wherever they went, night and day,' he said. 'When they went into the forest, we followed them too. If they were sleeping when they should be feeding, we would ask, are they sick? We looked at them as we did our cows.'

So what pushed Keleshi into killing rhino is not clear. He says it was because of an argument over expense allowances from when he spent a month in Malawi, helping a national park track rhinos—but the logic makes little sense. In any matter, the trigger is not the point; what matters more is that he felt he could kill a rhino and that people around would turn a blind eye. People were not in support of poaching, but Keleshi judged they might no longer report him to the police if they suspected he was guilty. That was the tipping point for action.

Keleshi says he reached out to men he knew in Isiolo, quietly asking about rhino horn dealers. His message was passed on upwards—and eventually a dealer made contact. Keleshi is vague on the details—still scared, apparently, of the consequences. 'I knew exactly where the rhinos were,' Keleshi said. 'I wanted to get the money. That was all I could think about. I organised for them to get inside the fence, and showed them where the rhinos were. I said the only thing I would not do was shoot a ranger.'

* * *

Protecting the rhino became like a war. In 2011, a group of men spotted creeping towards the fence opened fire when rangers rushed to stop them. In the firefight, two of the gang were killed. A year later, a large group were found inside Lewa, firing on the rangers. In the messy battle in the dark, four poachers were killed. Firefights were intense and deadly.

In 2012, seven rhinos were killed on Lewa. In 2013, six were shot. Within three years, seventeen rhinos were massacred. The slaughter was not on Lewa alone—nor indeed, just in Kenya. It was a continent-wide problem driven by market forces from outside— but it was bringing Lewa to its knees.

With elephants, there was a critical price point where the cost of ivory on the black market rose so that it outweighed the risks, and poaching soared, driving chaos. A boom in an economy on the far side of the planet swiftly sent ripples of impact across the world.

Rhino horn prices fluctuated too, but they were always danger-ously valuable—and now demand was soaring even higher. The market in the mid-2000s had rapidly expanded. Traders in Vietnam fed rumours that rhino horn was a cure for cancer. They charged astronomical prices, exploiting people's desperation for a magic medicine. Yet it was a cynical marketing ploy spread through social media without any basis even in traditional remedies. The traders were well practised, adding the horn to the long list of endangered animal products for sale, often in markets crammed with live ani-mals packed in together. They were even advertised as a health elixir for hangover cures, or as an aphrodisiac for the wealthy to brag about, an old man's hope to get hard. Rhinos, once native in Vietnam, had been hunted to extinction there by 2011. Organised crime gangs looked to Africa.[2] Once the easy targets were taken, conservancies like Lewa were next on the list.

So Lewa brought in more rangers, with more guns, posted to act as soon as they heard a shot. The poachers responded by fitting silencers onto rifles. One group of poachers even stole a dart gun used by vets to knock animals unconscious—so that the rhino fell asleep in silence without a shot. The gang hacked the horns off—and the rhino later awoke, only to die slowly in agony with his face sliced in two.

Lewa used every technological advancement they could—but the poachers used them too. The rangers used thermal or infrared night-sights to spot intruders—but so did the poachers, to know where the rangers were. The poaching networks had powerful contacts able to source the most up-to-date kit. In time, police helped track phone signals to locate the gunmen, and track the associates of the gang through their calls. Yet as soon as poachers suspected that, they simply left their phones behind, taking out the sim cards before they crossed the border into the conservancy.

Security was tightened, but the Lewa teams knew something bigger was wrong. The poachers stayed one step ahead of the rangers. It did not take long for men like Edward to see that the attacks could not have taken place without inside knowledge.

* * *

All the rangers were investigated, and slowly, the net closed in on Keleshi. He lived in a village alongside several other rangers, and they noticed he had more cash to spend. He bought a motorbike, and a diesel generator for electricity. He purchased new cattle for his herd at home, then a plot of farmland. Keleshi said he had taken out bank loans, and some thought that was plausible—but when he began smoking a more expensive brand of cigarettes, suspicions grew he had money to waste. Each rhino that he gave information for and that was successfully killed netted him about half a year's salary, although that was nothing compared to the profits the dealers higher up the chain would eventually make.[3] If invested wisely, it could have made a difference, but the money was soon spent.

The signs pointing towards him mounted. There were reports he was spotted in Isiolo with two Somali men, who travelled in an expensive car. There was strange behaviour; a few days after the killing of a rhino, he was seen beside the remains of the carcass, left to be eaten by the hyena and lion. There he was seen sprinkling herbs as ritual invocations to avoid evil spirits. His movements were tracked; during some attacks, Keleshi was on leave—and so could have carried out the killing. In other attacks, he was on duty. He could not have shot the rhino in that case—but then the information he radioed in about where the gunshots were heard seemed to direct the rangers tracking the poachers in the opposite direction. It was all, however, circumstantial. For the police to act, there had to be a smoking gun.

* * *

In the end, it was the community that came together—and put a stop to it all. 'The elders called me and asked what I had been doing,' Keleshi said. 'I wasn't afraid of being killed when I was after a rhino, but I could not lie to them.' Respect of the elders is equated with respect for the Maasai god, Nkai, and to disobey them, to bring down the wrath of the divine. The elders threatened Keleshi with the one thing that terrified him: the painful and dishonourable isolation of being ostracised from the community he comes from. He had desired money to buy status in the eyes of his peers through his cattle and motorbike; but the respect he craved had turned sour. It had only brought him shame.

The elders brought in someone who, more than anyone, held power over Keleshi: a man he called his *Nkiyu*. When young men become warriors through elaborate coming-of-age ceremonies, the ties they make are unbreakable. One rite includes sacrificing a cow and feeding a chosen friend a special cut of meat—the chest of the cow, known as *nkiyu*—as a symbolic commitment to a life of sharing. The friend then takes the position of Nkiyu, a relationship like a blood-brother. It is an almost sacred position. For Keleshi to have gone against his Nkiyu would have brought down a curse upon his head. 'I had to tell the truth to him,' Keleshi said. 'So I told him everything I had done.'

The elders had to report him to the police, and he was imprisoned for two weeks. Charges, however, were eventually dropped—because Keleshi refused to confess in court. Without that, lawyers said a conviction was unlikely. So the elders struck a deal with far more symbolic power than a jail sentence: a public judgement whereby Keleshi confessed at a community meeting.

Perhaps, if he had gone to jail, he could have cast himself as the victim—but not when he was humbled in front of a huge crowd. There, the stigma stayed with him. Keleshi hung his head in shame, and admitted to killing two rhinos, and to being involved in the poaching of at least six others. The meeting was attended by the police and his former colleagues from Lewa. He handed over his ranger's rifle, and was dismissed from service. He had escaped prison, but not the condemnation of his peers.

'I cannot forget how the elders were crying and crying, asking me why I had done such a thing,' Keleshi said, his voice quiet, and his eyes downcast. 'I cannot ever get that out of my head. From that day on, I stopped completely.'

Today, he struggles to make a living from his farm and a few cattle, a man who has lost the trust of the community and the respect that he once had as a ranger. As for the money he got from killing rhino, it was mostly squandered. A large part of his herd of goats and cattle were stolen. His motorbike broke down. Keleshi was left only with his small plot of farmland. From the hilltop beside it, with sharp eyes, between the scattered clumps of whistling thorns, you can see the rhinos grazing on the grass peacefully in the distance.

Some in his village say Keleshi believes a curse will come down upon him if he sets foot on Lewa again, but the ex-ranger shook his head at that suggestion, and did not want to talk. Since his confession, he has not stepped back onto Lewa. Keleshi still seems angry, but with a sense of bitter regret at the past. Would he, if he could turn back time, do it again? His eyes narrowed, and he pulled out a cigarette. He had already half smoked it and had saved it, relighting the stub. He drew his tattered, fake leather jacket in tight around his thin shoulders from the chill wind. 'No,' he said, slowly, after some time. 'I wish now that I had not killed the rhinos.'

* * *

Stopping Keleshi slowed the poaching, but if the conditions remained, then another man would have stepped into his shoes. The dealers circled, looking for the weakest they could peel off and persuade to guide their gunmen in to find a rhino. But Lewa had learned a tough lesson—and took action. They put the needs of people at the centre of the conservancy, to show why the rhinos mattered.

For Malele Abdi, the businessman from Leparua, it also proved to be a tipping point. Poaching brought in quick cash, but the risks were high. Friends of Malele had been killed when on poaching trips. Then, in his home in the Leparua conservancy, Lewa raised donor funds through the charity Tusk Trust and renovated a school, building a dozen classrooms, a science laboratory, creating a well-stocked library, teachers' houses, a dormitory for children whose herding parents moved with the livestock, a canteen and kitchen garden, and a medical dispensary. It was a government-run school, but conditions were poor. The investment helped it provide a far higher quality of education. In the middle of the playground, the builders had used spare concrete to make a waist-high statue of a rhino.

'This school is why I stopped poaching,' said Malele Abdi, whose four children all attend, patting the rhino's head fondly as if it were real. 'Before, we didn't see value in a rhino,' Malele said. 'But then they came and rebuilt the school here, and I saw the impact that wildlife can have.' The concrete rhino provided a daily reminder of where the funds for the school rebuilding came from. The children, who incorporated it into their playground games, loved it. A year after the school was built at Leparua, the poaching of rhino on Lewa had stopped.

'The money you get from poaching will run out, and it will not give you a school for your children to get education,' Malele said. 'I tell the herders today: protect the wildlife, and it will provide for you.'

Edward Ndiritu puts that advice into practice every day. He rose through the ranks of Lewa's rangers to become head of anti-poaching operations. The teams he leads are better equipped now than ever before: thermal imaging cameras on a helicopter, specialised sniffer dogs, alert systems and satellite maps have all helped boost security, adding layer upon layer to protect the rhino. But while technology plays its part, far more critical is the investment in recruiting the right people whose heart lies truly with conservation and communities, and giving them training, skills and opportunities. In the end, the best protection was the one that money could not buy: the backing of the community. He runs operations according to a simple rule. 'Support the people that support us,' said Edward.

The other conservancies also took the message to heart. One of the most visible signs was the creation of specialised ranger teams aimed not to protect wildlife alone like guards, but focused instead on supporting the communities themselves.

11

THE NINE TEAMS
(HOW TO BUILD PEACE)

Captain Losas Lenamunyi pushed through the tangled thorns, the black curved hooks of the 'wait-a-bit' tree trying to snag his jacket like a cat's claws. Then he ran weaving past boulders and up a gravel slope in a quick, loping trot, his assault rifle seemingly light in his hands. The sun was so fierce it glared up into the eyes from glinting fragments of glass in the desert. Looking up the steep hill, the air shimmered in the heat, radiating off rocks with a temperature not far off a cooking stove.

Losas, a towering soldier with a stern face, stopped at the top of the hill, sweat leaking through the back of his dark-patterned camouflage jacket. His second name, Lenamunyi, comes from the word for rhino in Samburu—and he looked about as strong. He crouched down, resting his rifle on his knee. The 32-year-old was the commander of an elite ranger team, a rapid response unit known by its radio call sign, Nine-Four.

The seven men following him fanned out quietly in line. They did it without command; each knew exactly what to do. All were police reservists with the power to arrest and carry a rifle, and were well trained and fully equipped. What had begun with Lenadokie and the joint Samburu-Borana unit in the early days had developed into a network of specialised mobile rangers at the sharp end of building peace. They were recruited from across all the different areas they operated. It made each team a multi-ethnic unit speaking several languages, with local knowledge, contacts and cultural ties. That meant it was seen as a community patrol, not an outside military force. Many had served first as rangers in their home conservancy, and had then been hand-picked to join the team, brought together under the conservancies' umbrella body, the Northern Rangelands Trust.

These men were tasked with the hardest of jobs—making peace a reality. Their work was to prove that each conservancy was not a paper park that existed in theory, but something that had a physical impact in practice. Like Losas' 9–4 team, each were called by their radio code—from 9–0 up to 9–5. Together, they were known simply as the Nine Teams.

The scramble up the hill had been to use its height as a lookout. There had been a bandit attack on a livestock lorry just days before, in which the rangers were shot at dozens of times. Kneeling down beneath the low trees, the rangers positioned themselves to face all directions, rifles cradled in their arms. Some sipped water from tubes draped over their shoulders connected to a small bladder on their backs. Floppy bush hats shaded their faces, so even from just a few steps away, they faded invisibly into the scrub. It was a break from the speedy pace zigzagging up through the rocks, but no one was resting. Each man listened carefully for what was around.

The animals gave out their warnings. Above, on the tops of the acacia trees, a pair of white-bellied go-away birds with cockatoo hairstyles, screamed their alarm call of *g'way, g'way*, the watchmen of the wild. A pair of black and white hornbill birds with their curved orange beaks joined in too, with their strange laughing cries. Within a few minutes, a pair of knee-high dik-dik antelope pottered past, their big dark eyes staring hard. Their long snouts wrinkled at the scent of the men, making their soft whistling *dzik-dzik* warning sound to each other that gives them their name. Then they too moved on quietly. The rangers shrank into the shadows. Everything seemed peaceful, but everyone was on guard.

* * *

The Nine Teams went on constant patrol into the toughest of areas, making their presence felt. Each team deployed for a month at a time. As the number of conservancies had grown, so had the ranger teams. It created a different security dynamic—and sometimes a solution to one problem can cause another issue elsewhere. Conservancy boundaries often reflected territorial control by separate ethnic groups. A key problem was that when raiders stole livestock, they would take them from a neighbouring land. If local rangers chased the thieves, they could end up on a next door conservancy. In a worst case scenario, it could even end up starting battles between two different communities.

So the Council of Elders of NRT met to solve one of their first big challenges: how to create a security force that could work across the borders of several conservancies. The solution was to create multi-ethnic teams made up people from all across the lands they patrolled. They did not replace the community scouts of each area, but acted as an additional support. Having the rangers come from different communities was not simply an important symbolic message, that teams backed neither side. It was crucial when you were trying to stop battles along ethnic fault lines.

'We come from all over,' said Galgalo Dati, at twenty-three the youngest in the 9–4 team, from a Borana family from the northern conservancy of Jaldessa. 'That is our strength.' Just the 9–4 team alone included five different ethnic groups who could speak at least eight languages—and across all teams, there were nearly two dozen different languages spoken, crucial skills for intelligence gathering and negotiation. 'If we were not mixed from different places, then it would be very dangerous indeed,' said Lkiparia Lekango, a Rendille who grew up in a cattle-herding family in Songa, on the flanks of the mountains of Marsabit. 'They could look at us as the enemy. People would even attack. Instead, when we arrive in a community, they look at us and say "this one is our son". So then they welcome the rest of us.' Their ability to move freely into any community was far more valuable than almost anything else. 'One time, we came into Borana lands, and they were hostile. They said they would have burned our car—and even us,' Lkiparia said. 'But then they saw one of us was a Borana, so they listened. So we helped them, and then they even came and brought a goat to eat to thank us.'

Within a few years, there were half a dozen units with nearly a hundred combat-ready men. All the rangers were chosen after a series of aptitude tests and teamwork exercises—and passing a gruelling physical selection course that would test the hardest of soldiers. Many applied, few were chosen.

Facing them were fierce men with plenty of guns. Yet the rangers knew very well who they were up against; they were their brothers.

They came from the same communities. If any men knew how a cattle raider or a poacher might think, and where they would run to when chased, these men did.

'We know the routes the cattle rustlers would take,' said Galgalo. 'We lived in the bush before. So we can follow where they go, what they do.' Galgalo, a thoughtful young man, was taken away from looking after the goats as a boy by his brother, a policeman, who insisted education was important and paid his school fees. Since then, he'd tried various jobs: herding livestock, driving a motorbike taxi, and working as a building labourer, before passing the ranger selection test and starting training. 'We know where the wildlife goes, and where they hide,' he said. 'This is my home to me, so we understand it better than the police.'

Having teams of well-trained rangers was a massive deterrent to the poaching gangs. They were organised and well-equipped poaching squads—and to combat them needed a force just as strong. But the day-to-day monitoring of wildlife was best done by the conservancy rangers based on the ground, who stayed in one spot in their home area. So while the Nine Teams stopped poachers, the most important part of their job was different.

'We do not stand still and guard elephants,' said Lkiparia. 'What we do is about protecting human life, and their property—because that is what makes peace. That is what really matters.'

* * *

Losas pulled out a pair of binoculars from the heavy belt of canvas pouches around his waist, and scanned the wide plains. He swept around to face where the road ran north towards Ethiopia. It was close enough that you could just make out the sound of grinding gears of an old and clunking cattle truck packed full of animals. It braked as it approached a long S-bend on the road.

There had been a string of recent highway robberies here; major heists involving car hijackings with full frontal assaults using automatic weapons. Sometimes several people were killed. Yet security had slowly improved. Now the attacks had been reduced to a few small stretches of road.

The last attack had been the week before. Samburu moran waiting in the thickets had opened fire at a passing lorry coming from the market crammed full with goats. 'The attackers were hiding on that side,' Losas said, pointing to the brushwood bordering the highway. 'And they shot up the truck just before the curve.' The men knew the trucks would be coming from the weekly livestock market in the town of Merille, bringing the animals to the butchers in the Isiolo. It was the perfect place for an ambush. A lookout had scoped out the best truck to attack, and called by phone to let the gunmen know. The twisting road meant the vehicle was slowing down as the men stepped out from the bushes, shooting out the tyres and raking the cab with bullets. They fired shot after shot until the driver swerved and lost control.

'The truck rolled onto its side,' Losas said. The smashed windscreen glass still lay scattered alongside the road. A dark pool of sand was stained by the diesel that had gushed out from the bullet-riddled fuel tank. Remarkably, the driver survived. He was left for dead, unconscious in the baking heat. He was lucky no spark had turned the leaking fuel into a fireball. The attackers focused instead on rounding up the goats not left in a mangled mess by the collision, and herding them into the bush. 'We got here not long after, but the moran had already run off with the animals,' he said, pointing to a low hill far to the west. 'That is where they headed—we followed their trail.'

The bandits had based their attack on the assumption that most regular police officers arrived late and gave up early. So the getaway plan was simple: run hard and fast. When the sun grew too hot in the sky and the police ran out of water, the officers would turn back. But Losas and his team had not given up. The trail on stony ground was hard to follow, but Losas was born half a day's walk to the south and had spent his boyhood herding goats along the thin foot tracks and riverbeds that the rangers ran on. Just four hours after the attack, the 9–4 rangers surrounded a clump of trees where the gunmen had holed up. The bandits opened fire—but after the first few rattles of shots, the rangers had pulled back to safe defensive positions. They had time to watch and wait, and no need to prove their bravery. No one wanted a bloody last stand battle for a bunch of goats.

The raiders knew that the rangers had strict rules of engagement. Their weapons are issued for self-defence and they can only fire when fired upon first—but they also can only fire a strict limit of bullets each day. For those carrying G3 rifles, it is a maximum of two magazines—or 40 shots in total. For the lighter AK-47, it is one magazine of 30 rounds. The rangers were not the army; flick the switch to automatic fire, and they'd be out of bullets in seconds. The cattle rustlers, however, can fire as many bullets as they can afford. Ammunition was not cheap—around two dollars a shot, the same a labourer might earn for several hours of work—but there seemed always to be cash for bullets when the time came for a fight. The rangers had undergone long training on the police rifle range to fire their weapons accurately, but the herders were always going to have more bullets to fire. The rangers' success was not going to come from brute force, but from building trust.

Losas knew the men firing at him as well as anyone. He had taken part in livestock raids himself when he was a young man. In one attack three of his comrades were shot and badly wounded, and as he carried one of his friends, bleeding on his back through the bush, he had promised himself he would not change. So while he was now a captain, the men he faced were not his arch-enemies. They were his brothers and his cousins. They were his community.

So it didn't take long to find elders nearby who agreed to join Losas to persuade the herders face-to-face. He put his gun down, and walked in unarmed to speak. Allowing time to pass since the ambush had helped the hot-headed warriors consider their position. Escape seemed the sensible thing. They called a truce, gave up the animals and ended the standoff. 'They let all the goats go,' said Losas. 'They handed them to the elders, who gave them to us. Then we returned them to their owner.' The moran slipped away empty handed.

Losas put down his binoculars. The truck rumbled on peacefully. There were no shots this time. His radio, strapped to his chest webbing, crackled into life. He spoke briefly to the rest of unit, following in the dry valley below in the team's pickup truck. As he stood, so did his men. Then they continued on along the ridge with the same swift pace as before. They could keep it up all day long.

* * *

Losas ducked under the shade of an acacia tree, meeting the team's truck at the rendezvous point. It was time for tea. He took off his camouflage jacket, hanging it on a branch. 'Conservancy Warriors for Peace and Wildlife,' his T-shirt read. He also wore a sparkly beaded bracelet around one wrist in the colours of the Kenyan flag. He gathered up a bunch of dry sticks, starting a small fire in a scrape in the sand to boil a pot of water. As the flames crackled, Losas sat down to relax.

'There is always something happening, so we always have to be ready to move,' he said, recounting an operation the month before, when the team ran more than three marathons back-to-back over three days through a desert of volcanic rock—all while under fire from the raiders they were chasing. 'People call us, and expect us to be the first there to help,' he said.

He stopped the conversation briefly to call over a couple of curious herdsmen passing by. Losas poured them water into his battered tin mug. They gulped it down, refilling it over and over, until they had their fill. Then they shared news of what was happening, chatting as they waited for the giant saucepan of milk, sugar and some tea to slowly boil. The rangers welcomed those who passed by, and when not in a rush, gave lifts on their pickup. It is the nature of people here to show hospitality to strangers. For the 9–4 rangers, it was also a good way of improving relationships, and a useful way of gathering intelligence.

When a conservancy was just setting up, the arrival of the mobile ranger teams was one of the clearest signs of immediate change. People living day-to-day off their herds needed to see something happen. So here, with the rangers bringing back their stolen herds, was something tangible. Before, almost none of the animals stolen were recovered, and revenge attacks were a key driver of further conflict. Now, half of all livestock reported stolen were recovered by NRT rangers. Where they didn't succeed, their response made the gunmen think twice before raiding again.

Discussions in academic papers on the theory of 'peace dividends' can seem disconnected from what that means in practice. Better security had a knock-on effect far greater than the obvious but important one of sleeping peacefully at night. It was the foundation on which so much more was based. It opened up areas to building projects to put in infrastructure—clean water with wells and pumps, improved roads, school classrooms, or a health clinic. No one would want to come and build those in a war zone. It meant that children were more likely to go to school. It allowed people to better plan and protect their livelihoods—including providing the space for those who might seek different ways to earn money through small businesses.

'I don't want my children to have to be a ranger,' said Corporal John Lantare, recruited into 9–4 after showing his mettle working as a ranger for two years in his home conservancy of Songa. He was intensely proud of his job, but it was not an easy life. 'I want them to go to school and get jobs where they don't have to take the risks I do,' he said. When the 9–4 patrol passed close to his home, John asked if they could pull over to show his comrades his new-born girl, Olivia, his third daughter, holding her up to the cooing men. 'I miss my family because I am away on patrol so much,' he said. 'But I think it is important what we are doing. I don't see us as guarding animals. I see it as protecting my home and family for the future.'

* * *

At night, the men put bed rolls out alongside the truck, feet warm against a fire with glowing embers left over from cooking the supper of rice and beans. The first stars shone out, and the tiny dot of the planet Mars flashed red in the sky. The sounds of the day changed to become the calls of the night. Somewhere below, the sawing roar of a leopard echoed out. One ranger scanned the forests with a light, checking what eyes flashed back in reflection—yellow were likely grazers like antelopes, but red or green could be a watching predator.

The rangers had more immediate challenges, however. The teams were working to encourage peace, but the first gaps to be bridged were among themselves. Galgalo, the Borana ranger, lay straight up looking at the stars. Beside him was a man who would otherwise have been an enemy in a cattle raid. Molu Katelo was a former herder from the Gabra people in the neighbouring Shurr conservancy, where he had been a ranger for four years, before joining 9–4.

The Borana and Gabra often fought over livestock and grazing, in battles that still left many dead each year. But Galgalo and Molu had become good friends. They had been in 9–4 for two years together, living alongside one another in combat conditions in which both had trusted the other with his life. 'This job has brought us together; before, I would have feared to have gone to his land, because I would not have felt safe to have slept there,' said Molu. 'Now I would not even have to take my water and food, because I know he would look after me. I would even take my family, my children, my brothers, and they would be safe.'

Young goatherds in the bush didn't want to be footballers or musicians, who have such different lives. Instead they idolised the action men of the Nine Team who came roaring to the rescue with guns and smart uniforms. People looked up to the famous rangers who came to help in a crisis, seemingly unafraid of conflict in the area. 'When we come, people see me sitting alongside men who once would have been my enemy, but now are my friends,' Molu added. 'I think that has a big impact.'

The most difficult thing the rangers faced was when men from their own community had to be stopped. 'It is the hardest thing, when you have to go against your own people,' Molu said. 'So if my brother stole cows, then first we would talk. But if he wants to fight then we must do so too—because then he wants war. And war does not work, only peace does.'

* * *

The team had camped on the edge of the high Marsabit jungle. The mountain was chilly at night, with swirling clouds snaking between the trees. At dusk, the rangers had sat on the lip of an old volcanic crater, the cliffs tumbling below covered in thick forest clinging on with the strongest of roots. In the middle, as if a mirage, lay a huge circular lake surrounded by luminous green, Lake Paradise. It was an immense amphitheatre to watch the elephants emerge from lush rainforest to drink. The elephants of Marsabit had once been legendary for the size of their sweeping tusks. The biggest had all been killed, but the genes remained, and the population was growing again with the protection of the rangers.

When the men rested, Losas pulled out his phone, and on the small and cracked screen, played a video over and over that a friend had shot of him. It was his passing out parade at the government's wildlife ranger college, the KWS Law Enforcement Academy. The paramilitary training had covered everything from military tactics to radio communication, map reading, weapon handling, and law and order. 'The training was difficult,' said Losas, who had won the cup for 'best all-round trainee' at the college. 'But we learned so much.'

Out of the successful candidates, many had shown their commitment by first working as rangers in their home conservancy, and had then applied to join the special teams. But others had stolen livestock, and some had been poachers, expert trackers with unsurpassed knowledge of the movement of wildlife. Their names were put forward for the selection course by the community, in the hope that if chosen, they would dedicate their energies towards protection, not destruction. All, however, had to pass the tough training at KWS, and then from the police.

The Nine Teams are all registered Kenya Police Reservists. That means that while their salaries are paid by NRT, their licences to carry a gun, and ability to arrest, are granted with the approval of the government. Each mission is carried out with sanction of the police—and the teams often carry out joint operations. Their pay is similar to KWS rangers or local police, but they feel there is something special about the Nine Teams. They also take regular courses at the police academy too, to ensure each ranger is up to the standard of a police reservist, including practice in weapon handling, collecting evidence, and crime scene management. 'The last training we had was in human rights,' Losas said, when police trainers brought several of the Nine Teams together, turning a helicopter hangar in Lewa into a makeshift classroom. 'They taught us the legal processes and the responsibilities of a police officer.' When the men were not out on patrol, or on leave at home, they were training.

But it wasn't only classroom lessons. NRT brought in advisors to give the Nine Teams the edge they needed: Special Forces trainers who were experts on small and mobile teams in covert reconnaissance and counter-insurgency tactics, operating for extended periods far from base.

* * *

The green pickup screeched to a halt in a cloud of dust on the plains of yellow grass. 'Ambush on the right!' shouted the commander, standing in the track as a mock roadblock. Men leapt down from the benches on the back, running and rolling to the sides. They dived to the sand, then picked themselves up, crawling forward, setting out defensive positions, aiming their rifles ahead. The trainer shouted again, imitating the sound of bullets crashing into the dirt around. The rangers, now regrouped in orderly lines offering covering fire, shouted back as they advanced.

The 9–4 team had stopped off at one of the few fixed resupply bases for the teams, a basic bush camp. It was not rest time, however. A trainer was putting them through a two-day refresher course. Barry, a Kenyan brought up on the coast, had previously served as an infantry officer in Britain's Royal Gurkha Rifles. He had already led the men on a half-marathon at dawn, and then after breakfast, offered lectures in the relative cool of an open-sided grass-roofed hut began.

The topic was contact drill—or in non-military speak, what to do in a gun battle. Barry wrote on a board the long list of hand signals the men had to memorise to move silently through the bush. There were simple orders to move—halt, listen, look and single file. Then there were the commands of battle: enemy, assault, snap ambush and run. Barry showed the men how to react to an ambush and where to move.

He drew out the shape of the team's vehicle in the sand, placing squash ball-sized palm seeds he'd painted in bright colours to represent each man and their position on the truck—and where they had to run. The men, sitting around the drawing, took turns moving the seeds into the right place, then practising the moves jumping from the truck, until it became second nature.

Many could not read or write, so the trainers tailored infantry lessons. Planning tactics and troop movements needed some adaptation. 'To start with, there was no concept of maps,' said Pete, a wiry built former British Special Forces veteran, teaching tactics to the teams, who also went only by his first name. 'So we used a sandpit. With the sand we could make the hills, and use grass for woodlands and chalk powder for the rivers.' It didn't take long before new recruits were assessing contour lines, and giving grid references and

GPS coordinates over the radio. It was critical information if rangers needed support. With helicopter and aircraft based in Lewa, there was the capability of evacuating medical emergencies, bringing in reinforcements, or providing aerial reconnaissance.

Pete spoke to the men with an easy-going manner. He was well respected, setting up the fundraising organisation For Rangers, providing everything from socks and waterproof jackets for those in need, to supporting the families of those killed while on patrol. But he also had a quiet hard streak that gave him authority. He did not shout, because when he spoke, the men listened. His sense of pride in what the rangers had achieved was clear. 'If they'd been in the British army, some of them would have got medals for what they've done, no doubt at all,' Pete said. 'Some VCs, probably,' referring to the highest of British military medals for valour, the very rarely awarded Victoria Cross.

The drills were repeated and repeated in practical exercises out on the grasslands. When one team ran the wrong way, muddling left and right under pressure, the men waiting for their turn and watching from the side-lines laughed. Yet they all knew the importance of the training. In an attack, it could, quite literally, save their lives.

* * *

One of those carrying out the drills was Sergeant Machakos Lepore. He was a veteran, not a new recruit. He had learned the risks of the job in the hardest way. He had responded to a call from the community to the team to retrieve a dozen stolen camels. Picking up the tracks of the stolen herd at dawn, he followed them along a dry riverbed, which soon led into a narrow forested valley, with stony hills on either side. 'We went to get the animals back, the sort of operation we carry out all the time,' Machakos said. 'But they were waiting for us, and wanted to kill us.' An aircraft from Lewa had already scouted the area, spotting the camel, but the six gunmen had hidden from view. 'We approached the camels cautiously,' Machakos said. 'Then suddenly there was firing everywhere. Some were hiding among the camels, using them as protection. Others were behind rocks.' Fearing they would be shot in the back if they retreated, Machakos levelled his gun and charged forward. He was thrown backwards as if punched.

'That was when I realised something was very wrong,' he said, as he was lay stunned in the dirt. 'My leg felt heavy and slow, like it was a log of firewood. I saw there was blood everywhere, all over my trousers.' It was not the first time Machakos had been shot. In the days before he had joined the Nine Teams, he had taken part in a cattle raid himself, and a bullet had grazed his chest, slicing his skin like a razor. 'This time it was different,' he said. 'I couldn't walk. There was so much blood, and when I saw that, I was really scared.' Machakos sat back, showing where the bullet smashed into him, at the top of his right thigh. A close-quarters shot from an AK-47 could have been devastating. A fraction left or right would have left Machakos with a stump of a leg if it had hit a bone—or taken his life had it ripped into the main arteries in his groin. Luckily, the bullet passed through, only taking a lump of flesh.

But the training kicked in. Under fire, four men picked up their wounded sergeant, hauling him out beyond the fighting, and radioed for a helicopter to come for backup, calling in precise coordinates from their handheld GPS unit. A helicopter at Lewa took off, picking him up and swiftly taking him to hospital. In a crisis like that, seconds matter. Doctors stitched him up, and he was back on his feet within a month.

As for the raiders, this time they escaped. 'They went on,' Machakos said with a shrug. 'And that was it.' He didn't dwell on the injury; not every incident ended with a bullet wound that healed so well. Several rangers from the Nine Teams had lost their lives when bandits shot to kill. At the time, his daughter, Nabaru, was just a year old. His wife had much to say. 'She told me to leave the work because it is dangerous,' Machakos said. 'But I knew that before I began. If I always listened to my wife, I would be out of work. I wanted to come back. It is what I do.'

*　*　*

The drop to the riverbed was quite clearly a cliff, but it was the only way down. The 9–4 team driver, Charles Muthamia, shouted to the men in the back of the pickup to hold on, as he found a route that looked not much more than a goat track. The 9–4 patrol were all in the one vehicle, a dark-green Toyota Land Cruiser. It was a tough machine capable of the most extreme conditions the men could put it through. The thick wheels gripped on to crumbling soil, rocking from side to side like a rollercoaster, then rushed down the final section and onto a soft landing of beach. Then, gunning the engine, the pickup growled through the gravel that washed over the wheels. It pulled up the bank on the other side and, with a roar, set off across the desert plains at high speed.

Wherever the rangers needed to go on patrol on foot, the vehicle followed behind. 'Everything we need is with us,' Charles said. 'We can just keep going and going.'

The pickup was well equipped. Two benches ran the length of the back, with a canvas-covered roof rack, where rucksacks, mosquito net dome tents and sleeping bags were strapped. Rangers sat on benches facing out sideways from the direction of travel, four on each side. The benches lifted up and doubled as storage boxes for supplies; sacks of rice, beans and maize flour, tins of milk powder and bags of sugar for the super sweet tea they loved. It carried a second fuel tank, meaning they could travel double the distance without needing to refill. It was even fitted with a vehicle snorkel, a plastic tube reaching up to the roof, so that it could cross raging rivers after storms without flooding the engine. The team's smaller radios for talking between each other when on patrol were charged off the truck's battery, as were all their phones, used when there was network signal. Beyond replenishing their containers of fresh water and topping up the fuel tanks, the team could operate independently for weeks. In short, they travelled light, and could go far.

This also meant the rangers were also able to deploy straight away in hot pursuit. Regular police officers in a far-flung outpost did not have the capacity to send a team out into an operation that could take days—and be extremely dangerous. Government rangers, from the KWS, were caught up with the enormous job of defending over sixty protected areas. Their mandate—to conserve and manage Kenya's wildlife—meant that an operation such as chasing a herd of stolen cattle was usually low on their list of priorities. Charles knew the demands of the job well; he had served fourteen years in the regular police. He had retired from service for a more peaceful life farming, but after his crops were hit in a series of bad droughts, he began work as a tourist safari driver, and then after that, as the driver for 9–4. 'The police don't see us as taking away their work,' the old officer said. 'They're happy with us because we are assisting them.'

The 9–4 unit totalled fourteen men, at least half of whom were deployed at any one time. That meant the rangers could be continually rotated, so that as men took leave after a month, replacements hopped onto the truck. They needed to be always able to respond. 'Sometimes we have to get to places that it seems like no one else can get to,' Charles said. 'But it is important because that is where the raiders and the poachers go to. People can rely on us. They call us, and we will come. However hard it is, we will get there.' As the radio crackled, Charles twisted the scanning button on the dashboard to tune it for a better reception; headquarters was calling. Losas picked up the radio mic, and spoke to the officers on the other end of the line in the radio room in Lewa far to the south.

* * *

The howls of hyena hunting in the hills echoed for hours. The night had been cold, lying out beneath a dome of stars and a moon so bright you could see it against your eyelids when you closed them to sleep. The team had camped next to a herder's home, outside his thorn barricade, with his camels and cattle crowded inside. When the animals moved, so did the heavy bells slung around their neck; tinkling metal for cows, deeper wooden chimes for camels. With eyes closed, the peal of bells sounded like an English churchyard.

Long before the sun had even crept over the mountain peaks, the team were up and drinking tea with camel milk against the dawn chill. As light reached the camp, it was already packed up. The men passed around a brush to make sure all their army boots were polished shiny, and their uniforms neat. It was nearing a month on the road for some of the men, sleeping in the bush every night, but all were scrupulously turned out. 'What we look like, is what the people think of us,' said Losas. 'We are professionals so we have to look smart.'

Then they stood in a circle, offering a prayer for their safety and success. Half of the team, those who were Christian, stood with their heads bowed and bush hats on top of their rifle. The other half, those who were Muslim, raised their hands up in front of their chests. A different man from each religion alternated leading prayers at daybreak. Then 9–4 was off again, bouncing down the sand of a riverbed, pushing the pickup through the forests. But the driver suddenly braked. 'Listen,' Charles said, pointing to the waving branches of a tree, as a cracking of wood could be heard. 'And smell—there are elephants.'

The elephants had come down in the night from the hills, where they felt safe, into the plains where the people lived. Now they were heading back to the forests to rest in the cool during the day. A large mother elephant advanced to protect a wobbly-legged baby behind. Her ears flapped out wide, so she seemed to grow even bigger in size, with her head shaking her gleaming tusks from side-to-side. She reached forward with her trunk, smelling the ranger team with the waving grey limb, reaching forward so it was held almost horizontal. She could use that powerful trunk to pull down trees. Facing the rangers, perhaps she wondered if they should be treated in the same rough manner, but then she seemed to calm. The rangers posed no threat, she decided. Perhaps she had seen them before, and remembered them. In any case, the threat had passed. Her children had moved on, she had guarded them, and now she could follow too. She paused. At the very end of her trunk, two small finger-like tips were slowly being opened and squeezed together, as though she was reaching forwards to touch, in a far gentler gesture.

Her trunk flopped down, and with a final ear flap, she turned and pushed through the trees. Charles waited for a moment to let the elephants head off, then drove on slowly. The team was going south again, towards where the giraffe roamed the forests in the shadow of the misty mountains, to a valley of fig trees where the elephants gathered called Reteti. The rangers in the back of the truck clung on tight as the truck sped off. There was a long road ahead.

12

AN ELEPHANT CALLED POKOT
(HOW HUMANS AND WILDLIFE TRUSTED EACH
OTHER AGAIN)

It was too late to run. The trumpeting was wild and terrifying. It was the call of a herd of elephants stampeding at speed. The crowd of people standing among the trees stepped back in panic, looking at each other in fear. Adult African elephants, the largest land mammal walking the earth, can stand twice the height of a human, weigh in at seven tonnes, and rapidly overtake even the fastest sprinter. Smashing their way through the forest, the herd burst out of the bushes.

First there was an audible sigh, as people smiled in relief. Then they laughed in simple delight. The two dozen elephants were noisy, but nothing, after all, to be scared of. All were young orphans, or had been rescued after being separated from their herd. The elephants rushed into the open area where a keeper waited for each animal, holding out a bottle of milk the length of their arm with a giant rubber teat. Some keepers were almost knocked over by the enthusiasm. The older ones took matters into their own trunks and took the bottle themselves, lifting and drinking. Two litres were gulped down in a few seconds. For a few minutes, the elephants stood with their trunks curled in play around the necks of their keeper. The animals gently sniffed their faces.

Their home is Reteti, the first community-owned and run elephant sanctuary in Africa, in the forested foothills of the conservancy of Namunyak. It is a unique refuge, giving the rescued elephants a wild future. The sanctuary brings income and jobs, and funds for the conservancy to provide education and health. 'We look after the elephants,' said senior keeper Dorothy Lowakutuk. 'And the elephants are taking care of us.'

* * *

The youngest elephant was barely a month old. She was still wobbly on her feet, with her thin trunk whipping from side-to-side like a hosepipe. Tiny Samburu was weak from losing her family, having been swept downstream when rains turned the sand and rock into roaring torrents of fierce brown water. Now she ran with ears flapping to keep up with her newly adopted siblings.

The orphans all came from across northern Kenya, from the conservancies of the NRT, national parks and more. Some were orphaned because their mother was killed by poachers, or by herders in a fight over grazing or water. Others had been found fallen deep down a well and got stuck, having to be dug out by hand. The youngest rescued was just two days old.

They were only taken to Reteti as a last resort. The best outcome is for the calf to be reunited straight away. An elephant mother does not easily abandon a baby she has already carried inside for 22 months of pregnancy. So when a calf was pulled out of a well, even after hours of digging, the rescue teams stepped back and left it for a while. Often the family hide nearby, and then rush out to greet it.

Yet there comes a point where the baby will die unless it is fed. Then the keepers took the orphan to Reteti, often first by road to a bush airstrip. Pilots had several times squeezed a small elephant in beside them, a sleeping Dumbo in the skies. Even the youngest can weigh more than a man, and the older they get the heavier they are.

The oldest that charged out of the bush was four years old. She was called Shaba; like most of the elephants, named after the place that they were found, inside the government's Shaba reserve. She was rescued after her mother was shot in the head by poachers. Little Shaba was one of the first arrivals to the sanctuary, but she nearly didn't make it. She was traumatised, and fearing humans, had refused to eat. The keepers spent hours tempting her with everything from milk to tasty seed pods. They stood inside a roll of car tyres inside her stable, in case she was angry towards humans, until she was finally won over. She had suffered at the hand of man, but learned that not all humans were her enemies.

Shaba was still a child in elephant society. Her tusks were just tiny nubs barely poking out. Like humans, elephant's brains are roughly only a third of their full adult size at birth—and so they depend on family units for their survival for the first decade.[1] Yet in the absence of older elephants, Shaba had taken it upon herself to lead her adopted family, becoming the matriarch of the herd. She was protective of the other elephants, guarding them and teaching the new arrivals how to stay safe. Shaba also kept order amongst an otherwise unruly bunch, chivvying on dawdlers to make sure the herd stayed close together, and pushing them with a bossy head shove. In calmer moments, she reached out with a reassuring trunk to let the youngest know they were not alone.

Alongside her was Pokot, found abandoned aged just six months old. Perhaps he fell behind during the intense drought, or maybe he was lost when cattle herders and his mother fought, and he got separated. Either way, he had been severely dehydrated, and it had taken days of intensive care to nurse him back to health. A keeper was alongside him all the time, for it had been touch and go as to whether he would survive. He spent days shaking under blankets, a thin, wheezing breath rasping out of his trunk. Keepers placed hot water bottles on his flanks, and another behind the ear, to help circulation with saline drips going into the veins. Now Pokot was one of the most playful. After feeding and throwing the bottle down, he bounced over to play football, kicking it with the keeper. Then he headed to a small pool for a breakfast bathe in mud. It was heaven for an elephant.

The rescued elephants, when returned to the wild, would help boost numbers in the area. Yet that was not the crucial point of the sanctuary's work. Reteti was also changing people's mindset towards elephants—from one of outright fear and hatred, to one where people could see the value in protecting them. Getting to know the orphans as individual animals helped change views about the whole species. 'Before the sanctuary began, people could not imagine feeding an elephant,' said Dorothy, showing photograph after photograph on her phone, displaying how the elephants had grown under her care. 'It is changing the way that people see elephants, and how they behave to them.'

* * *

As the conservancy in Namanyuk flourished, elephants returned to lands they had been too fearful for many decades to visit—and problems grew. There had always been conflict. Humans had always killed elephants in defence, and to protect their farms from their hungry appetites. Elephants had also always been scared of people, trampling them down if they were surprised in the bush. There was fear on both sides, rooted in the very real danger that each could cause the other.

Yet in the past, it was also a fear tempered with respect. Old men spoke of how, when they were young boys herding the cows, they would move among the elephants without worry. Some elephant herds were always more used to having humans around; others were more wary. The men described how as boys they had played games of seeing who could get the closest—and then tap the elephant's ear in play. Perhaps the elephants realised they were only children, for the animals would tolerate them, or at worst, swing a lazy trunk to warn them away.

Herders in the past didn't give elephants individual names like the orphanage did, to remember where they came from. They didn't need to; they could judge the elephants on sight. They had names to differentiate between the types of elephants they met—and that helped them assess the risks they posed. There were the fearless *sangalai* bulls guarding the herd who rarely retreated in the face of a threat, and the solitary males called *laingoni*, out looking for adventure or mates. They knew how to react when confronted with the mothers of the herd, the protectors called *ngamitoni*, who were aggressive in defence of their children, and the oldest grandmothers, the *narikoni*, retired as active defenders, but who serve as wiser matriarchs of the family. People could judge if elephants were skittish, frightened of attack, and more likely to respond with aggression. They could also see if they were calm and peaceful, ears gently flapping and at ease, and so more tolerant of having a human around. Elephants were seen as moral creatures, capable of hurting—and of being hurt.[2]

The violent decades from the 1970s on and the waves of poaching had shattered that. The tolerance by elephants of man was broken by bloodshed. Like humans, and unlike many other animals, they live long lives and have few children. Each child takes many years to become independent, with the community of the herd investing time and effort in helping them grow. Yet elephants were now traumatised by the wholesale obliteration of herds. The great animals live in close-knit families, so that the impact of killing a single animal sent waves of shock across the group. The oldest matriarchs had the biggest tusks, and so had been shot down first. In the societal breakdown, elephant teenagers became guardians of disturbed youngsters. Many had actually witnessed the killing of their relations by humans. Researchers saw their reactions as similar to the post-traumatic stress disorder symptoms that humans had after war: abnormally startled responses, unpredictable behaviour and hyper-aggression.[3] A whole society needed healing. For elephants, it did not take long for their old wariness of man to be replaced with open hostility.

When the killing waves began, the great herds were easy to find, for the defence of the elephants was in their strength together, not in hiding. Yet as the massacres continued, the last survivors became wild, nocturnal and dangerous—which benefited their survival. They became experts at hiding away in the thickets of forests, avoiding the tracks that humans used. The young generation of herders had grown up rarely seeing an elephant up close—and when they did, because the elephants were often angry, they saw it as something to fight off first before it attacked. The first reaction of a herder was to reach for a rifle.

It was as if the diplomatic relations between two great nations had broken down. Stopping poaching was one thing, but learning to live with wildlife again was an even bigger challenge. Some people shrugged, and said that it was a change that could not be halted; that the world had grown too fast and gone too far to have elephants and man living alongside each other in the future. The problem is, our lives are intertwined. Without protecting nature, our lives suffer too. Lose wildlife, and we will lose ourselves. A reset button was needed.

* * *

So in 2016, the conservancy at Namunyak opened the sanctuary as part of its work. With the conservancy rangers providing security, poaching for ivory had become rare. But elephants were still dying in conflict over water. 'Fights between herders and elephants are the big problem,' said Joseph Lolngojine. 'The community dig wells, but you can't tell an elephant not to drink there too—and then they collapse them.' Joseph had every reason to hate elephants; his step-mother Noonkutot had been trampled by an elephant, killed when she walked out at dawn to milk a cow. Yet Joseph trained as a veterinary nurse, and now worked at Reteti caring for the elephants. 'Before, if I just saw an elephant, I would run,' he said. 'But something changed in me. I saw how they have different personalities—some are timid and some are playful. Of course these little elephants are not like the grown ones. You must be careful, and you can get problem animals that are angry. But we learn their behaviour; that they like to go to this place to drink water, or to that place because there is salt. If you remember that, you don't have to scare them.'

In practical solutions, the sanctuary brought in investment to mitigate conflict. Community members set up a system of pipes stretching high up in the hills, bringing water from pools on the mountain tops down to the plains—partly for the sanctuary and the elephants, but also for livestock, which pleased the herders. Then a small dam in the hills was made to store water from a spring, so that elephants drank in that pool, rather than come into the settlement. With income from visitors coming to see the elephants benefiting the community, and jobs through the conservancy and tourism, people's opposition slowly faded.

The same herders angry at the elephants that had collapsed their wells now said that during the worst droughts, the elephants used their tusks to smell out springs hidden deep beneath the dust. Elephants have more genes dedicated to smell than any other animals recorded—double even sniffer dogs.[4] They used their strong tusks as tools to dig out the first wells. Once, if herders had found an abandoned elephant, they would have dragged it out of the well before it polluted it, but they would have then left it to die. Now they called for help to rescue it.

As for Joseph, he brings his two daughters and son to see the elephants whenever they can—as well as their fellow classmates from school. 'I had always feared them when I was a boy,' said Joseph. 'But now the children love to come and see them, and learn what they are really like.'

* * *

Reteti, nestled between high hills, was named after the wild fig trees found there that spread with thick roots. The trees are sacred, a connection for the Samburu between the world we live in and the divine. The valley is dotted with the trees, and offers a place of sanctuary. Herders who found injured animals began to bring them to the orphanage too. A kudu antelope, a gazelle, and even a giraffe ambled through the unfenced grounds.

The orphans spend their days wandering in the woods—watched by a keeper but free to roam. They seem to have less reverence for the sacred figs. They like them best for scratching awkward itches on their backs, or sniffing out wild fruits dangling within trunk reach. The elephants delight in a midday bath, wallowing in the mud pool like a spa. The dirt helps both as a sunscreen, and when it dries, to remove pesky parasites by scrubbing on the trees. Around the sanctuary, the trunks of the trees are left polished shiny and the bark smooth, where the orphans have rubbed themselves each day. Yet while the figs are useful scratching posts, the herd seeks out another tree to nibble branches for its bark—an acacia species used as a local remedy for fevers and stomach sickness. Perhaps the calves also know of its healing powers.

At night, the elephants sleep in a hexagonal stable with stalls radiating out, with their heads together at the centre. They can reach between gaps in the log walls to touch trunks together and calm each other. They are covered in blankets, since they do not have their mother's warmth. Their keepers—who they follow like parents—sleep on a platform directly above, ready for feeding shifts in the night.

Communities were rightfully wary of elephants. But the little orphans were changing people's opinions. Rather than shoot a gun on sight, herders were returning to the ways of the past—where a cautious respect could be found. In time, the elephants also became calmer and less aggressive. While there were always rogues— among the elephants, as well as humans—each species became more tolerant of the other.

For living with elephants was not an outside idea brought in by well-meaning but naive foreigners, but something entwined in people's deepest beliefs. It was a concept that lay in the heart of the culture of the people. Elephants, so different in appearance from us, had so much in common to our lives.

* * *

The Samburu tell folktales about the origin of the elephant: that once they lived in the home as family. Far, far in the past, the mother of the house, used to sending children out on errands, did the same to the elephant. She asked for wood to make a fire to make tea. So the elephant went to the forest, and returned with an entire trunk of a tree he had torn down. But the mother was angry, saying it was too big. She did not have time to split the wood with an axe. She needed a fire now. So the elephant went back and returned with tiny twigs. The mother dismissed it again, saying now that it was too little to boil the water.

Infuriated, the elephant lost his temper. 'I have helped you in the home,' said the elephant. 'But now I will leave and live free in the wild. We will separate forever.' As he stormed out of the hut, the leather cow skin covering the doorway wrapped around him, and it stuck to his head to become his wide ears.

Yet though the years have passed, and the elephants no longer live with people, the old connection between humans and elephants has not been forgotten. So even as the elephant left in anger, he also had a message for his old human family. 'We will remain friends,' the elephant said. 'I will extend my goodwill when we meet, and always come to your aid if you ask for it.'

Such tales are legends, but stories have power. They shape how we see the world, and how we treat it too. It is a relationship that goes far deeper than with any other animal in the bush. Elephants are still seen as related to humans, as if a wayward cousin. The language used by the Samburu to describe elephants echoes the common connections, rather than highlighting the differences; so tusks are described as 'teeth', and the long trunk, an 'arm.' It was for that reason eating elephant was taboo; because to do so was considered akin to cannibalism. It was against the government's laws, but more importantly, against the laws of nature. In the past, ivory was valued not for the money it brought, but because it absorbed the power and protection of the elephant. Parents placed an ivory teardrop pendant on a necklace around babies as a talisman to stop them from dying, while many men had ear plugs dangling from their lobes. The Samburu can kill an elephant in self-defence, but killing one for its ivory and to cut out its tusks is regarded as murder—and brought down a curse.

The modern world with motorbikes and mobile phones meant that many of the old traditions—values of respect reflecting the interdependence between humans and wildlife expressed through culture, custom and belief—had faded out of use. Yet, climb up high in the forested hills above Reteti, and the powerful old connections between nature and man remain.

* * *

The heavy skull was bleached white by the sun, and poked out from a tangle of grass. The elephant had been speared by an angry cattle keeper in revenge for killing a cow, a furious thrust with a tusk in a fight over water, when the grass had grown thin and brittle in the dry season. Now, less than a year later, the skeleton was already half-swallowed by the bush. The bones lay scattered where the hyenas had dragged them to devour her body, hidden in a narrow valley.

Yet it was not forgotten. Others had passed here before and marked the bones in memory. As if it were a human grave, flowers had been laid on the skull. Poking out the hollow space of the eye sockets, sprigs of tree branches stuck out. Their green leaves had been baked brown by the sun, and rustled in the gentle breeze. The empty hole where the elephant's trunk had once waved was garlanded with faded blossoms.

Lobik Lesasuyian, a Samburu cattle herder, led the way. He pushed through snaking paths in the tangled thorn-trees, with his long legs making a fast-paced loping stride. He stopped abruptly at the sight of the bones. Reaching up to a bush, he broke off a bunch of branches covered in small white buds. Then, hitching up a bright red tartan blanket wrapped around himself against the morning cold, Lesasuyian bent down beside the bones. He pushed the new blooms in alongside the old, laying fresh flowers in memory on the grave. His friend was dressed in the rolls of rainbow-coloured beads and a white feather headdress of a young warrior. He tucked his spear and a furled umbrella, that he carried in case of rain later, under his arm. He drew his forefinger across his braided hair, gleaming in the ceremonial maroon paste of a moran. Instead of laying flowers, he ran his finger with ochre from his head across the elephant's skull. It left a wide blood-coloured stripe. There were older, faded streaks from others who had done the same before. 'It is to say sorry,' said Lesasuyian. 'We have to live together.'

When people pass the graves of their relatives, they place small rocks on the memorial to make a cairn, pour offerings of milk onto the ground, or place a ball of tobacco on top. Or, they simply push green branches or flowers into the cracks in memory. Elephants are accorded similar reverence, the only animals to be given the same rites as humans. The great animals could threaten lives and be terrifying in a rage—and yet people still laid flowers on the bones to assign them respect even in death. The Samburu call it *asai*, the blessing of the dead.

* * *

Remarkably, elephants do the same. We think we are unique in our funeral rituals for mourning our dead, but the placing of flowers on bones is an act of respect not confined to humans alone. Biologists have exhausted long hours watching their behaviour. Elephants spend hours standing by the bones and ivory of fallen comrades, turning the skulls over and over, sniffing with their trunks, and touching gently with sensitive soles of their great feet. They are fascinated by the fallen bodies, and not just of their direct family, but of any elephant carcass they find.[5] They fall silent as they stand in a circle around the bones, slowly blowing out with heavy breaths. Sometimes, they tear down green saplings to lay the leaves gently over their fallen friends.

Even more surprising, elephants do that not just for their dead. There have also been many times elephants have been documented laying leaves in the same manner on the bodies of humans. Those who died in the bush have been found covered in green branches, the footsteps of elephants all around. Sometimes elephants have even covered the bodies of those they have trampled down in anger and fear, just as they did to the elephants that humans had killed in conflict. One herder, alone, sick and resting beneath a tree, described how he played dead when he saw elephants coming towards him. Terrified, he lay frozen as the elephants reached forward to touch his body with their sensitive trunks, investigating why the human was lying in the dust. Then he watched as the elephant family snapped off branches time after time, laying the leaves over him, until a green bower of fronds covered him from the sun. Afterwards, the elephants stood still, watching as though in a vigil, before moving on gently into the trees. Many can tell such stories.[6]

Zoologists have recorded the astonishing behaviour multiple times, but they are careful to stick to measureable data. They are wary of assigning emotions like compassion to animals, and fearful of anthropomorphism and drawing parallels between animal actions and human cultural behaviour. Animal altruism does not sit well with theories of natural selection, unless such action can benefit the wider family in some manner. So scientists stop short of saying it is an actual mourning ritual practised by elephants.

Yet it is clearly an extraordinary connection. All signs indicate elephants are complex social animals with an understanding of death and, like us, an awareness of their place in nature. Humans and elephants both honour their family who have died; and, in the same manner, recognise the dead of the other too. 'My sister,' Lesasuyian said, as he paid his respects laying the blossoms. 'Sleep in peace.' It is far more than a simple ritual. It shows the vital respect between people and the wild. The air smelt of crushed herbs, sweet in the dew of the dawn.

* * *

The rumble was deep, a sound so powerful it seemed to be more felt in the chest than heard in the ears. There was a sudden splintering crack of tree branches, not even a stone's throw down in the valley below. Lesasuyian pointed towards the bushy tangle of trees using his mouth, pursing his lips to the bushes. He stopped, every muscle tense, crept forward, then froze again. 'Ltome,' he mouthed silently in Samburu. 'Elephant.' His grin went right across his face.

He kicked his foot gently into the ground. The brown dust scattered in the wind, showing the direction that it was also taking the scent of sweat. He headed up higher. There was a flash of grey in the trees, and then, silence. Not one, but an entire herd of the largest land mammal, slipped through the trees with the softest of footfalls. The grass and leaves rustled as they rushed on, but soon all was still. They had vanished like smoke on the wind.

'Elephants don't want to meet us,' Lesasuyian said. 'They don't want trouble.' Lesasuyian led the way upwards on a lung-busting hike, winding up on the ridge of the mountain. 'When you see an elephant in front of you, you might feel fear because of their size,' he said. 'But it is the elephant who are more scared of you. So many of their family have been killed.' In time, the footprints faded into the heavy scrub. He pointed to fresh football-sized mounds of elephant dung, and to footprints as big as a pizza in the sand. In the softest dust, you could even make out the wrinkled folds of the spreading feet and toenails on the ground. Lesasuyian followed each turn like a story etched on the earth. 'We are relatives,' Lesasuyian said. 'They cry in pain too. They have emotions. When a baby elephant dies, the mother grieves. Look at their feet: they have toenails like a human, and a mother has breasts like a woman.'

As he pushed through the forest, Lesasuyian found a ball of dried grass not much bigger than the size of a fist. It was dung dropped by the smallest of the elephants. He poked at the bundle with the iron tip of his spear. 'The first fire a couple make after marriage in their home together should be lit from this,' he said, rubbing his hands together to mime the traditional way of making sparks from sticks. The elephant grass was used as the kindling for a symbolic blaze to mark the new lives as husband and wife. Since elephants eat fragrant herbs also used for medicine, burning the dung was seen as a way to release the healing properties and cleanse the new home of ill spirits. A fire from elephant dung is also lit as a burning blessing at the entrance to the thorn stockade to welcome the cows back after weeks away looking for grazing. 'Elephants are part of our culture,' he added, interweaving his fingers. 'Our lives are twisted as one, like creepers around a tree.'

* * *

In Reteti, in the sanctuary's elephant kitchen, Dorothy oversaw three keepers whisking up jugs of milk. They are big animals with hungry appetites, needing feeding every three hours, night and day. Calves are not weaned until at least two years old—and often much older when hand reared. 'They need strong bones,' said Dorothy. 'We have to make sure they get all the right minerals because their mothers would go to find the salts they need.'

Feeding elephants, however, is far from straightforward. They are intolerant to cow milk, so a special recipe is needed. Much of the first research was done through a long process of trial and error by Dame Daphne Sheldrick in Nairobi in the 1970s, when she was handed an orphaned calf. It was thought impossible to hand-rear, but she could not face the prospect of letting the little creature die for want of trying. Obtaining elephant's milk was not possible, so each day she tried new ingredients to mimic the milk. Nothing worked; the little elephant grew weaker, with sunken eye sockets and pronounced cheek bones. Then at the very last minute, she discovered the secret that brought the calf back to life—coconut oil.[7] Since then, the formula has been refined and developed, through the work of the Sheldrick Wildlife Trust, whose pioneering orphanage in Nairobi has raised and rehabilitated over 260 orphans through the decades. Reteti would build on that foundation and experience.

The needs changed as the calves grew, but the most challenging was to keep the very youngest alive. All too often, it was the littlest that got lost from the family. The keepers experimented time and time again—and then tried goat's milk. When their reports came back that it seemed to be working, research scientists from the Institute of Conservation and Research of San Diego Zoo—a key supporter of the sanctuary project—tested the milk. Together, the partnership between the keepers' practical testing and the scientific analysis provided the missing ingredient for the youngest. Before, the weakest orphans sometimes died despite the best efforts of the keepers, but the goat milk had a dramatic reduction in the numbers lost.

In the very beginning, the upmarket health food stores in Nairobi's swanky shopping malls were surprised when their shelves were swept clean by the bulk orders for giant tins of dried goat milk power placed by a faraway Samburu community.

But soon the Reteti team recruited herders to bring fresh milk from goats to supply the smallest. Even a little elephant can slurp through impressive amounts, needing a herd of two dozen goats to supply daily milk for each of them. The milk money earned soon provided an important income for the herders, especially the women, who did the milking.

On the wall of the kitchen, a board detailed ingredients: two litres of water whisked with formula milk powder with wooden spoons—no one likes their milk lumpy, after all.

Then there is a long list of additions: a cup of ground millet flour, a dash of probiotic powder to boost the body's defence against sickness, a pinch of salt and tablespoon of glucose, and whey powder to build muscle. Some also got a pinch of bicarbonate of soda to reduce gas—an elephant fart can be, well, enormous. Then the keepers sprinkled in vitamin-packed powders from the local moringa and baobab trees. This made it taste like mother's milk, Dorothy said, as she carried the giant bottles outside for feeding.

The expense of feeding an individual animal was gigantic, though contributions from visitors helped offset the costs. However, rescuing individual elephants was not about trying to save a species one by one. It was helping change how people saw elephants and the wild animals. The orphanage drew in visitors from far. It was not only tourists, but also schools and locals. Most had never seen an elephant in such a setting.

* * *

Standing behind the keepers, a line of visitors watched. The crowd came from two conservancies, Pellow and Masol. Both were members of NRT, in the north-western Pokot region of Kenya. Over fifty members of the two Pokot conservancies had travelled by bus on a trip to see how the sanctuary worked—and to meet a specific elephant. As the orphan family rushed in for the milk, the visitors called out to the keeper to show them a special animal to them—the mischievous Pokot.

'He came from our lands,' said Roselyn Lokorkilen proudly, the treasurer of Pellow conservancy, and a politician in the county government. 'We have seen elephants as wild animals, but never so close up as this; or if we did, we'd be running away.' The Pokot conservancies were working to stop their own conflicts between herders and elephants. Coming to see the work at Reteti showed the possibility of a different future. Beside her, Solomon Todoo, the headteacher of the school in Pellow, nodded. His phone was full of videos he had made to show the children back in class. 'We have many wild animals in the bush,' Simon said. 'But to see them interacting with humans, playing football, that is something we could not have imagined unless we saw it with our own eyes.' He said he would be bringing back his entire school to see the elephants at Reteti.

'It shows that wild animals can become kind, depending on the way you treat them,' said Duncan Mading Kanyakera, a Pokot student finishing a degree in environmental science, one of a new generation of young Kenyans growing up and seeing wildlife through different eyes.

'We humans always want more than we need,' Duncan said. 'More cows, more goats, more cars, more money. But seeing the orphans at Reteti showed me that we can't always keep doing that without causing harm. If we do, we will lose our wildlife, and then we have lost something we can't replace. When it has gone, it is gone forever.'

Yet it wasn't only the young elephants that were changing people's minds. Close to Reteti, in the neighbouring conservancy of Sera, rhinos were returning too, bringing an animal that once stood on the brink of extinction back to its homelands. One of the key people involved in that incredible return was Pauline Longojine, the lady who had done so much to build peace.

* * *

When Pauline was growing up, the stories of rhinos were the tales of history. 'When I was young, we never saw a rhino,' said Pauline. 'They were told as the stories of the past.' At school, she was taught all about the wild animals that roamed around, from antelope to zebra. At home, over supper, she was told what to do if she met them while out in the bush: back slowly away from an elephant, give a buffalo space, don't go near where the lions were meant to be. But she only learned about rhinos through drawings in a book. No one told her how to stay safe if she met one, because there was no point. None of the animals were left.

For a while, in the quietest corners, the rhinos had clung on. Herders, who travelled to the most distant places too dry for cattle except right after the rains, came back and spoke of glimpsed movements in the trees, a flash of vanishing grey as the massive barrel-bodied creature charged away. They repeated the sounds of puffing snorts of anger they'd heard as the animal stamped into the bush. Occasionally, the distinctive wide print of their three-toed hooves were found, pressed down into the soft sand of a dry riverbed. There were still a few individuals, doing all that they could to avoid the scent of man, seeking out the harshest lands far from disturbance. In time, like their tracks left in the dust that were washed away in the rains, even those rare stories were no more. The final frightened rhino hiding in the bush northeast of Archer's Post was thought to have been eventually cornered, shot and its horn hacked out from its face, sometime in the late 1980s. A species safe on earth for 50 million years had been intentionally exterminated. It did not take long before the history of rhinos faded into fireside fables. 'All of them were killed,' Pauline said. 'None of them were left.' There was every reason to despair.

* * *

It had not been Pauline's ambition to work to help bring the rhino back—at least, not to start with. After all, it was not as if she missed them; she'd never even known the animals growing up. But after Sera conservancy was formed in 2002, the idea of returning rhinos slowly grew.

It was only the start of a very long process. It would take more than a decade of debate before a final decision was made. Since poachers remained an all too real threat, rhinos would have to be kept in a fenced sanctuary. That worried many in the community. 'Many people were doubtful what it would all mean,' Pauline said. 'Some didn't see the need to bring back the rhino. Some said, "No! Rhinos don't listen, and the only way to control them is with a spear."'

After Pauline was elected head of Sera conservancy in 2012, she was determined to push ahead with the work. The first step was to convince people to support it by explaining exactly what it would entail. The area proposed was of little interest to a herder. There were enough woody plants for rhinos, but the grass and water was usually too poor for cattle. Rhinos, like elephants, had the strength to dig down to drink from the water that seeped out of the sand. So plans included concrete wall dams across narrow seasonal rivers. They were deliberately designed to fill up with sand, because the precious water was retained in the gravel for far longer than open pools.

In the end, the financial argument won over most; over two-thirds of the respondents asked cited economic gains for their backing of a return of the rhino.[8] 'Eventually, even those who were opposed changed their minds,' Pauline said. 'People wanted the rhino to come back.' Sera conservancy stretched over 200 sq miles, or 500 km sq. A fifth of that was fenced off to become the rhino sanctuary.

It was a massive undertaking. The electric perimeter fence alone would stretch across the English Channel. The project required substantial external investment. The bulk of core operational costs were borne by the US government's development arm, USAID, as well as other donors.[9] But the money was not being spent as a payment to protect an animal; donors saw it as an investment to make lasting economic change. Use the cash to assist the wider community—and the people who benefit will protect the animals themselves out of self-interest.

In 2015, rhinos returned to Sera. Ten rhinos were successfully moved in batches, the bulk coming from Lewa where numbers were expanding successfully. Lewa's plan had worked, and the dreams that had seemed so unlikely in the 1980s were coming true, for the descendants of the rhinos rescued from the clutches of poachers were finally going home. Three decades after the last rhinos were killed, the animals were back.

It is the first community-owned and run black rhino sanctuary in East Africa, showing others what can be done with determination. Tourists come to track the rhinos on foot, with the revenues raised going into the conservancy. Some pays wages and running costs, but the rest goes to a community social fund, for school bursaries, water projects and health infrastructure, however the community chooses.

A year after the first returns, in 2016, a black rhino calf was born. Rangers called her Ntangaswa, the 'first born.' Several more calves have since been born. The rhinos were safe and happy, and their numbers, for the first in a very long time, were growing.

* * *

Joseph Lesanjore bent under the drooping branches of a tree, where broken smaller shrubs were pressed down to the earth. 'She rested here,' he whispered. 'She is with her calf, so she'll be nervous.' Joseph, dressed in the neat green uniform of a Sera rhino monitor— the special rangers tasked with tracking the rhino each day—kneeled to point out the tracks: dinner plate-sized hoof prints of the mother, and a side-plate sized circle of her baby trotting behind. As he got nearer to where the rhinos were, even the whispering stopped. Instead, he used hand signals, pointing ahead. A pair of handsome silver-backed jackals wandered past, a giraffe chewing a tree top watched with curiosity, a flock of sand grouse fluttered in to land, while antelope chased and played by 'pronking', leaping with all four legs into the air, jumping for joy in the shining morning dew. Yet it was the animals beyond that Joseph was creeping towards.

About the length of a bus away, a black rhino and her daughter browsed in the bush. It was close enough to see the thick folds on her slate-grey skin, and her long and pointed ears flick forward. Joseph could recognise each rhino by sight from the shape of notches and rips on their ear. He pointed to the calf; he had named her himself, Nteekwa, or 'Early', because he had been the first ranger to find her after she was born, and had spotted her at dawn.

Tracking rhinos on foot must be one of the greatest thrills there can be. It is one thing to spot a rhino from comfort inside a vehicle, and quite another matter to hear it snorting hard from inside a bush just steps away. With a potentially lethal spiked horn leading a tonne of muscle with the weight, power and acceleration of a car, they are not animals to be trifled with. The senses come alive. Every sound sends the blood racing. There was a sudden grunt. Then they passed through the thorns as if the softest grass, and backed away deep into the forest.

* * *

The wailing sound of mewling carried far into the night, as though a baby was crying in pain. The black rhino called out for his keeper—and a bottle of milk. The calf, a year and a half old, three-quarters grown, but already over half a tonne in weight, was still too young to fend for himself. His smallest horn was just the size of a fist, and his front horn, not even the length of a forearm. The rangers had named him Lojipu, meaning the 'second born', because his mother had already had a calf a couple of years before. Born in Sera, he had been abandoned by his mother the day he was born. So he was taken to Reteti, growing up alongside elephant brothers and sisters. It was not clear why his mother had left little Lojipu behind, but he was doing well now. In fact, he was growing visibly bigger almost every week. He still reached up hardly higher than his keepers' waists, but he had the strength of a small tractor.

This was his first night back in Sera. He had been driven in a container all day from Reteti, on the start of the slow process of return to the wild. Rhinos are weaned at around three years old, but Lojipu would likely take a little longer. Until he was old enough to be on his own, rangers slept alongside, camping out under the stars, protecting and keeping him company. In the dark, they and the rhino stayed safe inside the thick log walls in a large stockade. In the day, keepers took him further and further out into the bush, trekking down the dry riverbeds and finding the puddles left from the rains to wallow in. He loved the mud, and in the rains, slid down riverbanks on his belly to splash into the cool pools. He played in the grasslands, and then followed the keepers back for feeding time. For the first few months, on walks following rangers into the bush, he would sniff the dung left by wild elephants—as if he were hopeful of finding his old friends. When he smelt rhino's dung, he would paw his hoof, as if fearful. In time, that would slowly change. He was transitioning, step by step, to surviving on his own.

Mary Lengees had brought Lojipu up since he was the tiniest of babies. At the beginning, when he was the size of a dog, she could just about carry him in her arms. She came with Lojipu on the move to Sera, and would stay for the first few months of transition. She unzipped the mosquito dome over her camp bed inside the enclosure. The moon was bright and full. It was still too early for his bottle of milk, but the rhino needed something. As she turned on a small light, the rhino trotted forward, snorting like a horse, and with his small tail wagging. He pawed the dust. The crying stopped, and turned into snuffling. 'He just wants to play,' Mary said sleepily, reaching forward to scratch him behind his hairy ear. 'He gets lonely.'

The mewling had become high squeaks of happiness. It was a surprisingly gentle sound. As the rhino tried to nuzzle her, Mary laughed too. After a few minutes, Mary pushed his heavy head down, telling him to stop his fooling, before he knocked her over by accident. She chided him to move like a mother talking to her child, turning him away before he got too excited and bashed over the camp beds. As Lojipu headed back towards his nest of dried grass to go back to sleep, he grinned with what could only be described as a rhino smile.

* * *

For a rhino monitor like Joseph, the most direct benefit of the rhinos was his job. 'Having a salary guaranteed every month makes a difference,' he said. 'And the health insurance is important too.' Joseph, a 25-year-old father of three, also looked after his two younger sisters. It was a stretch on his ranger's salary and there would always be demands he could not pay. Sera employed around ninety people, including as rangers, rhino monitors and radio operators. The impact of regular paid work in a land where few hold salaried jobs was spread wide. 'Before, we didn't see much good in a rhino, because what did it bring?' said Lekanaya Lkilayno, the veteran rhino ranger chief. 'Now they bring us our daily bread, so we protect them.'

Yet the animals were not income alone; they are a symbol of change, and of success. Lojipu had won over hearts in a way that no amount of community education efforts could ever do. Lojipu has carved out a soft spot.

There was shouting from one ranger as Lojipu wandered through camp, poking his wrinkled nose in curiosity—or a constant hopeful search for food—deep into a plastic bowl of water being used for washing, before ambling on. The other rangers laughed. 'Jipu!' one called out, shouting his nickname in a sing-song voice, encouraging the rhino to move away from the cooking hut. 'Jipu! Jipu!' If some rhino earned a reputation of being bad-tempered and not very bright, Lojipu was challenging that stereotype in every way. There was clearly deep affection for the calf. He was more than a mascot; he had brought people together.

Rhinos remain endangered, and the animals inside Sera are at constant risk. They are as safe there as they can be, but poachers would still shoot them all dead in minutes if they could. As long as people buy horns, the animals are threatened. Rangers have to remain on endless guard, but nowhere can be guaranteed entirely secure for ever. The location is good; being remote with few roads means those who do come can be more easily monitored, but no fence is impregnable. But with the community supporting the rhinos, they provided protection.

'If I compare today with the time before, there has been a very big change,' Joseph said. 'Before, people could kill any animal, because they were seen as belonging to the government, not to the community. Now, the animals are secure, because they belong to all of us. The animals bring in money for the people. In hurting the rhino, they are damaging us.'

As for what would happen if a poacher did kill a rhino in Sera, Joseph shook his head. 'We would be angry if a rhino was killed,' he said. 'Really, really angry. And if someone killed Lojipu…' His voice trailed off. He looked towards the dozen rangers, queuing up with tin mugs for tea, their rifles neatly lined up against the wall. 'No,' he then said firmly. 'We just would not let that happen. We'll protect him.'

For the children in the area, they no longer need to learn about rhinos from school books alone. 'They are real, not just pictures,' Pauline said. 'Now children come and see the animals themselves.'

* * *

The sanctuary at Sera was set up for rhinos, but they were not the only wildlife to have found safety there. Two dozen Grevy's Zebras from Lewa were brought in to establish a new population of the endangered species, after global numbers fell from some 15,000 in the 1970s, to just over 3,000. But Sera also became the first point of release for the elephant orphans from Reteti.

In May 2019, the keepers at Reteti quietly gathered around the padded box on the back of a truck, gently blowing into the trunks of three bull elephants inside, to reassure them all would be fine. Some leant back to pose for selfie photographs on their phones, a final shot of the keepers and their elephant friend, then reached in to touch the forehead, a mix between a little scratch that they liked, and a gentle, final pat.

Sosian, Warges and Il Ngwesi, aged between three and four years, were the first three elephants to be released. It was planned to be a gradual process, with the elephants put first into a holding pen inside the sanctuary, with bottle feedings on offer. The elephants, however, had their own idea. When let out to walk, they did not come back. They took their chance at a wild life without hesitation.

But collars with satellite and radio trackers had been put around their necks. Researchers were able to track their movements, and on an online map, little elephant symbols showed where they moved. For a while, they were on their own, exploring, but sticking close together. Then the symbols came close to another group of elephants, who had also made the sanctuary their home. Step by step, the orphans were accepted by a herd of some thirty elephants. Their new family picked up where their human guardians had left off. It was a ground-breaking achievement. Not only had the elephants been raised by the community conservancy at Namunyak, they were now released happily into another community conservancy, at Sera.

* * *

Six months later, another three were released in Sera—the young matriarch Shaba, and two others, Mpala and little Pokot. Like the first returns, they were also released in a temporary pen, a half-way house to being on their own. They did not need it.

For a while, they stood outside the pen, tired after the bumpy journey to reach Sera. Everything was new. They wandered close by the pen, sniffing the ground and the air, listening to the sounds around. Then, minutes later, they headed off, on a fast but steady trot through the forest. They had never seen the rolling hills in Sera, but it was as if they knew where they were going. The rangers lost sight of them as vanished into the trees.

Yet when the researchers later looked at the movement from the signals sent from their collars, they had, within a matter of a few hours, met up with their fellow orphan siblings. Elephants have been recorded sending sub-sonic rumbles, a powerful base too low for human ears. Other elephants, however, can hear it far across the plains. It seems Shaba, Mpala and Pokot had sent out a message, and their old friends had come running.

While no one saw them meet, the tracking signals on the computer screen were clear. The symbols showed the six young elephants meeting up, circling around and celebrating, then heading off together to explore their new home. The new arrivals were introduced to the bigger herd. Camera trap photos show them happy and healthy. The elephants were orphans, but they were not without a family. They had each other. The little team was back together.

Since then, more orphans from Reteti have joined the herd in Sera. When they are ready, they will leave the sanctuary to head out on adventures. Somewhere out on the great rangelands they might, just perhaps, find their old family that they were separated from as tiny calves, and happy trumpeting will echo over the hills. Elephants, after all, never forget.

13

THE ELEPHANT ROADS
(HOW DATA HELPS IT WORK)

The small airplane turned in a tight circle low over a clump of palm trees on the great plains of Biliqo Bulesa. Sitting in the co-pilot seat, David Daballen scanned the ground. One eye searched for movement in the trees, the other watched the screen of his phone. It showed a satellite map of the land below, covered with colourful elephant icons. Each marked the position of an animal with a tracking collar, slung on a giant cloth band around its neck. Locating that one animal meant finding the whole herd—and that could be as many as a hundred. Behind each moving symbol lay a much bigger story. 'I can see a herd of about twenty beneath the palms,' David told the pilot, his face pressed against the window. 'But I can't see a collar on any of their necks. Let's try again, and this time, can we go a little lower?'

David, a zoologist and head of field operations for Save the Elephants, was searching for a particular animal. The GPS satellite signal from the collar had brought the plane in close, but even with that, a herd can still be hard to spot. Elephants shelter from the sun in the shade of trees, though when the plane buzzes in close, they often scatter. So a radio scanner helped narrow the search, with H-shaped aerials attached to the plane's wing struts picking up the signals. The squelch and squeals of the VHF radio filled the cockpit.

'We're looking for Nyiro,' he said, taking photographs with a long-lens camera, and then zooming in on the image to check. 'He's trekked down here from far to the north.' He wanted to see if others were with him.

David had been watching elephants since he could remember, herding goats in the Rendille community in the northern forests of Melako. Once, out collecting firewood as a boy, he had pulled at a fallen log sticking out of the ground. Instead, he found it was a huge tusk hidden by a poacher. As a reward for telling the police, he was given a trip to see the wildlife inside Marsabit National Park. The forests were home to tuskers famous for their long ivory. While David had grown up with wild animals all around his home, seeing elephants up close left him astonished. 'I realised what wildlife could be, and it amazed me,' David said. His enthusiasm was encouraged—like so many of the new generation of Kenyans supporting conservation efforts—by his school's wildlife club. 'From then on, I wanted to work with wildlife,' he said.

He was unsentimental about elephants, for he knew the terror of a raiding elephant smashing fences or driving cattle from wells. Yet he had also spent enough time around them to see they were sensitive and intelligent animals, and had become fascinated with the complexity of their lives. Now, working with Save the Elephants, he used pioneering data gathering techniques to track the herds as they moved. The research and campaign group worked all across Africa, but its main study base had for decades been a simple thatch-hut camp on a slow bend of the river in the Samburu reserve. It was surrounded by NRT conservancies. The researchers and the conservancies worked hand-in-hand.

Save the Elephants also teamed up with some of the world's leading technology companies and experts, including from Google and Vulcan, a philanthropic company created by Microsoft co-founder Paul Allen. They developed sophisticated software to map where, when and how the elephants moved. 'We collar elephants because by understanding their movements we can understand their decisions,' said David. 'If we know that, we can understand what they need.' It is about as close as we can get to being able to explain how an elephant thinks. The conservancies would become a testing ground for some of the most advanced monitoring of elephants. It provided the data for decisions to help at the vast scale needed across entire landscapes. 'We're looking for solutions to create a tolerant relationship between elephants and humans,' David said.

It was not just about the elephants. The herders' way of life across the open rangelands faces so many of the same threats as the elephants: the loss of space, changes in land use, and soil degradation. Herders must be able to move huge distances, so that when drought hits one area, they can travel to find the grass and water needed. Elephants are the same. They evolved to wander far. Maps of elephant movements show that the lower the rainfall of an area, the bigger the range. Elephants are a keystone species, one on which the ecosystem depends. Ensuring elephant populations are healthy is about sustaining the ecological integrity of the places they live. Healthy elephants equal healthy ecosystems—and that is good for the people whose home it is.

It was now more crucial than ever. The grazing rangelands have become less productive as human and livestock populations have increased, combined with a changing climate, as rainfall decreases and temperatures rise.[1] As the impact of the heating planet worsens, all will need more space, not less. Trying to solve that conundrum was a challenge that required cooperation, planning, mapping and every bit of technological support available.

David looked down as the plane twisted, following the snaking route of a dry riverbed. The wingtips were nearly level with the tops of the trees. Beneath was a mighty bull elephant, with skin dark from mud from the fresh rains. The animal paused for a moment. He appeared to consider the noisy buzz of the plane above as if it were a fly. His trunk was raised, and ears were wide. Just visible around his neck was a collar. 'There, in the valley, crossing the rocks,' David said excitedly. 'It's Nyiro. He's come back—and he's not alone.'

* * *

Nyiro was a survivor. He was born in the peak of the poaching wave of the late 1980s. Researchers can only guess at his past; all they know of his story is from when he was first spotted. It was in a place where, after nearly half a century of absence, few thought an elephant would ever be seen again.

Mount Nyiro is a green island in the desert that rises up from the scorching hot valley. The misty peak of bamboo forests is sacred to the Samburu. The last elephant officially recorded there was in the 1970s. Then in 2015, reports filtered out that a small group of bulls

217

had been spotted. 'It was an area deserted by elephants—or driven out—decades before,' David said. 'We could hardly believe it; the elephants were pushing back into their old ranges.'

The scientists were sceptical. The elephants were too young to have visited before, and the way to the peak was hard and harsh. The brutally hot volcanic plains around look like the moon, and while it led to the glittering emerald waters of Lake Turkana, that was salty like the sea. It would only be the most adventurous of animals who would test a route there, unless a map was somehow passed down in the memory of the herd. On top of that, more people had fenced in land or blocked tracks with settlements. The old migration routes were harder than ever for wildlife to navigate.

Yet the reports were real. On an initial aerial survey, David spotted possible tracks. Then, when an elder reported a new sighting, a collaring team rushed up by helicopter. Running through the scrub were seven bull elephants. They were crowded together, unusually for males. It was a sign they were nervous.

Collaring an elephant is risky, for both the animal and darting teams. A vet dangling out the door of a helicopter fires the knockout drugs, but get it in wonky and it becomes slow to act, and then the elephant can panic. Even if the animal does go down in a good place, the rest of the herd can linger close. In their eyes, it looks like a poacher has killed their comrade, and they want to defend their family.

When an elephant is tranquilised to have a tracking collar fitted, for the few minutes as they sleep with great trunk-shaking snores, it is possible to look close up into their eyes. Their large ears, floppy in sleep, are folded forward over the sensitive eye to protect it from the sun's rays. Yet if you lift the ear up gently, the eye is open, surrounded by long black lashes, as thick as electric wire but still delicate. The pupil of the eye is jet black, and the surrounding iris is a golden amber streaked with radiating dark lines. Those lucky enough to have stared into an elephant's eye say they have no doubt it is a sentient being of intelligence and emotion.

As David's team darted Nyiro, there was another complication. Everyone wanted to come and touch the sleeping giant. 'As we worked, the community came out in big numbers,' David said. 'They'd never seen an elephant like that on the ground. Everyone was so very excited and wanted to see him.' People were fearful, but also fascinated. 'The very fact that the elephants had returned showed there had been an attitude change,' he said.

The collaring was completed, and Nyiro stood up, woozy from the drugs. Then he charged off. 'The big question was: where would he go?' said David. For a while, he didn't move far, hiding on the high top of the mountain. Then, as the rains came, he packed his trunk and charged off at speed. He headed south-east, in about as straight a line as he could. He trekked eight marathons back-to-back over three nights. The research team watched his icon move in astonishment. 'He moved like a ghost,' David said. 'How he navigated at night over the mountains and through valleys at night was incredible. He has a GPS on his collar, but the way he travelled, it was like he had a GPS in his head.'

Nyiro headed to Biliqo Bulesa, seeking the company of females in a herd. Then, after two months socialising, he was off again, back to the valleys where he had been collared, a journey that became a regular route for him. This time, on the fly-by assessment from the airplane, he appeared to have switched the company of his adventurous bulls for time with females again. 'The collars have given us so much information,' David said. 'Even though I have spent my life around elephants, something always surprises me.'

* * *

Nyiro is one of some forty elephants collared across northern Kenya, drawing a spider web of stories. Mapping how the elephants moved not only provided data on a single species—it provided a way to measure the health of the wider ecosystem. Through that, it became a key tool to assess if the conservancies were actually effective.

Financial audits showed how the conservancies were running, and opinion polls and surveys indicated how people felt. Yet the collars and tracking maps provided a unique assessment from the viewpoint of the wildlife itself. The results were clear; the conservancy model had made dramatic changes to how elephants behaved. It gave scientific backing to NRT's work.

'Anyone can say, "things are better today", but the collars give hard data,' David said. 'Since the inception of these community conservancies, we have seen a big change in the range of the elephants and how they behave. The more we see elephants using community conservancies in a relaxed and calm manner, then the more we think there is something positive happening. More people are informed about why elephants are important, and are beginning to accept and tolerate them. Through that, the elephants are slowly trusting people again.'

The Nature Conservancy, one of the world's biggest conservation organisations, was a key funder of many of the conservancies in NRT, as well as supporting the elephant tracking programme. They asked Save the Elephants to see how the animals acted in different conservancies. 'We rate the conservancies as to how the elephants behave in them,' David added. 'It can show the elephants' relative degree of tameness, or wildness, in the different areas they are in.'

The herds were moving further than they had for generations. 'For decades these places were only transit corridors—elephants were running through scared to get to another safe place, only using them in the middle of the night,' David said. 'Now they are stopping in these former problem places, and they are staying to rest.' The collars could even measure 'tortuosity'—or how twisty their route was. Run fast and straight, and the area was not good. There was no dawdling in a place where you might be shot. But stop and sniff the flowers, and the land was somewhere the elephants felt secure. If an elephant starts to 'streak'—a sudden stampede out of an area—it could indicate panic after an attack by a poacher.

* * *

The plane circled around again. This herd was heading east, to where the winding waters of the Ewaso Nyiro entered the Lorian Swamp, where the river ends long before reaching the sea. Much was impenetrable high-growing grasslands and thick forest of acacia trees. Elephants love their seed pods. Herds of well over a hundred elephants are common; numbers in the wider Biliqo Bulesa have more than doubled since the worst days of poaching at the end of the 1980s, to some 7,500 elephants.

'In the dry season, they are clustered around where they can get water,' David said. 'But in the wet season, the elephants go deep into areas they do not usually go—and so at that time of the year we take extra care. We share that information with the NRT rangers, because when the elephants are roaming far they are happy—but they are also exposed to more risks.'

New cameras for aerial surveys use digital processing programmes to count animal numbers far more accurately—and cheaply—than the old ways of spotting and estimating by sight from the air.

But the work also involves the miserable but important tracking of carcasses. NRT rangers help gather data from the ground, while aerial surveys locate others in more remote places, for the bodies are marked by rotating spirals of vultures visible from afar. Each carcass is then assessed on foot. It is a highly organised system. All deaths are recorded, whether from old age, sickness and accident, or those killed for ivory or by herders in conflict over water. This provides an index of poaching pressure by comparing natural deaths with those killed, called the Proportion of Illegally Killed Elephants, or PIKE. 'The higher the PIKE ratio, the more elephants are being killed,' David said. It is an extremely sensitive barometer of change.

In NRT conservancies, the ratio tumbled. From a grim PIKE score high in 2012 of 76 percent, by 2019, that had dropped dramatically to just 30 percent. It pushed past the tipping point where births exceed deaths, turning the population decline of the previous decades into gradual growth. It was a big endorsement for the conservancy model. The conservancies had significantly more elephants—and much lower levels of killing—as opposed to neighbouring community land without a conservancy framework.[2] As for poaching for ivory, the conservancies had almost stamped it out entirely. The number of elephants in NRT member conservancies killed for ivory dropped 96 percent from 2012 to 2019. It was a staggering transformation.

* * *

For Iain Douglas-Hamilton, the founder of Save the Elephants, it was a change he had spent decades working to bring about. He had been in northern Kenya since the very beginning of the NRT conservancy movement. Elephants, predictably, were his passion.

'That's Matisse,' the British scientist said, sweeping back his flowing silver hair and waving in response to a gently raised grey elephant's trunk, as if both were greeting an old friend. He leant enthusiastically out of the pickup he was driving, as he bounced down a narrow track past the 'Artists' family of elephants. 'There's Rodin,' he said, naming one wallowing in mud, as he identified each of the twenty-three animals grazing among the bushes. 'And Goya is there,' he added, pointing to another, pushing a tree down. Since elephants live as a family, researchers had named each herd after a different subject for easy identification. That meant the messages on the crackling radio could include conversations about Blizzard and Breeze from the Storms family, Jericho and Jerusalem from the Bible Town herd, or Cleopatra and Catherine from the Royals. Each elephant had their individual character. In one lucky escape, zoologists watching two bull elephants—named Rommel and Abe Lincoln—were caught up when the rivals turned and fought. Rommel, the loser, flipped their vehicle in angry defeat—punching arm-sized holes in the metal with his tusks. The researchers only climbed out to safety when Abe returned for another bout. The rusting wreck of the truck sat at the camp as a warning.

Iain began studying elephants in 1965 for his doctorate at Oxford, camping for five years beside Tanzania's Lake Manyara. To understand family relationships, he developed an extraordinary technique to recognise hundreds of individual elephants on sight. He learned the profile of each animal's ears and the shape of their tusks by photographing 450 elephants head on. Unfortunately, since elephants flap their ears out wide often as a warning sign, it was not always the safest of pictures to take. He was an eager pioneer of collaring and radio tracking.

With his wife Oria, the Douglas-Hamiltons would dedicate their lives to elephants. Oria loved elephants just as much. She grew up in Kenya amongst the wildlife, where her Italian and French parents had settled. The letters her parents wrote home inspired their cousin Jean de Brunhoff to write the story of Babar, the King of Elephants. The books were read to Oria as a child.

But the real elephant story the Douglas-Hamiltons documented was a darker one. In the 1970s, they criss-crossed Africa to assess the continent-wide massacre of elephants. Everyone could see the species were in crisis, but without facts and figures, some said it was exaggeration. Their data provided hard evidence that could not be dismissed. Gathering it was not without risk, however. Flying a small plane to count carcasses, they were often shot at by the poachers—so they took to sitting on a flak jacket to protect themselves from bullets from below. 'We saw only bones, day after day, and I realised that we were just clerks of death recording yet another holocaust,' Iain wrote. He and Oria were determined to do something to make a difference. They wanted to understand what elephants needed, in order to find a solution to secure a peaceful future for them.[3]

In 1997, the Douglas-Hamiltons considered setting up in Samburu for their research—but the area was dangerous then with poachers and bandits. They called an old friend for help.

'I've known Ian Craig since he was about twenty years old, and he was always passionate about wild places,' Iain said, describing how he had seen the changes over the years. 'I saw him in his various stages; in the early days, Ian just had this idea, that wildlife and humans should exist side by side. He was interested in rewilding his family's farm, Lewa, to make that into a place where wildlife could once again roam, which he did. Lewa was where it began. From there, his vision was literally a straight line from where he lived looking north to that beautiful, sacred mountain of Ololokwe. I remember him telling me what an incredible area it was underneath the mountain, and how many elephants there were there—elephants always played a very important part for him. He had an idea, and he is very convincing; but a lot of the key to his success is how he talks to people. He is quiet and unassuming, but also he listens.'

Ian Craig calmed the Douglas-Hamiltons' worries about security. He said the newly founded conservancies would give the researchers a safe space to work in, and the rangers to protect them. It won the Douglas-Hamiltons over. They set up in Samburu, in the shadow of Ololokwe, beginning one of the world's longest-running monitoring projects of elephants.

It was a collaboration that developed and deepened over the decades. 'There is a huge amount of talk of the principle that you must not only protect wildlife, but must also engage the local communities,' Iain said. 'In most places it stays just as talk, but NRT has been different because they made it happen. They started by asking people what they thought, and how they would they engage in conservation had they the means. So it has been built from the bottom up, and they took it to a whole new level.'

The cooperation helped with a key tool. Mapping the elephants provided data that also fed into the NRT's operations room, in the lush green heart of Lewa.

* * *

From the outside, it looked like a tin-roof cattle dairy, as if left over from Lewa's days as a farm. It was tucked into the bush, with monkeys swinging from the creepers that hung off the yellow-barked fever trees.

Inside, there was a very different atmosphere. Banks of flat screens were attached to the wall, with three lines of desks with computers. Phones rang, and radios crackled with messages. The men and women on duty in the Joint Operations Control Centre— or more simply, the JOCC—coordinated ranger movements across a massive region, night and day. They provided the oversight to link both rangers from the conservancies and the NRT's Nine Teams, as well as cooperation with regular police and KWS wildlife officers.

On white boards at the front, summary reports radioed in from across all the conservancies were listed. 'Sighted: ARMED GANG,' one message read. Above, in red pen, an officer had added, 'CONTACT', the military term for gunfire. There was an ongoing operation to stop cattle raiders, and the Nine Teams were chasing them. They were catching up rapidly, but the bandits were firing back to stop them.

'Everything that happens, we can see here,' said Yusuf Kurtuma, the JOCC commander, as he tapped a giant touch-screen monitor to zoom in closer on the map. An icon showing a Nine Team transposed onto a satellite photo of the harsh desert south of Marsabit could be seen. 'The raiders fired on us,' Yusuf said. 'And we responded.' Across the map, an aircraft symbol showed where a small plane flew, scouring the plains for signs of the raiders. The JOCC teams relayed information from the pilot to the rangers.

Technology had revolutionised the conservation landscape. In the early years at Lewa, Ian and Jane used to scribble down messages from a sputtering radio in the farmhouse. Then, as the rhino sanctuary grew, operations were coordinated by the radio room in Lewa with dedicated operators putting pins on maps to mark positions. Still, for a long time, once on patrol, the rangers were effectively on their own.

Then in 2016, Paul Allen, the philanthropist and brains behind the elephant mapping programme from Vulcan, offered his help. He had been horrified at the alarming results of his Africa-wide Great Elephant Census. It showed that numbers had dropped by nearly a third in recent years, with an annual loss of around eight percent. He estimated that an elephant was killed on the continent every 15 minutes.[4] To try to stop that, he expanded support from Vulcan for a new system to help a conservation organisation's coordination. Using Save the Elephants' tracking systems as a basis, Vulcan's tech-experts developed an online mapping and management system they dubbed 'EarthRanger.'

In 2016, Vulcan put the first such system in place for NRT. It collated streams of information from multiple sources, and displayed it on a constantly updated satellite map: locations of ranger radios, vehicles and aircraft—as well as the position of animals fitted with collars. Situation reports from each conservancy, or tips from intelligence assets, were tagged on the computer screens linked to the map. There were dozens of icons to indicate different threats: a gunshot heard, cattle stolen, a wounded animal, or suspected poachers. 'It is a command and control solution for conservation,' Yusuf said. 'We have a minute by minute oversight of what's happening. It helps us see patterns too. If we map where there are attacks, and where the bandits were last seen, we can start to predict where the risk spots are. Then we can see where they might strike next.'

The officers read the terrain like a book. They knew the gunmen soon had to take the stolen herds to water. On the dry plains, there were only limited wells to go to. 'They have sighted the animals,' radio operator Martin Leperere said, after the Nine Team rangers called in their latest report. Yusuf took note of the position, and used his fingers on the flat screen to expand the photograph of the landscape. He was worried about a potential ambush site he could see. He feared that the raiders could use it to attack the rangers. 'The main gang are heading for the hills here to hide,' Yusuf said. 'So we have to stop them before that.'

Yusuf said the system provided rangers with an edge, calling it a 'force multiplier' by adding to the rangers' strength. Using the maps, it was easy to calculate ahead and find the shortest route to cut the raiders off. So two hours later, another Nine Team had positioned themselves between the hills and the raiders. With rangers on either side, the raiders let the stolen animals go, sneaking away to hide amid the maze of rocks. The Nine Teams rounded up the herds, and sent messages to the owners they were bringing them back.

While the job of the rangers had not changed, the support behind them had. Still, the most modern technology is only ever as good as the teams on the ground at the sharp end of carrying out the work. Well trained, motivated and dedicated rangers with good kit remained as critical as ever.

* * *

The system has been a major success. Vulcan's EarthRanger system, developed in NRT lands, is now a key monitoring tool used by over 100 protected areas in thirty countries across Africa, Asia, Europe and North America.

Technology continues to add new techniques to the toolbox. There are plans for listening devices placed on hills to monitor gunshots, sending a warning signal pinpointing the location moments after the trigger was pulled. As plotting the movements of animals becomes ever more sophisticated, the system helps provide management of the animals. It can sound the alarm if a known troublemaking elephant approaches a fence put up to protect settlements or farms. Rangers can be sent to head them off before they get into trouble.

The next generation of motion-sensor camera traps are also changing the game. Just as computer programmes can be used for facial and speech recognition, analysts are applying that to wildlife. The potential implications are enormous.

Before, each camera trap had to be visited in person once a week or more—and then it could be even longer before the thousands of photos were looked at, logged, and the information collated. Now cameras can be taught to recognise specific subjects of interest. So the cameras are able to distinguish not only whether an animal is a goat, a rhino or an elephant, but by using identification programmes focused on ear notches, horn shape or tusk size, which particular animal has been seen. The cameras can even recognise the shape of an AK-47.[5] Since the cameras have to operate in areas far from internet connections, and because sending thousands of photos by satellite is expensive and slow, the smart cameras send brief text message alerts.

Of course, technology cannot operate alone—and some of the best work combines high-tech support with old ways of monitoring. The conservancy structure helps provide the platform for scientists to work.

For researchers from San Diego Zoo worried about dramatic declines in giraffe numbers, that has meant putting in place over a hundred motion-sensor cameras and collaring giraffes with GPS units. But it has also meant recruiting conservancy members who came forward to join the Twiga Walinzi—the 'Giraffe Guards'. Reticulated giraffe, a beautifully patterned species unique to northern Kenya, had seen a 70 percent drop in recent decades. Numbers fell from 36,000 to fewer than 9,000, largely on account of habitat loss, land fragmentation and poaching. A tower of giraffes—the communal name for the graceful long-necked giants—went from being a common sight to being put on the international endangered 'Red List.'[6] The Giraffe Guards monitor the herds, as well as maintaining the cameras and carrying out community outreach programmes, to help persuade people to protect the giraffes. At the same time, online volunteers worldwide help sift through over a quarter of a million photos for the researchers, to identify individuals and log their position. Together, the research data and community scouts help the scientists better understand giraffes' habitat preferences, and how they interact with livestock.

Similar programmes are used by the Grevy's Zebra Trust, a close partner of NRT. Just as we have unique fingerprints, each zebra has their own stripe. A digital stripe software system identifies each animal photographed. Community scouts—the majority of them women, and many of those widows or single mothers, with their salaries providing key income—patrol remote areas. They monitor the highly endangered Grevy's Zebra, taking photos with a camera that saves each image with a GPS location. Patrols in more distant areas head out for days on camels. The data helps show where the animals are struggling, and to identify what can be done to change that. The work has helped stabilise populations of one of Africa's most endangered large mammals.

When a problem is understood, then there can be hope of finding a solution.

* * *

Inside the JOCC, one screen was dedicated to the elephants alone. 'If you see elephants suddenly moving and scattering, you think—this is not normal, and so perhaps there have been gunshots,' said David. 'Or if an animal doesn't move for a few hours, an alarm is sent to our phones.' It was simple to radio map coordinates to the nearest ranger team, so they can take a look in person.

When collars relied on the old system of radio tracking alone, it was hard to exactly pinpoint a location. It was not known whether the collar had fallen off, or if the elephant had been killed. So sometimes when an icon stopped moving, 'ghost' signals would be left, a virtual memorial to a lost animal, until the battery died years later. Now, with a combination of accurate GPS and mobile Nine Team rangers, someone can be at the site within a matter of hours. It is time enough, if the poachers have killed the elephant, to use sniffer dogs to track the trail.

Still, not every alarm is a tragedy. Elephants rarely sleep for more than a couple of hours at a time—but there is always one that likes a longer snooze.[7] 'Sometimes it is a false alarm,' David said, smiling. 'Because the elephant has taken a nap.'

The programmers developed algorithms to measure anomalies in movements. Collars were fitted with similar devices to those that allow phones to know which way up you are holding them. They measure the angle of the elephant's neck to indicate if it is feeding or resting. Or, if they show that its head is up, and the elephant is charging, that it is in trouble.[8]

The technology has radically changed things. In the early years, using radio tracking, it was considered lucky to find one or two animals a day. In the 1990s, Iain Douglas-Hamilton even strapped an extraordinary box contraption including a video camera—complete with automatic windscreen wipers squirting water to clean the lens—around an elephant's neck. For a few hours, it provided a constant video diary of the elephant's movements, but batteries and tape soon ran out. He called it the 'Ellie Tellie.' Now there is a nearly continuous flow of information on each animal's location. The data is key to another piece of the puzzle; keeping the wildlife corridors open.

* * *

The map looked like Vincent van Gogh's painting *Starry Night*: swirls of light scattered across the canvas, but all connected with dramatic bright lines. As well as day-to-day maps, tracing elephants over time helped provide long-term planning. Each swirl marked a place of refuge, showing where the animals had spent time. The lines marked the routes elephants trekked across the rangelands, from wet season ways to dusty tracks in times of drought. The lines on the map were the elephant roads. The problem was, those roads were being blocked.

Elephants don't just wander aimlessly. Like humans, they follow ancient trails long since cut along the contours of the land. Often, the wide tracks became the basis of human roads; it was easier, after all, to follow where an elephant had bulldozed through tangled jungle than blaze a trail. We still move on the old elephant ways; even in Europe and North America, where the forgotten forebears of elephants are found only as fossils, the ghost trails of elephants still remain, for the origins of some roads in use today were those torn open by tusk and trunks many millennia ago.[9]

With the space left in the world shrinking, many places will soon become too crowded for elephants. As homesteads merge into villages, and villages sprout into small towns, the open land is divided with buildings, fences and tarmac highways.

Elephants need space—and they are increasingly living in pockets, sprinting from one place of refuge to another. Like all animals, elephants weaken when kept in isolated, genetically separate 'islands'. Government reserves acted as vital sanctuaries of safety, but they could not operate alone. When elephants were confined, their foraging had a massive impact, pulling down almost every tree. When they burst out, they made enemies by raiding adjoining agricultural land for food. That added to a spiral of destruction. Scientists have mapped how the smaller the area of land wild animals have to roam, the fewer are able to survive. That is not just a matter of population size, but even of numbers of species present. For wildlife to flourish, they need the freedom to move.[10]

The work of the conservancies had helped put a stop to the worst of poaching. Yet that was only the immediate threat to wildlife. The far bigger threat was competition and conflict with people. Northern Kenya still had great spaces left to roam—but it needed planning to protect that. The next question for the conservancies was how to manage the land. For as much as humans were a threat to wildlife, they also held the solution.

'There are resources that come in to defend nature, as well as to destroy it,' Iain Douglas-Hamilton said. 'If you take it as a given that nature is worth saving, in order to accommodate the human changes that are definitely going to happen, then what you can do is rational planning.' The mapping tools offered a high-tech way to protect the oldest routes. It was like building bridges across an archipelago. 'You can't stop wanting to lift people out of poverty,' he added. 'But there is no need to develop destructively in every case.'

When a new road was built, ribbon development along the route would potentially divide wildlife populations. The maps marked out exactly where the elephants liked to cross. 'With the facts ahead of the time, you can go to a community with a map of elephant movements,' Iain said. 'Together we plan crossing points.'

* * *

At their simplest, elephant crossing points were just signposted corridors left free of obstacles, like a road junction between humans and wildlife. In other places, they needed more effort. One of the most important routes had been closed for years—and its reopening was critical in linking the herds back together. Africa's first dedicated elephant underpass connected otherwise fragmented populations on the high forests of Mount Kenya, via a long corridor through farmland, to the great plains northwards beyond.

Some 3,500 elephants on Mount Kenya had been slowly cut off by farms, roads and settlements. Once in a while, the biggest bulls still charged through. They smashed through farms, trampled down the golden fields of corn, or were hit by fast traffic. They left anger and destruction in their wake. The rest lived in isolation among the chilly and misty forests. Sometimes they ventured up so high they had been seen grazing in grass white with frost. The remains of one lost soul was found frozen close to the snow line, beneath the 17,057 foot (5,199 metre) high peak. He was dubbed Icy Mike.[11]

Letting the elephants out so they could move freely to the plains would channel them away from raiding tasty crops, the thinking went. So, in 2011, two large commercial farms let a wide strip of their land be fenced in an 8-mile, or 14-kilometre, corridor. From the highlands, it connected through the NRT conservancy of Ngare Ndare, then to Lewa, and then on to the network of conservancies beyond. In places, it was wider than the length of several sports pitches laid together, a wildlife reserve in itself. But as it approached the fast highway, the fences narrowed, until it squeezed through a concrete underpass. It was a truck-sized passage three men tall, high enough for the biggest bulls.[12]

Building the corridor was gamble. After the enormous effort, no one was even sure the elephants would use it. Several people were sceptical. The key thing was to get one elephant to lead the way and show it was safe. So to start with, the tunnel was strewn with hay, and lined with elephant dung picked up from Lewa, to entice them through. Then, the secret ingredient was added: drops of vanilla essence—a scent apparently irresistible to elephants. Perhaps it smells like bananas.

Within days of it opening, the first elephants came down from the mountain. The first grey trunk was seen poking out of the underpass, sniffing the scent of freedom on the other side. He put out his head to make sure all was safe, then moved out entirely. Moments later, the camera captured another elephant, a set of white tusks glinting in the gloom, and then a third.

They came through one by one. Soon, more than a thousand crossings were being made by elephants every year. Many more species of wildlife used it too, a safe passage through the farmlands and villages of humans either side.

Today, if you head out from the bustling streets of Nanyuki, you will cross it after passing through the market town of Timau. It is sited just after the road north drops from the highlands of lush green farmland, down towards the sun-baked plains of rangelands far below. The slope plummets so fast through the cedar forests that, with bad brakes, your ears pop multiple times.

It is easy to speed above the elephant road without even noticing it. It is a sign of how the changes needed to let wildlife and humans live alongside each other need not be a huge imposition and hinder development. It only needs a bit of forethought and planning. If you're lucky, elephants may be using it, trumpeting safely on their migration north below.

* * *

David Daballen, back from the airplane survey, stood in the camp beside a long pile of elephant jaws, collected for research. 'To win the hearts of local communities, people have to see the benefit,' David said, recalling how he, as a child, had been won over to wild-life after visiting Marsabit National Park. 'That's why it's so impor-tant to go into schools to explain the value of elephants—and then to bring children to visit them for real,' he said. 'The children are the ones who will decide the future of elephants here.'

He lifted a bleached shoulder bone once belonging to an elephant called Ebony. A bullet hole from a poacher's gun went right through it. It was a sad reminder of the cost of failure. 'When I first started working with elephants, going out day after day in the bush to rec-ognise them by the notches in their ear patterns, people at home thought I was crazy,' David said. 'But then, I come from a herding family. So I replied, isn't it similar to how our people cut different ear marks on their cattle, so we can tell which cows belong to them from hundreds of others?'

David remains optimistic, trusting that the young generation growing up will see the importance of free ranging herds in the future. 'The pastoralist people, the Samburu, the Rendille, the Borana, we have always known that elephants live in a group,' he said. 'But I don't think many people knew of the real depths of their complex family and social life we discovered in recent years of research,' he added. 'So when I tell communities about what we know about elephants now, they are absolutely amazed.'

He described the blessing of leaving green branches on the skulls of elephants in respect, and the old relationships between wildlife and humans. 'We have so many stories from our elders about how we shared the landscape with them,' he said.

He looked out over the river, where elephants splashed in the shallows. 'Everywhere in the world, our cultures are being diluted by the modern changes within our environment,' he said. 'We are trying to remind people of the old connections, to not forget that bigger and deeper relationship that we have with wildlife and who we share the land with. It is so important.'

14

THE RAREST ANTELOPE ON EARTH
(HOW IT WORKS IN DIFFERENT ECOSYSTEMS)

Dawn was breaking with red skies as the exhausted rangers pulled into the small police station in Masalani. It was a hardscrabble tin-roof town on the banks of the snaking brown waters of the Tana River in the far south-east of Kenya. But the rangers had been out on patrol for 10 days in the furnace-heat forests along the troubled border lands with war-torn Somalia, and it felt like coming to the big city. They were a mixed team combining conservancy scouts, an NRT Nine Team unit and Kenya Wildlife Service officers. They'd been tracking poachers in the silvery-grey thornlands in the conservancy of Ishaqbini.

It was a land of huge herds of buffalo, as well as elephants, lions and leopards. The rangers had even come across the area's legendary residents, a trio of white giraffes, animals seen so seldom they seemed like a myth. The pale skin was startling, strange and spectral. The giraffes had crossed the quiet track just ahead of the team, looking back in apparently as much astonishment as some of the rangers. For a moment, the rangers and the giraffes stared at each other. The white skin was not caused by albinism, but a loss of pigmentation—a condition called leucism. So the giraffes' gentle opal eyes were dark, framed by long white eyelashes fluttering. It was easy to understand how the Somali people who lived here saw them as a sign of good fortune, and wanted to protect them. Perhaps unexpectedly, the white was good camouflage. They blended into the thorns bleached pale by the sun. Stepping back from the track, they soon vanished. It was if they really had been an apparition of the mind.

But the rangers had also seen something else: two young men on a motorbike, racing at midnight through woodlands. The rangers had blocked their tracks, and the pair skidded to a halt with shouts and screams. The two men, aged eighteen and twenty-two, sat handcuffed to each other, dazzled in front the truck's headlights. Faced with the threat of prison, they sobbed like little boys. The ranger's commander gave them a cup of sweet tea, and they soon spilled out information on the poaching network.

They said they had been heading out to meet a poaching gang that had caught a giraffe. The motorbike men had been called to help butcher it with machetes, and to take back haunches of meat for sale in the market. It was not about a hungry family hunting an animal for the pot. It was largescale and commercial poaching for bush meat. They used sharp wire snares, with nooses that bit deeply into an animal's leg or neck. The rangers had been tipped off by an intelligence source in the village, and they had lain in wait. But the big dealers had slipped out on a different route.

'Next time, we'll catch them,' said Omar Hasan Harrow, a member of the NRT's 9–3 team. 'Arresting these two sends a warning sign.' Omar came from the fishing and farming Pokomo people, who live in the mangrove forests of the Lower Tana Delta. 'So much of the wildlife has already gone,' Omar added. 'If we weren't stopping the bush meat traders, all would disappear.'

Omar's home on the wide and winding waters of the Tana Delta was one of seven conservancies who had joined the NRT umbrella in Kenya's coastal region. Communities had seen the changes being made in northern Kenya through the conservancy movement, and set up their own too. Some were inland, forests deemed of global importance as biodiversity hotspots.[1] But others were marine communities, wetlands and estuaries accessible only by sea channels that weaved through the dense walls of mangrove trees. Flocks of birds there fill the sky, and some of the last dugongs of Africa, the gentle sea cows whose faces inspired legends of mermaids, still held out in the quietest creeks.

Beyond, communities had set up conservancies on the scattered archipelago of Lamu, islands with ancient tower houses with elaborately carved wooden doors, architecture with echoes of trade with Arabia and India. The sparkling blue waves of the Indian Ocean crashed through the coral reefs onto soft sand shores, where the turtles came to nest. They were far from the original cluster of NRT conservancies, entirely different ecosystems to anything found in northern Kenya. Yet the principles of community engagement were common to all, and the same system of conservancy rangers and NRT Nine Teams operated.

The rangers had earned a reputation for stemming once out of control poaching—and the two men in handcuffs shook in fear as the team drove into the police compound. Eventually, they'd be let off with a caution, but the rangers thought a stern warning might be the shock needed to put them on a path towards something more constructive.

* * *

While police took the fingerprints of the two men, the rangers wandered through a scrapyard of crashed vehicles in the parking lot of the police post. Some were rusting, and had been abandoned there for years. One, however, was new. It was a green-painted army troop carrier, or what was left of it. The wreckage was caused by a roadside bomb a few months earlier. Its front left wheel was ripped off, the metal cab frame crumpled, and its chassis twisted. The amount of explosives needed to throw a heavy truck full of men up into the air was huge. The rangers said that two soldiers had died in the attack, and that several others were wounded. Dark brown flecks were spattered on the paintwork.

These were dangerous parts. The big threat here was not armed poachers, nor cattle raiders like in northern Kenya. It was guerrilla fighters from al-Shabaab, the Somali-led East African franchise of al-Qaeda. In Somalia, they controlled swathes of land, dealing out their hard-line interpretation of Islamic law. Al-Shabaab was fighting across the porous border in this corner of Kenya too. The jihadis rejected the authority of Kenya's government, and took revenge for Kenyan troops sent to Somalia to fight them. Kenyan soldiers here were based in fortified garrisons, surrounded by deep ditches and earth piled up as defensive walls. These were needed; the jihadi fighters had attacked army bases, including storming an airfield and blowing up a US surveillance plane and killing US troops. A favoured tactic was turning trucks into suicide vehicle bombs and ramming through defences. They regularly staged ambush attacks on soldiers, or laid landmines on the roads. At night, they crept out and moved among the villages. The army tried to track them down, and there were heavy gun battles. But al-Shabaab was ruthless in response, torching villages and executing dozens of civilians. Gangs of gunmen prowled through the remote forests inland from the Indian Ocean, surviving off the animals they shot—buffalo, antelope and giraffe—and supplies from the people they had threatened.

The rangers touched the jagged holes in the truck. They knew the risks, but the sight was still a shock. Their job was not to fight al-Shabaab, but to support their community and to protect the wild-life. But they were no supporters of the guerrillas. They feared for their children. In Arabic, al-Shabaab means 'The Youth', and they targeted teenagers for recruitment. Sometimes the fighters used slick propaganda to brainwash children. Boys from the area had sneaked off and joined the fighters; the tales of those killed fighting the army were repeated in shame as a warning to others. But it was a deprived and marginalised land, and false promises of a glorious escape out of poverty through death in jihad were powerful. When that didn't work, al-Shabaab resorted to kidnapping. They abducted the young cattle herders out in the forest and forced them to fight, and kidnapped the schoolgirls as slaves for sex.

The rangers clambered back onto the truck and roared off. They were off to find a shady site to brew tea and cook up breakfast and rest for a few hours before another night-time patrol. As their pickup drove along the dusty track, children were walking to the primary school in the village of Kotile. Three twelve-year-old girls wearing headscarves and neat-pressed long skirts chased each other in play on the road. They were late for assembly, and waved the rangers down. The team slowed down, and squeezed up to give them a lift. One of the girls, Ayan Ibrahim, said she dreamed of being a doctor when she grew up. Her satchel bulged with biology and mathematics books. 'I want to help my people,' she said. 'I want to make sick people better.'

She was a bright girl with big dreams, but she represented some-thing more remarkable. Al-Shabaab insurgents were strict oppo-nents of girls going to school and learning. They were a real threat, and operated in the Boni Forest close by, where the herders took their livestock to graze in the dry season. Yet as the rangers pulled up outside the schoolyard, and the girls hopped off, over 400 children were standing in lines as assembly began. Education was changing the children's lives.

The school was supported through the Ishaqbini conservancy, with funding for construction and support for students. 'It's providing opportunities for the children,' headteacher Hassan Farah said. 'The bursaries are allowing children to study who might otherwise miss school completely.' On the wall of his office, Hassan had written a quotation of Nelson Mandela. 'Education is the great engine of personal development,' the sign read. 'It is through education that the daughter of a peasant can become a doctor, that the son of the mine worker can become head of the mines, that a child of farm workers can become the president.'

The conservancy at Ishaqbini began because of a remarkable antelope. Conservation efforts to protect the species had brought the community together, offering a more hopeful future that did not involve al-Shahaab. The antelope species is called a hirola, and if you have not heard of the animal, it is not surprising. They are the rarest of the rare. They are the most endangered antelope in the world.

* * *

For a brief moment, the herd of a dozen hirola antelope paused. They have elegant, ridged horns and a beautiful tawny coat. Between their dark eyes is their most distinctive feature, an inverted white chevron stripe. It crosses their face, and circles their eyes. It makes it look like they're wearing a pair of spectacles.

'They're shy animals,' said Ahmednoor Abdi Maalim, the conservancy manager, as he pointed to the antelope bounding away into the bush. 'But they mean a great deal to us; this animal is connected to this community. In the past, there were very many across a big area. Now they are only found in this part of Kenya.'

They're related to hartebeests, but in the scientific naming list of all living things, the hirola are in their own genus. That's the branch that ranks above species, but below family. The herd of hirola were not only the last few of their species, but the last of their genus too. Their future was precarious, and without action, they would have vanished—or have been left in such small numbers their extinction was inevitable.

'The loss of the hirola would be the first extinction of a mammalian genus on mainland Africa in modern human history,' the International Union for Conservation of Nature warned.[2] They have the hirola on their Red List as a 'Critically Endangered' species, the final warning step before extinction. 'The sole survivor of a formerly diverse group,' said the Zoological Society of London, the ZSL, adding they are 'often referred to as a living fossil.' The ZSL included the genus on its EDGE list, short for 'Evolutionarily Distinct and Globally Endangered'. The list was designed to raise support to protect some of most remarkable threatened species with few close relatives on the tree of life. 'They represent a unique and irreplaceable part of the world's natural heritage, yet an alarming proportion are on the verge of extinction,' ZSL said.

Once, hirola were common in the arid forests and savannahs of East Africa. Their scientific name Beatragus Hunteri, or Hunter's Hartebeest, came from the zoologist who found them in 'large numbers' in 1887. They galloped away with 'more vitality than any other antelope' he had killed.[3]

But the hirola's range soon shrunk. In the last century, it was found only in Kenya and Somalia. Then from the 1970s to 1980s, the population crashed. Numbers tumbled from some 15,000 to 2,000. They were devastated by drought and disease, including one of the last waves of rinderpest. The hirola struggled to recover. The elephants that once roamed between Kenya and Somalia were decimated by poachers. Without them the grasslands turned into twisted bush, reducing the grazing for the antelope. On top of that, hirola were easy prey for poaching gangs. Numbers never recovered. In Somalia, the antelopes are believed to have been entirely wiped out. The last stronghold was in eastern Kenya. Numbers dropped to fewer than 500 individuals, surviving in tiny scattered pockets.

Its extinction would be a loss to the world, but those who would mourn its loss the most were those who lived with the antelope. To the Somali people, especially the Abdulla clan who shared the land of Ishaqbini with the antelope, the animal held a special place in their hearts. For generations, they had grazed their herds of cattle in peace alongside the antelopes. At night, the antelopes came close to homesteads for protection from hyena, leopard and lion. In turn, the people used the antelope as guides in drought. They said the wild herds could forecast when rain was coming, and would move to be under the showers when they fell. In Somali, the antelope is called *arawale*, or brown, from the colour of its coat. It was the mangled pronunciation of outsiders that turned that into the name hirola. The people knew of the value of the arawale long before scientists came to tell them how rare the hirola was.

* * *

'The hirola are the most beautiful of all the antelopes,' said Harun Bulo Hassan, an elder in his eighties dressed in an embroidered cap, and stroking his red-hennaed beard. 'They are special to us, because they are a sign of good health.' Harun, sitting outside his small home in a neatly swept compound in Ishaqbini, poured cups of cardamom-spiced tea, his granddaughter sitting on his knee. 'We didn't know that the hirola could become so few,' he said. 'We thought they would always be here.' He had seen the land here change over his eighty years of life, through war, and through waves of poaching that had decimated the wildlife. He remembered the days when elephants were common, wandering through the villages, and rhinos still hid out in the bush.

Much of Ishaqbini is made up of arid plains of grass and thorn, sandwiched between the acacia bush and the thick coastal forests. In the dry season, when the grass is poor, people move their cows. They seek grazing in the Boni Forest, the wild, wooded reserve along the border with Somalia. Then when the rains return, they come back to the open rangelands at Ishaqbini. It is a slow rhythm of back and forth that has gone on for centuries. The antelope grazed happily behind the cows, for they preferred the short grass the cattle left behind after eating.[4]

But at the end of the dry season, the hirola moved first. They smelt the showers before they fell. 'Hirola can sense the rain to come, so they show us where there are good pastures,' Harun said. 'We believe that without the hirola, the livestock will not do well— and without livestock we will not survive. For the livestock to grow and be successful, the hirola must be there.'

241

The community is proud of the hirola. It symbolises the wider importance of protecting the natural world among which they live and depend. Just as the Samburu in northern Kenya see elephants as an indicator of good health in the environment and their loss as a warning of the problems ahead, so the Somali people in Ishaqbini see the antelope as a measuring gauge for the health of their livestock.

When Harun was a young man, and the elephants were being massacred, the elders had warned that if the community killed the wildlife, they would pay the price in the end. 'They said that if the elephants all go, then the cattle would suffer,' Harun said. As young men, they saw the elephants as only a threat to their cows, and laughed. But when the elephants were slaughtered, the forests grew back, and so the grass for grazing went too. 'What they predicted was right,' Harun said. 'Now I am an old man, and I warn that we must protect the hirola like we do our livestock, or we will suffer again.'

It can be easy to profess care for wildlife, but his promise to shelter wildlife was not just rhetoric. As Harun spoke, dusk was falling. Three wild ostriches came in from the bush, to sleep inside the thorn walls of his compound for shelter at night. He repeated a passage from the Qur'an. 'The Prophet, Peace Be Upon Him, said that even if you fear your life is coming to an end, even if you only have one minute left, then you should take that time to plant the seed of a tree, for you can never know the future,' he said. 'The Qur'an says that we must protect the forests and the wild animals.' A pair of wild warthog trotted into the compound too, their tails upright like aerials. At times, he said, zebras even slept just outside the fence. 'To kill the hirola is wrong,' Harun said. 'To protect them brings us blessings of God.'

* * *

There is a controversial history of outsiders trying to protect the hirola. In the 1960s, people feared the antelope would not last long in their natural range. Hirola were rounded up, darted and captured, then taken to the national park of Tsavo East, where some twenty animals were released. In 1973, the government declared the Arawale National Reserve, a 200 sq miles, or 54 km sq

44. Harun Bulo Hassan from Ishaqbini, who said the health of livestock and wildlife are intertwined. © Peter Martell

45. Randa M'ikiugu, a beekeeper on Mount Kenya, shows Ian Craig a picture of Mau Mau comrades. © Peter Martell

46. Lake Paradise on Mount Marsabit – a 'sky island' with lush forests above sweltering rangelands. © Peter Martell

47. Rangers in the Nine team units are self-contained and can operate for weeks without needing to return to headquarters. © Pete McBride

48. A rhino on the slow process of returning to the wild in Sera, the first community-owned and run black rhino sanctuary in East Africa.
© Pete McBride

49. Bead workers, who sell their jewellery internationally through the support of NRT, check payments sent to the bank accounts on their phones in West Gate Conservancy. © Pete McBride

50. Mount Kenya, the 'mountain of brightness'. © Peter Martell

51. A hirola stands alongside a zebra in Ishaqbini Conservancy. © Ian Craig

52. Jumbo bottles. Elephants at the Reteti sanctuary drink a special formula of powder and vitamins whisked into goat milk to mimic the nutrients from their mother. © Pete McBride

53. Lenadokie Leterewa, who helped start the first multi-ethnic ranger patrols, in his former operational base in Sera. © Peter Martell

54. The age-old way life of the pastoralist animal herders is uniquely suited to the dry open rangelands. © Pete McBride

55. Osman Maro, community ranger in Ndera, on the banks of the Tana River. © Peter Martell

56. Iain Douglas-Hamilton, of Save The Elephants, standing beside a research vehicle battered by a bull elephant. © Peter Martell

57. The view from Ololokwe, or Sabache, towards Sera. © Peter Martell

area for the antelope. Yet it was little more than a park on paper alone, and many antelope lived outside the reserve anyway. Otherwise, little else was done to safeguard the hirola on the ground, and numbers slumped by as much as 90 percent. In 1996, following an aerial survey that counted barely 300 antelopes, many feared the hirola were a lost cause. So a capture programme arrived to round up some of last remaining animals to take to bolster the antelope herd in Tsvao. A total of thirty-five were captured, bringing numbers in Tsavo to around 100.[5]

Then the work stopped. People saw hirola as a blessing; so when the government began to take them away, there was anger. 'We saw the hirola being taken from their motherland,' said Abdikadir Sheikh Hassan, a local elder. 'We said they should stay here with us.' Abdikadir was so angry he took the case to the High Court in Nairobi. 'The plaintiff asked for orders restraining the removing of a rare and endangered animal called "the Hirola" from its natural habitat... on the grounds that it is a gift to the people of the area and should be left there,' the court paper read.[6] Abdikadir won; the judge issued an injunction. Yet while that kept the hirola at home, there was still nothing to protect them. Numbers continued to decline.

The community heard of the changes made in northern Kenya, through the conservancy network of NRT. The inspiration spread, and in 2007, the community came together to create the Ishaqbini Hirola Community Conservancy, across 350 sq miles, or 900 km sq. 'People now realised that the hirola they thought were found everywhere, were now only left in this area,' said the conservancy's manager, Ahmednoor Abdi Maalim. 'They accepted that land could be given to help their protection.'

NRT provided advice and helped them fundraise. Rangers were recruited, and hirola monitors tracked the herds. But numbers still declined, partly because of levels of predation by lion, leopard and wild dogs. 'So people agreed to build a fence for a sanctuary,' Ahmednoor said. 'Of course, the other benefits of the conservancy helped win over those who were fearful.' Those included jobs for rangers and management, as well as the security that they brought. The rangers were recruited from the community, so they were not seen as an outside force.

In times of trouble, people were fearful of relying on the regular police or army, because that could bring down reprisal raids from al-Shabaab. The conservancy rangers acted as a home-grown force that could help where the army could not, including working as an ambulance service to bring people to the clinic. Al-Shabaab appeared to tolerate the rangers—since their mission was to protect the hirola and support the community, not fight them. In the early stages when the conservancy was beginning, elders were even handed a message from al-Shabaab: 'Change the colour of your cars.' The pickup trucks the rangers used were the same dark green as the army—and the guerrillas were worried they'd attack one thinking they were soldiers. The conservancy spray-painted the vehicles a sandy green. A message was sent back from al-Shabaab—the colour change was good.

The conservancy brought in veterinary experts for the hirola, but who also provided free cattle vaccinations for livestock. It also put in infrastructure, including a water pipe pumping from the Tana River far into the rangelands for the cattle to drink.

'School bursaries and water; that's why I supported it,' said Hawo Selel, a mother of seven, busy serving cups of tea at her stall in the market. 'If it wasn't for the piped water, the children would be spending all their time fetching it, but now with bursaries, they are at school.' Hawo, one of three women elected to the conservancy board, had also received a soft loan through the conservancy to set up her small business. It was enough to build her stall, a grass roof hut with woven thatch walls, and buy a gas cooker and a large kettle, with a dozen chairs and tables for customers to sit. 'If it wasn't for the conservancy, life would be much harder,' she said. 'The security would still be bad.'

The work the conservancy was doing was to protect a rare antelope, but the impact it had was felt all across the community. It allowed the conservancy to raise funds not only from donors keen to ensure the hirola did not become extinct, but also from those who were more interested that such lands did not feel abandoned. The best defence against the extremism of al-Shabaab was not a costly military operation, expensive both in terms of soldiers' lives, and the price of bombs and bullets. The best defence was to offer a better future. It was more effective to ensure the stability, security and safety of a community, than to try and cope with the chaotic consequences of collapse and war. Rebuilding a society was slow, expensive and had a high chance of failure. Keeping the community together in the first place was a win for all.

* * *

The 10 sq miles, or 27 km sq sanctuary with a predator-proof fence was completed in 2012. Some hirola already lived in the sanctuary, but others from the surrounding area were herded up, and driven into long nets laid out in the bush. From there, they could be flown by helicopters into the sanctuary. The sanctuary opened with forty-eight antelopes, a tenth of the entire species.

The numbers doubled in just three years. By January 2016, an aerial and ground survey estimated 97 hirola in the sanctuary, bringing the total population to some 500 antelopes. By 2020, numbers had grown so that nearly a quarter of the entire species were protected inside the sanctuary, with the community working to extend the fence and size of the area for the antelope. In time, it is hoped to release antelopes to restock areas outside the sanctuary and allow the species to flourish.

Species are listed as endangered all too often, and once on the list, rarely come off. It is a term that has become so common that many of us feel that while regrettable, nothing can be done but to sadly accept it. Yet the story of the hirola shows that it does not have to be so. Hirola remain at acute risk, but there is hope ahead.

'If the sanctuary had not begun, I think the hirola would have gone by now,' said Ahmednoor. 'But it matters more than the hirola, much more. The hirola have brought us all together, and together, we are stronger. Without the conservancy, things would have been very different. There would be less opportunities, less jobs, less security, less education, less everything—apart from the numbers who would be joining al-Shabaab. There would be a high rate there.'

* * *

Bordering Ishaqbini is Ndera, home to the Pokomo and Warderi communities. There, the open grasslands turn into a band of lush riverine rainforest. The trees hug the banks of the Tana River. Inside, the jungle is thick, almost impenetrable in places, with creepers like nets blocking the tracks. On the deep leaf-litter floor, it is dark even on the sunniest of days because the canopy is so dense. Above, the calls of monkey chatter rang out loud. A Tana River Mangabey, a nimble monkey with elegant grey fur and dark eyebrows, peered down from the trees. It screamed its warning call to its troop. 'Go-go-go-go,' the mangabey yelled. It leapt from through the treetops like a trapeze artist.

The narrow strip of tropical forest along the river is home to two of the most endangered primate species in the world. One is the mangabey, the other is the Tana River Red Colobus. It is a more sedate species, with a fine head of red fur as if wearing a cap. As their names suggest, they are found only here. There are estimated to be fewer than 1,500 of each species remaining. At one point, the International Union for Conservation of Nature listed both species on its Red List of 'The World's 25 Most Endangered Primates.' The mangabey shouting and swaying in the canopy of the cathedral-like forest of Ndera might seem to be happy, but their home is shrinking fast.

Their biggest threat is habitat loss. Trees are being cut down at terrifying speeds, with the land turned into farms, and the wood used for timber or burned.[7] For the colobus and mangabey, the more patches of forest that are left—and the more corridors of trees connecting those areas—the better chance the monkeys have of survival.

The people have always farmed alongside the thick woodland here, but in the 1990s, there were moves by the government to declare their forest a national reserve—meaning they would have to leave the land they depended upon. It sparked fury, and there were pitched battles between government rangers and the farmers.

'The land by the river had always belonged to our people,' said Muntu Ali, squinting up at the calls of monkeys, somewhere in the tall trees of the rainforest that bordered his small riverside plot. 'I feared if it became a reserve we'd be forced to go.' So some, like Muntu, turned to destroying the forest. The ancient hardwoods were solid like iron with bases too wide for small chainsaws. 'I lit fires around the base of the trees to fell them,' he said. Each tree could take days to burn, but the even the tallest, which soared like skyscrapers, came crashing down finally. Muntu replaced the forest trees with bananas and mangos. 'In the past, if you wanted to cut a tree, you first had to seek permission from the elders,' said Omar Mohammed, a neighbouring farmer and fisherman. 'But when we thought we'd lose it all to the government, people didn't care.'

But neither Omar or Muntu wanted all the forest cleared entirely. 'I only wanted enough land for my farm,' Muntu said, a seventy-year old former headmaster, hoeing the lines between his sweet potato and maize crops. 'If all the forest goes, the land is bare. The trees bring the rain. Where all the trees have been cut, the fertility of the soil does not last for long. For a while, we'd be okay—but then we would all end up with nothing.' Above his head, bright yellow weaver birds chattered, hanging in their straw ball nests from the branches of a mango tree, as though using their home for a swing. Muntu went into the forest for deadwood for cooking fires, to gather fruits and roots to eat, and herbs for medicine. The forest was communally owned, but there were special palm trees he claimed as his, the sap of which he tapped to brew a powerful moonshine wine. 'This place is called Awalamunyo,' Muntu said. 'It means, the "forest of the people."'

What people wanted was to use the forest—not destroy it. So while people blocked the government plans for a reserve, in 2010, they created the Ndera conservancy. They had seen the changes made next door at Ishaqbini, and NRT offered to walk the community through the steps needed. 'You can't order people to protect wildlife,' said Osman Maro, head ranger of Ndera. 'You tell them to "move here" and they will refuse, and it will bring fights, because it has always been their home.' Osman commanded a dozen rangers. They patrolled the 325 sq miles, or 850 km sq, conservancy both by boat, nosing up the jungle river on the metal skiff, and by motorbike, zooming through the narrow forest tracks. 'People only want to destroy it if they are not allowed to use it,' he said. 'They want to protect it.' The conservancy structure also meant that the forests were safer from commercial loggers. It was easy to pay off individuals to chop down the trees, but far harder to win over the entire community.

But with populations increasing and demand for farmland growing, people needed land. The easiest plots to carve out were beside the river, because there was access to water. Creating farms there destroyed the riverine forest—the same tree cover the monkeys need to survive. So to encourage people to use land beyond the forest back from the banks, the conservancy set up dozens of water pumps and irrigation pipes. 'There is lots of land to farm away from the river if you can get the water to it,' said Osman. 'But you need to be organised, or before you realise it, all the forest is gone before your eyes.'

Farmers close to the forest struggled to guard their crops from the wild animals, from buffalo and elephants crashing through their maize, to baboons raiding their potatoes. It was a constant battle, but the cost of the wildlife to the people's crops was offset by the support of the conservancy, through school bursaries for the farmers' children, and micro-loans for entrepreneurs. The conservancy was also working with mango farmers to help bring their crops to market. 'Mango farmers were being taken advantage of by brokers,' said Ndera manager Malika Maro. 'People were forced to sell their crop for cheap or risk it rotting.' Malika was working to link up remote Ndera directly with buyers in town. 'We can help as a community to support each other,' she said.

People respected the monkeys as part of the jungle—as they did all the species that lived in the rainforest—because if the primates were safe, then so too was the forest.

* * *

The boat keeled against the wind, the much-patched triangular sails straining in the gusts. The creaking timbers of the dhow sliced fast through the creek in the mangroves of the Dodori Forest. From the thick tangle of jungle on shore, a single, lonely male buffalo stared out with a sullen look. His horns, wet with mud and dripping like dark blood, looked as though they were made of wrought iron. He slowly turned, but only after showing he was not afraid. The boat was far enough away in the channel, and it was not worthy of his energy for a fight. He thumped away through the creepers to find a place he could be undisturbed. The sailors pushed on, back out into the main channels, and passing empty white sand beaches that seemed to stretch on and on. Eventually, they swung back around, through the white horses on the waves of the open sea, safe to port on the island of Pate.

Fuzz Dyer, who had helped turn Lewa from a ranch into a rhino sanctuary in the 1980s and then supported the first conservancies at Il Ngwesi and Namunyak, had since set up a beach hotel on Manda, the island just northeast of Lamu. He had seen communities struggling in the fallout from the conflict in neighbouring Somalia, with al-Shabaab threatening people, and pirate gangsters even kidnapping tourists. 'Much of the northern Kenya coast was largely forgotten in terms of government,' said Fuzz. 'I'd been involved at the start of NRT, and I had seen the differences that could be made. So with the communities, we helped bring in some of the ideas that NRT had put in place in northern Kenya.'

The coast was an entirely different ecosystem, but the fundamental principles for making a change through conservation were the same. In 2013, four communities—Pate, Awer, Kiunga and Lower Tana Delta—all established their conservancies. Maritime rangers patrolled the community's fishing zones by boat, monitoring catches and helping to identify the biggest problems, so people could find ways to tackle them.

A key challenge was that the fish stocks on which people depended were threatened. The fishing areas closest to shore were being overexploited, and fish populations were in rapid decline. People's existence depended on the fish. So Pate focused on one of their most important resources—the octopus.

* * *

Low-tide in the knee-deep waters glittering off the island of Pate, the fisherwomen were out hunting octopuses. They scouted for the fine string of bubbles, the sign of a hiding octopus. With a long pole, a wriggling octopus was tickled—then grabbed and pulled out. It was a way of life they had lived for generations. But after worrying years of seeing catches decline, the community heard of a project that had revolutionised fishing communities further south in the Indian Ocean, on the great island of Madagascar. People there had been struggling from many of the same problems, but marine biologists suggested they cordon off blocks of a community's fishing grounds. It resulted in stunning increases in the number and size of octopuses caught. At first, it didn't seem to make sense; fish less, but catch more.

So Pate community members went to Madagascar to learn what had been done. 'They shut fishing zones for three months,' said Firdhaus Yakub Athma, a Pate ranger and radio operator. 'The octopuses they caught afterwards were much bigger, and many more.'

Octopuses grow fast but die young. The bigger they are, the more eggs they produce. So even limiting fishing for a short period can mean huge increases in catches. In Madagascar, the suggestion of closing off fishing grounds had initially sparked opposition. What, after all, could people eat if they could not fish? But scientists from a marine conservation organisation called Blue Ventures had mapped out a plan. People in the village of Andavadoaka backed a trial test, to close a fifth of the fishing area and allow octopus stocks to regrow.

There were years of data to prove it worked. A study by Blue Ventures, carried out over eight years and in dozens of sites, found closures of just three months could reap returns far greater than the cost of not fishing. Since people could still fish in remaining areas, their income did not decline during the closure. In the month following the opening up of an area, villagers more than doubled their income. The weight increase of octopus landed overall was greater than 700 percent.

For Alasdair Harris, the British marine biologist who set up Blue Ventures, it had exceeded his wildest hopes. A decade before, as a young and idealistic zoology student crazy about coral, he had begun work to map Madagascar's reefs by scuba diving along them. If people knew what there was to lose, he reasoned, they would help protect them. Yet while he and colleagues gathered reams of research, that alone was not going to make the changes needed. It had not worked. After all, the fishing communities already knew all too well the state of the reefs and the fish stocks upon which they depended.

As a scientist, he had made earnest appeals to communities to set up no-fish zones. Set aside the healthiest reefs as no-catch areas to allow time for stocks to regrow, he argued, and the reserves would replenish the fished areas outside. The science was sound, but the proposal was dismissed. It had not worked either. People did not want conservation advice telling them where not to fish. They wanted help to catch enough fish to survive.

But the test case of an octopus closure had a bigger consequence than boosting catches in one small area. The experiences of running the fishery closures united people. The successes gave people confidence, and proof that community action could make a change. So the community set up a 'locally managed marine area.' It was, in effect, another name for a community conservancy.

With a governance structure in place, they began to make larger changes. They outlawed destructive fishing methods such as poison, and they banned the use of mosquito nets for fishing, since the fine mesh caught the youngest of fish. They even set aside permanent no-fishing refuges around coral reefs and mangroves. It was the very same proposal Blue Ventures had proposed years earlier, which had been dismissed. Those protected areas saw fish numbers rise by almost three times within six years.[8]

'The real magic went beyond profit, because a far deeper transformation was happening in these communities,' Alasdair said. 'Spurred on by rising catches, the closures sparked community interest in broader conservation initiatives. It was a democratic system for local marine governance that was totally unimaginable just a few years earlier.' After the first village of Andavadoaka, two dozen communities followed the same path. Together, they declared 600 sq miles, or 1,550 km sq, of marine protected areas. They called it 'Velondriake'. It means 'to live with the sea.'

'We were the very first to do the octopus closures,' said Bridgit Finy, a fisherwoman from Andavadoaka. 'When others saw how well it worked, everyone around Madagascar decided to copy what we did.'

Conservation proved to be the catalyst for far wider social change for good.[9] Just as NRT saw in its support of conservancies in Kenya, so in Madagascar, the achievements by one community inspired another. The communities came together, establishing a civil society umbrella organisation called Mihari, an acronym in Malagasy for 'marine resource management at the local level'. It included over 70 communities, covering nearly a fifth of Madagascar's inshore waters. It was nearly a third larger than the total marine area under Madagascar's national parks system. But it spread beyond Madagascar too, and was adopted in countries across the Indian Ocean, adapting to the different environments and conditions in each new place. The ripple caused by the example of one small fishing closure spread wide. 'A handful of fishing villages taking action sparked a marine conservation revolution for hundreds of thousands of people,' Alasdair said. 'I've learned that our goal has to be to win at scale, not just to lose more slowly.'

So when the conservancy team from Pate saw the project in action, they came back keen to give it a try. 'We saw what they had done in Madagascar,' said Firdhaus, the Pate ranger. 'So we brought the idea back home.' In January 2019, three villages agreed to stop fishing in an area of sea about the size of 100 football pitches. When it opened in May, there was disappointment. The results were not dramatic—and people admitted that some had not been following the rules, and had sneaked in to fish. So the zone was closed again, and this time, the rangers increased their patrols.

At the second opening in September, people were sceptical there would be change. Yet, as the fisherwomen came back to shore bearing heavy loads of octopus, there was celebration. It had surpassed even the highest of expectations. In five days of fishing in May, people had caught 186 kilograms (410 pounds). In September, in four days, they caught 868 kilograms (1,913 pounds) of octopus. The amount was more than four and half times the weight hauled out before. 'People were excited,' said Firdhaus. 'Before they'd walk far to find a few octopuses. It had really made a difference.'

Buoyed by the octopus catch successes, the community have also put in place no-take zones, and expanded the temporary fishing closures elsewhere. The mangrove forests, important nurseries for young fish—as well as a key carbon store, and a storm barrier from flooding—are also being protected. Communities are also working to replant areas once cut for timber and charcoal. One small change inspired many more.

The challenges ahead are enormous. The global outlook for the health of our planet is grim; the horrors of the impact of environmental damage in a rapidly heating world. But the successes made by communities are small victories to prepare them for an age ahead of ever increasing extremes. Conservancies have brought people together. Even the best organised community may be overwhelmed by forces not of their making. Yet against such change, the best chance the communities have is to unite and face it as one. It is an example that those on the frontline of change can offer all of us, wherever we are in the world.

15

FROM THE SACRED MOUNTAIN
(HOW IT OFFERS HOPE FOR OUR FUTURE)

From the high forests of Mount Kenya, Randa M'ikiugu stared out towards the plains of the north far down below. Randa was a farmer and a beekeeper, though he was elderly now, and he did not often come up this far into the forests to see how his hives were doing. The high slopes are sacred. For farmers living in the foothills, they pray facing the colossal mountain with arms outstretched, calling out the lord of nature who lives on the snow-topped peak. Its title *Kiinya'a*, as called by the Kamba people, or *Kiri Nyaga* by the Kikiuyu—the Mountain of Brightness—was what gave the name for the nation of Kenya itself. The mountain forest brings rain and feeds rivers that snake out across the land, bringing life to so much of the country.

Randa was from the Meru community, who lived on the fertile and green lower slopes, and he had spent a lifetime on the mountain. He pulled tight a chunky hand-knitted wool scarf around his neck and tugged in his thick jacket against a breeze straight off the ice above. 'We have always looked after the forests here,' Randa said, listing the ways that each bush, herb and plant had special properties as a medicine, food or as a way to sustain life. 'Every tree has a use.'

The old beekeeper rested on a roughly carved walking stick. Now his grey hair was thin and his voice was wobbly, but the great-grand-father still stood strong at the age of ninety-six. Dusk was approaching, and wispy clouds snaked around the tops of the trees like wreaths of smoke. There were clear tracks where an elephant had pushed through the trees, and piles of fresh dung. The forests of Mount Kenya were protected, but so much of the land around them was not. The last century Randa had experienced had seen more change than in any other century of human existence: the growth of cities, development of infrastructure and land turned into farms. Since he was born in 1924, Kenya had undergone a demographic explosion. The population multiplied some twenty times over.[1] It was a century that also saw more destruction of the natural world than ever before. That damage was not, of course, only in Kenya. It is clear in the ruins found in every corner of the world. Nature works in long cycles, and it is far easier to destroy than to protect. The trees that take decades to grow are chopped down in minutes.

'There were elephants and buffalos everywhere,' Randa said, remembering what life was like when he was a boy herding goats. 'The animals were as many as the trees in the forest, or the blades of grass on the plains.' Back then, rhinos were still common even high up on the mountain. Randa craned his head up towards where the summit of Mount Kenya lay. The once thick glaciers have all melted, with only sorry relic memories of ice left in the deepest shadows of the gullies. The dusting of snow at dawn has often gone with the burning equatorial sun by noon. The land is changing, and fast. 'There were no roads back then,' he said. 'Only paths for people walking. To find our way, we faced the sun for the direction we were going. We had the snow on Mount Kenya as a signpost. You looked at the shape of the hills, and you knew which way to take.'

As a young man, Randa had joined British troops in the King's African Rifles, sailing east and fighting Japanese forces in Burma in World War Two. It was a brutal jungle war, with close quarters fighting in horrific conditions. 'It was a bad time,' he said. 'The battles in the jungles were dreadful.' He made it safe home, but on his return, he refused to accept a continued status of political exclusion. He had fought for others; now he would fight for his own rights. He became a Mau Mau soldier, battling to overthrow colonial forces. 'The war here in Kenya was much worse,' he said. 'We lived in the bush for years.' Randa used the skills he had learned in the army to craft homemade rifles. He'd earned a terrifying reputation, staging raids on police posts and farms, attacks the British responded to with violence on a far larger scale. Neither side showed mercy to their enemies. He pulled out a much-folded piece of paper from inside his coat, a copy of a photograph from Kenya's independence in 1963. It showed the Mau Mau generals standing in front of a pile of the improvised guns that Randa had helped make, stacked as a symbol of their struggle. 'We fought hard and achieved our objective,' Randa said. 'We won. We got our freedom.'

Ian and Kinyanjui sat alongside Randa. They were driving in the forest, and had met Randa on the side of the road. They had known each other for years, and they greeted each other as old friends. They had first met when Ian came to construct a thick-walled log cabin out of fallen trees, high up on the shoulder of Mount Kenya, a fishing hut called Rutundu. Randa had often stayed nearby, tending his honey hives, and staying in secret caves hidden in the hills. Randa had at first been deeply suspicious of Ian, worried that he would disturb his beehives, and fearful that outsiders would take the land. Over the years, however, they had become friends. They rested on the soft grass in the clearing of the forest to talk.

The once-fearsome guerrilla was now a softer, older man. Randa was thoughtful with the understanding of age, reflecting on what he had seen, and what was ahead for when his young great-grandchildren grew up to be as old as him. The century past had seen a transformation almost unimaginable in the life of just one man, but Randa feared that the century to come would see a revolution even greater. 'Once we all knew how to live with wildlife,' he said. 'We protected it because we depended on it. We got everything we needed from the forest.' He had watched the land alter, and he worried about the future. 'I never went to school, and the young people now have more education than I ever did,' he said, but then paused. 'But they are forgetting about nature.'

He looked north, down to the hot plains, towards where Lewa began. Beyond, in the mist, was Il Ngwesi, and after that, the mountain revered by the Samburu, the round headed summit of Ololokwe. He had seen the changes made since Ian and Kinyanjui— and all the many others in the team—had started work four decades before to protect the first rhinos and turn the old cattle ranch of Lewa into a sanctuary. Randa had observed how over time the idea of conservancies had spread from community to community, as people came together to assert their control over their land. 'It has helped support the schools, the health clinics, and created jobs,' he said. 'But it has protected the land too.'

His sight was failing, and he stood without speaking for several minutes, staring across the flanks of the fierce mountain that he knew so well. He knew what it was to fight for land, and to protect the rights of the people who lived there. Randa had no time for saving wild animals just so that wealthy visitors could enjoy seeing them; he did not care about that. He cared because he knew that when the natural resources were stripped and gone, it would be the poorest people who would suffer the most. 'The land here could all be farms—but the land does not go on forever,' he said. 'If we had a land without wildlife, with all the trees gone, what would we have left? It would be terrible.'

* * *

Ian and Kinyanjui helped Randa into the truck. They gave him a lift back to his village, a cluster of tin-roof houses on a junction of the main road. He waved as they headed onwards, for the next stop, to drop off Kinyanjui at his farm. Night was falling.

Kinyanjui stopped at his home, just outside the boundary of Lewa. It was close enough that when Kinyanjui walked around his farm amongst his cattle, he could see the wild animals roam on the conservancy. Kinyanjui's voice broke out in laughter. 'I saw the biggest herd of buffalo today, and I thought of you,' he told Ian. 'In the old days, your legs would have been shaking with excitement to go and track them.' Ian smiled as they embraced goodbye.

Watching them, I thought of how much they had seen and done. What had begun as a friendship between two men looking for adventures had become a last-ditch effort to stop the extinction of the rhinos, and had then kick-started something far greater. From the seeds of those first steps had grown a gigantic network of nearly forty community-run lands. Some were direct neighbours, others lay further afield, but if the patchwork area were all placed together it would stretch across some 16,000 sq miles, or 45,000 km sq. They are home to nearly half a million people from at least eighteen ethnic groups—and spoke almost as many different languages. The conservancy movement continues to grow, inspiring others to follow the same path.

It is conservation at scale across landscapes that has created change to entire ecosystems. It is a story of relationships, of building bridges between communities, of developing trust, and of bringing people together to restore their connection with the land. But it goes far beyond just protecting nature. It paves the way for wider social change, so that the communities grow in confidence and take broader decisions to better their lives. It gives people the strength and the resilience to face the ever more extreme challenges of the forces our planet is facing.

I thought of the men and women who had risked all to protect the natural world around them. They live in harsh environments, places where people exist on the borderline between survival and struggle. They know what uncertainty and crisis look like. Drought and disaster, hunger and war; people had faced challenges that had often seemed insurmountable. Yet people had united, and had overcome them. There are many things they could teach others, but perhaps the most important is also the simplest. Even in the direst of circumstances, change is possible.

Driving back in the dark through Lewa, Ian was reluctant to take credit for what the work had achieved. 'If we didn't make it happen, who else was going to do it?' Ian said. 'I just didn't see anyone else going out to find money to put into projects in what were some of the most insecure places you could think of. I had the friendships, the connections, the history, the passion, the partnerships to help get it started. But it was the communities who did the work.'

Kinyanjui put it more succinctly. 'Our people always knew how to look after the land, but we had run into trouble,' he said. 'We just needed some support to get us going again.'

* * *

In recent years, Ian stepped back from the management of running NRT, keen to ensure it was in safe hands to continue beyond him. That role was taken up by smart young Kenyans, many of whom had benefited through the conservancy education bursary schemes the communities ran. Ian poured his time into other projects. He had done all he could to stop the poaching on the ground, but he wanted to work to stop the trade from the other side as well. The best way to stop the supply was end the demand. That required top-level political pressure, and he became a key player in the

Elephant Protection Initiative, which brought the presidents of eighteen countries with remaining elephant populations together. He also became involved in Stop Ivory, a global campaign pushing to end all trade and destroy government stockpiles of tusks. He'd been key in organising Kenya's giant 2016 burn of ivory of 105 tonnes, nearly nine times the size of the 1989 burn and representing at least 8,000 elephants, as well as 1.5 tonnes of rhino horn from over 450 rhinos.

He took a turn on the board of the Kenya Wildlife Service, supporting work to incorporate community conservation with government plans. He'd been honoured with awards, including one of Kenya's highest presidential orders, the Moran of the Burning Spear, as well as a medal for 'services to conservation and security to communities', presented to him by Prince William on behalf of the Queen. Still, he dressed in the same old shorts and sun-faded shirts, and outside meetings, if he was not with his grandchildren, he and Jane would be off camping, following the elephants as they moved with the rains.

Ian slowed the pickup. Just a stone's throw ahead, two young bull elephants ambled across the dust track. They turned to face the headlights, unhurried and unworried. Ian turned the engine off, and watched them play. The pair reminded him of what he had spotted the day before, while flying his tiny plane over the bushlands northeast of Sera.

'I came in low over a dry river and I saw a herd of perhaps fifty elephants coming out of the trees,' Ian said. 'They'd not been seen in that area in such numbers for generations. When I look at where the collared elephants are, there are more and more heading there—and why? Because they are safe. When one has gone and it is safe, another one comes in, and they find things are good there, then there is a knock-on effect. It is just like when the elephants were being badly poached and they came here to Lewa because they found it was good. It shows me that you really can protect wildlife at scale.'

After flying over the elephant herd, Ian had circled back and landed some distance away where the riverbed was not too rocky, then walked in closer. 'Everywhere I went there were tracks of lion and buffalo too,' he said. 'The full spectrum of nature was present.' If allowed to recover, nature does bounce back. The resilience of the land is extraordinary—but it has to be given the chance.

'Elephants won't hang out in a place that's not good,' Ian said. 'If elephants are happy, then so is the environment. It tells me that the security is good—and I don't just mean for wildlife. People will be safe there too. It's a place with a future.'

The elephants ahead on the road, still young but big enough not to be messed with, were playing with each other in the track. Ian watched them as they raised their trunks towards the car.

'Some argue that there is just not room for these elephants, and that might be the case in other parts of Kenya,' Ian added. 'But not here in the north. There are few people out in those areas. It's a land of pastoralists, big open rangelands without the issues of growing populations and crops. It's a place where the elephants are not under constant pressure or face conflict, so they start staying there for much longer. They've got the space to move safely as they want.'

The fate of elephants holds a mirror up to our lives. It can be easy through the generations to forget what we have destroyed. Step by step, the land heats, the forests are burned, the rivers dry; but over time each small loss can be hard to see. We grow accustomed to a gloomier, greyer, diminishing world of the wild. Animals such as elephants provide the warning bell to show us what damage has been done. It is, of course, not only elephants that are struggling. Yet if we cannot even protect an intelligent animal like elephants from our excesses, then we stand little chance of stopping ourselves from the demolition of our living planet itself. However, if elephants are thriving, then that is a sign the land is healthy not only for wild animals, but for humans as well.

Conservation is about protecting the very fabric of life. When we force a species extinct, we weaken the ecosystem it was part of—and like tumbling dominos, drive more to death. The extinction of species, habit loss, and climate change are all connected. The life support system of nature becomes increasingly unable to maintain a stable climate, or to provide freshwater and healthy crops, or to even protect us from natural disasters and disease. When we lose a species, we lose something of ourselves.[2]

* * *

This has been a story of the past, of what was done, of how people pulled their communities back from the brink. But it is also a story that shows us how it can help to handle the changes of what is yet to come. That is why it matters. It is easy to become disillusioned; the world is losing species at a horrifying rate. Reading reports of habitat loss and the extinction of species, it seems easier to turn our backs in despair. There are even some who say 'give up', and that the fading wild has no place in our modern lives.

Yet I tried to picture what the land would have been like if, so many years before, people like Ian and Kinyanjui had also not seen the point in trying. If Ian had stayed a farmer, Lewa would be today a failing dusty ranch. If the people of Il Ngwesi and Namunyak had not unified to protect their lands, and shown their neighbours what could be done, the situation would be grim. I had seen what that could have looked like. The neighbouring lands were so similar in terms of landscape and ways of life, that they showed what the alternative could have easily been.

As a journalist, across the border in Somalia, amid famine and in war, I had been caught in the dust storms whipped up after the desperate people burned the forests for charcoal to sell to survive, and met the angry and frustrated young men had joined extremist gunmen who ruled by fear and force. In South Sudan, I had witnessed the bodies of families murdered in cattle raiding violence, killed in battles over resources each year. There the trees were also cut down, and wildlife butchered for bush meat on a commercial scale.[3]

Northern Kenya could undoubtedly have become like that too. Yet it had taken a different route. People had peered into the abyss, and stepped back. They had been confronted by an existential crisis; they had no new land to move on to, no savings bank, no fall-back options, and no big state to rely on. They understood the need to unite to defend the resource on which they all depended. Cynics see humans as inherently selfish, but that has not been my experience of the people I met, and of the work I saw them carry out. Yes, there were crooks and cheats, killers and the corrupt. Yet there was also the balancing force of the wider community who could rein them in. In extreme conditions, the human instinct is not always to fight, but to cooperate. We can choose to help each other. Disasters can divide, but they can bring out the best in us too.

'We're much stronger and much more likely to find a solution if we are all united,' Ian said. 'As soon as you bring people together in any society facing a challenge—especially when poverty and real stresses are involved—then you can identify what the issues are, find some leadership, find a common purpose, and build it out from there. The fundamental foundation of a conservancy is applicable almost anywhere.'

Ian is no blind optimist, but keeps going with no sign of retiring or slowing down, determined to do what he can. He and Jane were recently nearly killed in an attack, when they spent New Year's Eve camping while tracking elephant. Scores of bullets smashed into their camp, pinning them down behind a tree, with chunks of bark splintering off with burst after burst of automatic gunfire. 'It was seriously heavy,' said Ian. He had his police rifle with him, but he knew he was hopelessly outgunned. 'I told Jane: this is it, it's game over, we're not going to get out of this one,' he said. 'I remember thinking, lying on the ground, so that's how all this ends, just some blood on the sand.' Jane said they had to try, and as the shots continued, they dashed to the aircraft, scrambling inside with bullets zinging past. There was no time to even untie the clothes line attached to the wing, trailing behind with belongings scattering as Ian pulled the plane sharply upwards. Somehow, they escaped without being hit. Months later, after sending messages through local elders, Ian and Jane went back to the same spot of the attack. There they met the group who had come close to killing them, a dozen teenagers who said they thought they were herders from a rival group. They shook hands as the boys mumbled an apology. 'It shows just how thin the "good" really is,' Ian said. 'But that is the world that NRT works in.'

He crept forward, flashing the truck's headlights. The largest elephant came to play with the pickup, nudging it with bravado, but when Ian revved the engine in warning, the bull stomped off to join his fellow elephant in the tall grass. Ian smiled, and watched them go in peace. 'Could we really, in our generation, allow the biggest mammal on earth to disappear?' Ian said. 'Then what next? The rhinos? Giraffes? Suddenly we would have an empty world, full of people, but nothing wild.'

* * *

I had come to learn whether the community conservancies had really made a difference to the people and the land. I had wanted to answer a key question. Is there still space for humans and wildlife to coexist alongside each other? From what I had seen in northern Kenya, the answer was yes. What I had seen seemed like a glimmer of light in an otherwise gloomy world.

But there are hard times ahead. In early 2020, what seemed the biggest cloud on the horizon in northern Kenya were swarms after swarms of hungry locusts. It was the worst outbreak for decades, but this time, according to scientists, they were encouraged by heating global temperatures. Warmer seas mean more cyclones that bring rain to usually dry deserts, and that provided perfect locust breeding conditions.[4] There were so many locusts they could make the bright sun go dim.

But another, even darker, test was coming. The Covid-19 coronavirus has provided the starkest of warnings that we are not invincible or separate from the environment we live in, and that human health is dependent on our relationship with the natural world. We are just one strand among the millions of species in the intricately balanced web of life. Pluck one thread, and everything reverberates. Damaging one part ripples through the whole system.

For Kenya, and for conservation work around the world, it created a profound crisis. Tourism made up nearly a tenth of Kenya's economy.[5] Cutting international travel hit nature-based tourism hard. People need income, and need to eat; but the warnings it would lead to a spike in poaching did not materialise, at least among northern Kenya's conservancies. The economy was based on livestock, and that continued the same as ever.

Dire warnings of climate change followed next, with the UN's Intergovernmental Panel on Climate Change in 2021 issuing a 'code red' for humanity, warning of increasingly extreme heatwaves, droughts and flooding. Stopping further catastrophe by slashing greenhouse gas emissions requires fundamental societal changes by the industrialised world who caused it, not the people here. Adapting to our heating world will require major cultural and economic revolutions. As northern Kenya has shown, if any system will pull through, it will be one with the backing of the community. Whatever the people will face, if they stand together, they will be better able to weather the coming storms.

* * *

At night, I dream about looking out high above the eagles from the mighty mountain of Ololokwe. I think of walking north through the lush forests and the open plains to the cool tumbling waterfalls of Namunyak, with the graceful giraffe galloping ahead. I take heart from knowing that somewhere out on the wide open rangelands, the herds of grey elephants roam as they wish, safe and free. Most of all, I remember how the Samburu herders bent down when they found the sun-bleached skulls, and how they broke off white blossom from the trees and placed it in the cracks of the bone, offering flowers for elephants.

It gives me hope. For the placing of flowers on the bones of the elephants is far more than a simple ritual; it shows the vital respect between people and the wild. The powerful old connection between nature and humans, for now, remains. So much of that which has been lost cannot be brought back—but some can, and that which we still have must be protected. Our relationship with nature is badly damaged, but it is not over. Repairing those bonds will never be easy. It takes time, as well as courage, strength and daring. We have no other option than to try.

VISITING NORTHERN KENYA

More information on the Northern Rangelands Trust can be found at www.nrt-kenya.org, but one of the best ways to support the work of the community conservancies is to visit them and hear their stories for yourselves. Climb up and camp on mighty Ololokwe, and sleep under the stars in Sera to wake at dawn to track a rhino. Swim in the azure jungle pools of Ngare Ndare, watch the orphaned elephants at Reteti as they are fed by their keepers, walk amongst the giraffes and lions at Il Ngwesi, trek through the tangled leopard forests of Warges, find Lake Paradise in the heart of misty Marsabit, or sail through the mangrove creeks of Lamu, out to white sand beaches where turtles dive into the Indian Ocean. A network of community-run sites catering for everyone from campers to those wanting top-end luxury lodges can be found at https://the big-north.travel, run by or supporting the conservancies. The roads are long and dusty, but adventure awaits.

ACKNOWLEDGEMENTS

The list of those who helped is long. My heartfelt thanks to HRH The Duke of Cambridge for his kind foreword.

Thank you too to photographers David Chancellor and Pete McBride, who kindly allowed their images to be included to showcase the stunning wonder of Kenya. Both have invested years documenting the work of community conservation. Their work can be seen at www.petemcbride.com and www.davidchancellor.com.

To Tom Lalampaa, thank you, as well as to Samuel Lekimaroro, Losas Lenamunyi, Frederick Ibras and all your fearless teams on the sharp edge every day, who watched my back and kept me safe. To Osman Hussein, for your vital organisation, Sammy Leseita for your invaluable insights, as well as Yusuf Kurtuma, Edward Ndiritu, Reuben Lendira, John Pameri, Bea Karanja, Joseph Piroris, Mike and Sarah Watson, Rob McNeil, Geoffrey Chege, and Adrian Paul, for always getting my wheels back on track. To all the many Craigs and Dyers, Susan and David Brown and Sue Roberts, but my very special thanks to Jane, who welcomed a stranger so warmly, and offered the best writing desk ever in an old rhino stable. For Garry Cullen, who made it happen in the first place, and Sir John Spurling, for your kindness. To those at NRT and in the conservancies who make it all work: Yusuf Odupio, Joseph Lolngojine, Juliet King, Mathew Mutinda, Fuzz Dyer, Titus Letaapo, Kieran Avery, Duncan Ndotono, Josphine Ekiru, Latif Boru, Fred Obiya, Patrick Ekodere, John Logeme, Burton Lenanyokie, Mading Kanyakera Duncan, Titus Peghin, and Joseph Lesonjore—for taking me closer to a rhino than I ever dared dream. To all the conservancy rangers and the Nine Teams, but especially John Lantare, Galgalo Dati, Charles Muthamia, Molu Katelo, Mohamed Huka, Lkiparia Lekango, Mujerin Lekuchan, Philip Lengerpei, Machakos Lepore, Butte Wato, Patrick Ngala, Omar Hassan Harrow, as well as Batian, Pete and Barry. To David Daballen, Iain and Oria Douglas-Hamilton, Frank Pope, Jane Wynyard, and all at Save the Elephants, who offer a future for a wiser animal than us. Lobik Lesasuyian, for your hospitality, and showing me the elephant roads through the hills of Namunyak. For all the expert advice, support and suggestions: David O'Connor and Jenna Stacy-Dawes at San Diego Institute for Conservation Research, Jonah Western, Hassan Roba, and Philip Winter, for his kind support once more, Charlie Mayhew, Dan Bucknell and all at Tusk Trust, Matt Brown, Martin Bucher at Zoo Zürich, Nigel Winser, Riccardo Orizio, Alex Rhodes, Mike Pflanz, Ed Ghaui, Allan Ward, John Nyaga at the East African Wildlife Society, Mordecai Ogada, the late Richard Leakey, Brendan Buzzard, Fred Nelson, Annie Olivecrona, Piers Bastard, and Mike Harkness at Durham University archives. From Nairobi to Nicosia and far beyond, to all who offered encouragement, advice and kindness, tea, read drafts or looked after Zanz when I was on the road: Hez Holland, Lisa Murray, Brian Harding, Carolina and Geoff, Rosie and Owen, Zoe Flood, Lauren McEvatt, Rajiv Golla, Emma Phillips, Mackenzie and Zoe, with huge thanks. For Al, Jonny, Nick, who were always there when I needed, and my parents, who welcomed us in lockdown, for Lucy and Sophie Martell—who drew the wonderful map, thank you. And last but most importantly, with all my love, Olivia and Bee, whose grandfathers taught me their love of nature—in the hope I can pass something of that on to you.

LIST OF ILLUSTRATIONS

1. Women meet in front of the sacred mountain of Ololokwe, also called Sabache. © David Chancellor

2. Blessing the dead: A Samburu herder places branches onto an elephant skull as a mark of respect. © Peter Martell

3. Lewa is a crucial wildlife corridor to Mt. Kenya, the peak seen on the horizon. © Peter Martell

4. Pastoralists in northern Kenya move with their livestock on ancient routes to the same areas each year to find water and grazing. © Pete McBride

5. An orphaned elephant is looked after at the Reteti community-run sanctuary, before being returned to the wild. © David Chancellor

6. A family 'manyatta' compound. Herders live across the community conservancies, grazing livestock alongside wild animals. © Pete McBride

7. The Samburu are nicknamed by some the 'butterfly people' for their love of colourful fashion. © Pete McBride

8. Boys play with a makeshift football. As cattle raids have diminished, more children are going to school. © Pete McBride

9. Mobile home, Samburu-style, West Gate Conservancy. Pastoralism is a sophisticated system of land management built up through generations. © Pete McBride

10. Ian Craig and Kinyanjui Lesderia, friends since they were both young men. © Jane Craig

11. In 1983, philanthropist Anna Merz provided the seed funds for a rhino sanctuary at Lewa. © Fuzz Dyer

NOTES

PREFACE

1. Karen Witsenburg and Wario R. Adano (2009), Of Rains and Raids: Violent Livestock Raiding in Northern Kenya', *Civil Wars*, 11(4): pp. 514–538; Carol Ember (1992), 'Resource Unpredictability, Mistrust, and War', *Journal of Conflict Resolution*, 36(2): pp. 242–262, June 1992.

2. United Nations Environment Programme (2005), *After The Tsunami: Rapid Environmental Assessment*, UNEP: Nairobi, pp. 133–4.

3. In 2021, the Notre Dame Global Adaptation Initiative listed Chad, Central African Republic, Eritrea, Guinea-Bissau and DR Congo as the world's most vulnerable nations, and ranked Kenya 148 out of 181 countries listed. Risk analysts Verisk Maplecroft had a similar list, putting Central African Republic, Haiti, DR Congo, Burundi and Eritrea in bottom place.

4. Wario R Adano, Ton Dietz, Karen Witsenburg, Fred Zaal (2012), 'Climate Change, Violent Conflict and Local Institutions in Kenya's Drylands', *Journal of Peace Research*, 2012 49: p. 65.

5. Halvard Buhaug (2010), 'Climate not to Blame for African Civil Wars', *Proceedings of the National Academy of Sciences*, September 2010, 107 (38) pp. 16477–16482; Ragnhild Nordas and Nils Petter Gleditsch (2007), 'Climate Change and Conflict', *Political Geography*, 26: pp. 627–638.

6. Rob Malley, International Crisis Group, 'Climate Change Is Shaping the Future of Conflict', Address to UN Security Council, 22 April 2020; The International Committee of the Red Cross (2021), *When Rain Turns To Dust: Understanding and responding to the combined impact of armed conflicts and the climate and environment crisis on people's lives*, Geneva, ICRC, pp. 5–15.

7. CNA Military Advisory Board (2014), 'National Security and the Accelerating Risks of Climate Change', Alexandria, VA: CNA Corporation, 2014, pp. 2–3.

8. Turner M.G. et al. (2020), 'Climate change, ecosystems and abrupt change: science priorities', Phil. Trans. R. Soc. B 375: 20190105.

9. Jean-François Maystadt and Olivier Ecker (2014), 'Extreme Weather and Civil War: Does Drought Fuel Conflict in Somalia through Livestock Price Shocks'? *American Journal of Agricultural Economics*, 96:4, pp. 1157–

1182. Their study on Somalia found that drought-caused livestock price shocks drove conflict; a one percent standard deviation increase in drought intensity and length raises the likelihood of conflict by 62 percent.

10. Clionadh Raleigh, Hyun Jin Choi, Dominic Kniveton (2015), 'The devil is in the details: An investigation of the relationships between conflict, food price and climate across Africa', *Global Environmental Change*, 32: pp. 187–199.

11. Germany; Gerardo Ceballos el al. (2020), 'Vertebrates on the brink as indicators of biological annihilation and the sixth mass extinction', *PNAS* 2020, pp. 1–7.; Dinerstein et al. (2019), 'A Global Deal For Nature: Guiding principles, milestones, and targets', *Science Advances*. 5 (4) April 2019.

12. IPBES (2019), 'Global assessment report on biodiversity and ecosystem services of the Intergovernmental Science-Policy Platform on Biodiversity and Ecosystem Services', *IPBES*, Bonn.

13. Scott Straus (2012), 'Wars Do End! Changing Patterns of Political Violence in Sub-Saharan Africa', *African Affairs*, 111. pp. 179–201.

14. David Western (1997/2002), *In the Dust of Kilimanjaro*, Island Press: Washington, pp. 288–9; David Western, Samantha Russell, Innes Cuthill (2009), 'The Status of Wildlife in Protected Areas Compared to Non-Protected Areas of Kenya', PLoS ONE 4(7): e6140. A 2003 study estimated 73 percent of Kenya's elephant range was outside government protected areas. J. Blanc et al. (2003), *African Elephant Status Report 2002*, IUCN/SSC African Elephant Specialist Group, pp. 88–89. Later assessments map an alarming decline in numbers, but the ratio of animals outside government parks is thought to remain the same, partly due to conservancies.

15. Pawlok Dass, Benjamin Z Houlton, Yingping Wang, David Warlind, 'Grasslands may be more reliable carbon sinks than forests in California', *Environmental Research Letters*, 2018; 13 (7): 074027; Dinerstein et al. (2019).

16. Rangelands occupy 54 percent of the world's land surface, according to a UN-backed 2021 estimate. International Livestock Research Institute et al. (2021), *Rangelands Atlas*, ILRI, Nairobi.

17. Some 268 million people across Africa depend on pastoralism, contributing between 10 to 44 percent of GDP in Africa's 55 plus nations. African Union (AU), 2010, *Policy Framework for Pastoralism In Africa*, Addis Ababa, 2010, p. 16.

18. Joseph Ogutu et al. (2016), 'Extreme wildlife declines and concurrent increase in livestock numbers in Kenya: What are the causes'? *PloS One* 11.9.

1. KINYANJUI'S CLASSROOM (HOW THE LESSONS WERE LEARNED)

1. For the Maasai people it is *'Ol Donyo Eibor'*, the white mountain.
2. National Museums of Kenya, Lewa Hand Axes, Early Pleistocene, Acheulean: Reference Number: GpJn1.4: KNM-2343–1.
3. Rinderpest emerged first in central Asia, and is thought to have spread to Europe in the thirteenth century with Genghis Khan. In Europe, previous rinderpest bouts meant people had developed the first attempts at disease control measures, including prompting the opening of the first ever veterinary school, in the French city of Lyon in 1761. Rinderpest would only be eradicated in 2011 after decades of hard work, becoming the second disease to have ever been deliberately exterminated, after smallpox.
4. Frederick Lugard (1893), *The Rise of our East African Empire*, Vol. I, William Blackwood: Edinburgh. pp. 525–527.
5. P Roeder, J Mariner, R Kock (2013), *Rinderpest: The Veterinary Perspective on Eradication*, 368 Phil. Trans. R. Soc. B.; Jeffrey Mariner (2012), 'Rinderpest Eradication: Appropriate Technology and Social Innovations', *Science*, Vol 337, Issue 1309.
6. Lugard, 1893: 359.
7. Dennis Normile (2008), 'Driven to Extinction', *Science*, 21 March 2008: Vol. 319, Issue 5870, pp. 1606–1609. F. Lankester, A. Davis (2016), 'Pastoralism and wildlife: historical and current perspectives in the East African rangelands of Kenya and Tanzania', Rev. Sci. Tech. Off. Int. Epiz., 2016, 35 (2), pp. 473–484.
8. Fred Pearce (2000), 'Inventing Africa: Which is more authentic: a game rich wilderness or cattle pasture?' *New Scientist*, Vol. 167, Issue 2251, August 2000, p. 30.
9. Jonathan S. Adams and Thomas O. McShane (1992), *The Myth of Wild Africa, Conservation Without Illusion*, Norton: New York, pp. 40–58. John M. MacKenzie (1988), *The Empire of Nature—Hunting, Conservation and British Imperialism*, Manchester University Press: Manchester, pp. 264–267.
10. Jomo Kenyatta (1965), *Facing Mt. Kenya*, Vintage: New York, p. 37.
11. The International Churchill Society (ICS), quoting, Ronald Hyman, (1968), *Elgin and Churchill at the Colonial Office 1905–1908*, New York: Macmillan, p. 356; Randolph S. Churchill (2007), *Winston S. Churchill, Volume II, Young Statesman 1901–1914,* Hillsdale: Michigan. p. 231; Winston S. Churchill, *My African Journey* (1909), Richard Clay: Suffolk, pp. 14–15, 85, 158.
12. Lotte Hughes (2002), 'Moving the Maasai: A Colonial Misadventure', D.Phil. thesis. University of Oxford, pp. 1–2; Lotte Hughes (2007),

'Rough Time in Paradise: Claims, Blames and Memory Making Around Some Protected Areas in Kenya Conservation and Society', Vol. 5, No. 3, 2007, pp. 307–330; Timothy Parsons (2011), 'Local Responses to the Ethnic Geography of Colonialism in the Gusii Highlands of British-Ruled Kenya', *Ethnohistory* 58:3.

13. Some 40–45,000 white settlers are estimated to have left Kenya in 1962–69, but at the same time, some 30,000 Europeans arrived. Of the original settlers, some 10–15,000 remained. Janet McIntosh (2016), *Unsettled: Denial and Belonging among White Kenyans*, University of California, p. 3; also Thomas Hoffman (2010), 'White Kenyan English', in D. Schreier, P. Trudgill, E. Schneider and J.P. Williams, *The Lesser-known Varieties of English*, Cambridge: Cambridge University Press, pp. 286–312.

14. R. Van Zwanenberg (1976), 'Dorobo Hunting and Gathering: A Way of Life or a Mode of Production?' *African Economic History* (2), pp. 12–21; Lee Cronk (2002), 'From True Dorobo to Mukogodo Maasai: Contested Ethnicity in Kenya', *Ethnology*, 41(1), pp. 27–49.

15. Sir Geoffrey Archer (1963), *Personal and Historical Memoirs of an East African Administrator*, Edinburgh, Oliver & Boyd, pp. 34–37.

16. Charles Chenevix Trench (1964), *The Desert's Dusty Face*, Edinburgh, Blackwood, p. 236.

17. Geoffrey Archer, government minute, written in December 1923— italics were originally underlined. Archer, then Governor of Uganda, was specifically referring to Uganda's Karamoja region, which borders northern Kenya, and treated by colonial authorities in a similar manner. In James Barber (1968), *Imperial Frontier: A study of relations between the British and the Pastoral Tribes of North East Uganda*, Nairobi, East African Publishing House, p. 209.

18. I.M. Lewis (2002), *A Modern History of the Somali*, Oxford, James Currey, pp. 164–5.

2. THE BUSH BANDITS (HOW THE ANIMALS WERE KILLED)

1. Lewis, 2009, pp. 202–4; Branch (2011), pp. 3–32.

2. Hannah Whittaker (2017), 'Frontier Security in North East Africa: Conflict and Colonial Development on The Margins, c.1930–1960', *Journal of African History*, 58.3, 2017, pp. 381–402; Hannah Whittaker (2012), 'Forced Villagization during the Shifta Conflict in Kenya, c.1963–1968', *International Journal of African Historical Studies*, Vol. 45, No. 3, 2012, pp. 346–363.

3. Michael Hodges (2007), *AK-47—The Story of the People's Gun*, London, Sceptre, pp. 37–43.

4. Hannah Whittaker (2015), 'Legacies of Empire: State Violence and Collective Punishment in Kenya's North Eastern Province, c. 1963– Present', *The Journal of Imperial and Commonwealth History*, 43:4, p. 650.

5. George Adamson (1968), *Bwana Game: The Life Story of George Adamson*, London, Collins & Harvill, p. 133; John C. Willoughby (1889), *East Africa and its Big Game*, London, Longmans Green, p. 82.

6. Peter Dalleo (1979), 'The Somali Role in Organized Poaching in North-eastern Kenya, c. 1909–1939', *The International Journal of African Historical Studies*, 12 (3), pp. 472–482.

7. Leakey, 2001: pp. 39–41.

8. Ivory carving factories were opened in 1958 in Beijing and Guangzhou. Demand dropped during the Cultural Revolution, 1966–76, but then returned. Yufang Gao, Susan G. Clark (2014), 'Elephant ivory trade in China: Trends and drivers', *Biological Conservation*, Volume 180, December 2014, pp. 23–30.

9. Iain and Oria Douglas-Hamilton (1975), *Among the Elephants*, London, Collins & Harvill, pp. 52–54.

10. Wilfred Thesiger (1994), *My Kenya Days*, London: Flamingo, p. 35.

11. Charles F. Mason, Erwin H. Bulte and Richard D. Horan (2012), 'Banking on Extinction: endangered species and speculation', *Oxford Review of Economic Policy*, Vol. 28, No. 1, Spring 2012, pp. 180–192.

12. The belief has since been proved wrong; the argument that trophy hunting 'strengthens' populations by selectively targeting old animals no longer applies, researchers argue. Hunters targeting the biggest male animals, with the largest horns, removes those with the strongest genes, scientists have found. When environments are stable, that has limited impact. But for a population already under pressure, 'harvesting rates' of just five percent of can cause extinction. Robert J. Knell, and Carlos Martinez-Ruiz (2017), 'Selective harvest focused on sexual signal traits can lead to extinction under directional environmental change', *Proceedings of the Royal Society*, B. 2017, 284: 20171788.

13. Anthony Dyer (1979), *The East African Hunters: The History of the East Africa Professional Hunters' Association*, NJ: Amwell Press, p. 91.

14. 'Kenya Bans All Hunting of Elephants Indefinitely', *New York Times*, 2 September, 1973; Douglas-Hamilton, p. 94.

15. Boyce Rensberger (1977), 'This Is The End Of The Game', 6 November, 1977, *The New York Times*.

16. CIA (1978) 'Africa Review, Kenya: Economic Stake of the Kenyatta Family', September 1978, CIA National Foreign Assessment Center, USA, pp. 9–13.

17. Dyer, 1979: p. 143.

18. Peter Jenkins (1983), *Lewa Downs: Rhino Sanctuary Project*, May 1983, pp. 1–4.

3. THE RHINO GUARDIANS (HOW A SPECIES WAS SAVED)

1. John Goddard (1967), 'Home range, behaviour and recruitment rates of two black rhinoceros populations', *East African Wildlife Journal*, 5, pp. 133–150; John Goddard (1968), 'Food preference of two black rhinoceros populations', *East African Wildlife Journal*, 6, pp. 1–18.
2. An adult black rhino can weigh some 1,350 kilograms, or 3,000 pounds, and have been estimated to reach speeds potentially as high as 35 mph/55 kph, some 25 percent faster than the 100 metre Olympic record.
3. Richard Estes (1999), *The Safari Companion: A Guide to Watching African Mammals*, Vermont, Chelsea Green, pp. 190–199.
4. Anna Merz died aged 81 in 2013. Her quotes come from her autobiography. Anna Merz (1991), *Rhino—At the Brink of Extinction*, London, Harper Collins.
5. 'Anna Merz, Obituary', 27 May 2013, *The Daily Telegraph*.
6. David Western (1982), 'Patterns of depletion in a Kenya rhino population and the conservation implications', *Biological Conservation*, 24, 1982, pp. 147–156; Mary Ashly, Don Melnick, David Western (1990), 'Conservation genetics of the black rhinoceros (Diceros bicornis), I: Evidence from the Mitochondrial DNA of three populations', *Conservation Biology*, 1990, 4 (1).
7. Western (1982), pp. 147–156.
8. Anthony Dyer (1996), *The Big Five*, Agoura: Trophy Books.
9. Jim Feely (2007), 'Black rhino, white rhino: what's in a name?' *Pachyderm, Newsletter of the African Elephant and Rhino Group*, 2007:43, pp. 111–15.
10. Elliot Fratkin (1991) 'The "Loibon" as Sorcerer: A Samburu "Loibon" among the Ariaal Rendille, 1973–87', *Africa: Journal of the International African Institute*, 61(3), pp. 318–333.

4. THE GREAT REWILDING (HOW NATURE WAS RESTORED)

1. Anthony R.E. Sinclair, Ally Nkwabi, Simon A.R. Mduma & Flora Magige (2014), 'Responses of the Serengeti avifauna to long-term change in the environment', *Ostrich: Journal of African Ornithology*, 85:1, pp. 1–11.
2. Northern White Rhino, a sub-species, are native to Uganda, DR Congo and South Sudan—but are thought to have been wiped out there entirely. All that remained were a lonely pair of females, the last of their species, in a reserve south of Lewa, called Ol Pejeta. Southern White Rhinos arrived in Lewa in 1993.
3. Michale Soulé and Reed Noss (1998) 'Rewilding and Biodiversity: Complementary Goals for Continental Conservation', *Wild Earth*.

4. A more detailed impact report on de-tusking elephants was carried out on Lewa in 2014. See Mutinda M., Chenge G., Gakuya F., Otiende M., Omondi P., et al. (2014), 'Detusking Fence-Breaker Elephants as an Approach in Human-Elephant Conflict Mitigation', *PloS One*, 9(3): e91749.

5. Lucy King, Iain Douglas-Hamilton, and Fritz Vollrath (2011), 'Beehive fences as effective deterrents for crop-raiding elephants: field trials in northern Kenya', *African Journal of Ecology*, 2011; Lucy King (2019), 'Beehive Fence Construction Manual, The Elephants and Bees Project', Nairobi, Save the Elephants.

6. Ogutu et al. (2016), 11.9.

7. Patricia Shultz (2003), *1,000 Things to See Before You Die*, New York, Workman, pp. 366–7.

5. FROM THE BLACK ROCKS (HOW PEOPLE GOT INVOLVED)

1. Katy Payne (1998), *Silent Thunder: In the Presence of Elephants*, London, Weidenfeld & Nicolson, p. 121; also Caitlin O'Connell (2007), *The Elephant's Secret Sense—The Hidden Life of the Wild Herds of Africa*, London: Oneworld.

2. Payne 1998: pp. 21–28.

3. Douglas-Hamilton (1975), p. 53.

4. The spelling of the mountains even varies, sometimes 'Matthews' with a double 'tt', and also with an apostrophe, Mathew's, as if it were his possession. One of the first references was in John Walter Gregory's 1896 account, *The Great Rift Valley*, when General Lloyd William Mathews was then British Consul-General for East Africa, based in Zanzibar. See also, Noel Simon (1962), *Between the Sunlight and the Thunder: The Wildlife of Kenya*, London, Collins, p. 111.

5. Western (1997/2002), pp. 99, 299.

6. Similar patterns were tracked in Guinea, where woodland around villages were created by people, not the last relics remaining of forests left standing. James Fairhead and Melissa Leach (1996), *Misreading the African Landscape: Society and ecology in a forest-savannah mosaic*, Cambridge University Press, pp. 2–4.

7. Wolfram Remmers, Joao Gameiro, Isabella Schaberl, Viola Clausnitzer (2017), 'Elephant (Loxodonta africana) footprints as habitat for aquatic macroinvertebrate communities in Kibale National Park, south-west Uganda', *African Journal of Ecology*, 55:3, pp. 342–351; F. Berzaghi, M. Longo, P. Ciais,.et al. 'Carbon stocks in central African forests enhanced by elephant disturbance', *Nat. Geosci.* 12, pp. 725–729 (2019).

8. From a combination of the Greek *ele*, meaning arch, and the Latin *phant*

meaning huge. There are other interpretations, including the Greek *ela-phos*, meaning an animal with horns. Doran Ross (1992), *Elephant: The Animal and Its Ivory in African Culture*, Fowler Museum of Cultural History, University of California: Los Angeles.

9. R.N. Owen-Smith, (1988), *Megaherbivores: the influence of very large body size on ecology*, Cambridge: Cambridge University Press; also P.W.J. Baxter and W.M. Getz (2005), 'A model-framed evaluation of elephant effects on tree and fire dynamics in African Savannas', *Ecol. Appl.* 15, pp. 1131–1341.

10. W. Robert Foran (1958), 'Edwardian Ivory Poachers over the Nile', *African Affairs*, Vol. 57, No. 227, April 1958, The Royal African Society, pp. 133–4; Marco Polo, Trans. Ronald Latham (1958), *The Travels of Marco Polo*, Harmondsworth, Penguin, pp. 302–3.

11. Verney Lovett Cameron (1877), *Across Africa*, New York, Harper & Brothers, p. 69; David Livingstone (1874), *The Last Journals of David Livingstone*, Vol. II, London, John Murray, p. 120; R. W. Beachey (1967), 'The East African Ivory Trade in the Nineteenth Century', *The Journal of African History*, Vol. 8, No. 2 (1967), pp. 269–290, Cambridge University Press.

12. Joseph Thomson (1885), *Through Masai Land*, London, reprinted by Frank Cass, pp. 313–314; Joseph Thomson (1881), *To the Central African Lakes and Back*, 1878–80, Vol. II, London, Sampson, Low, Marston, Searle & Rivington, pp. 16–20.

13. The Smithsonian, The National Museum of American History; Eric Scigliano (2002), *Love, War, and Circuses—The Age-Old Relationship Between Elephants and Humans*, Houghton New York, Houghton Mifflin, p. 159.

14. Keith Somerville (2016), *Ivory—Power and Poaching in Africa*, London, Hurst, p. 60; Cynthia Moss (1988), *Elephant Memories: Thirteen Years in the Life of an Elephant Family*, Chicago: University of Chicago Press, p. 270. 'A herd of elephants is located and the natives collect in large numbers, then they form an enormous circle and at a given signal fire the grass,' wrote Captain J.A. Meldon in in South Sudan in 1902. 'The circle of natives gradually closing in as the grass is burnt, the elephant rush madly in every direction, seeking to escape, and many are burnt, while those who do leave the circle half-blinded and suffocated, are speared.' Beachey, 1967: p. 281.

15. Thomson 1881: pp. 16–20.

16. Edward I. Steinhart (2006), *Black Poachers White Hunters—A social history of hunting in colonial Kenya*, Ohio University Press, p. 95. Beachey 1967: p. 280; Archer, 1963: pp. 37–8.

17. Theodore Roosevelt (1910), *African Game Trails: An Account of the African Wanderings of an American Hunter-Naturalist*, New York, Charles Scribner, pp. 284–285, 299–300.

18. Letter from the Marquis of Salisbury, the then British Foreign Secretary, dated 27 May 1896. Simon, 1962: p. 33.

19. Richard Leakey (2001), *Wildlife Wars—My battle to Save Kenya's elephants*, Macmillan: London, pp. 2, 36; David Western (2019), 'Kenya's Wildlife: A success story in the making?' Lecture, National Museums of Kenya, 21 February 2019.

20. A letter apparently signed by Somalia's dictator Siad Barre authorising ivory to be smuggled from Kenya was published in 1988 by reporters. Somerville, *Ivory*, pp. 116–118; USA Department of the Interior (1989), 'US Imposes Moratorium on Ivory Imports from Somalia', US Fish and Wildlife Service, 24 February 1989, pp. 1–2.

21. Leakey, 2001: pp. 36–37, 48.

22. Leakey, 2001: pp. 64–69.

23. From the late 1980s to the early 1990s, the price of ivory collapsed from $150 to $20 dollars per kilogram.

24. Jane Perlez (1989), 'Kenya's Government Fights for Control in a War that Endangers Tourism', *New York Times*, 27 August 1989.

25. Leakey, 2001: p. 68.

6. THE LAND OF GOOD BLESSING (HOW THE FIRST CONSERVANCY BEGAN)

1. In Yiaku, the phrase is *kutei tikuisi*, literally, 'everybody has their own thing.' See also; Jacob Mhando (2008), *Safeguarding Endangered Oral Traditions in East Africa*, National Museums of Kenya & UNESCO, January 2008, UNESCO, Nairobi; Lee Cronk (2004), *From Mukogodo to Maasai: Ethnicity and Cultural Change in Kenya*, Boulder, Westview Press. Also, R. N. Chakraborty, 'Sharing Culture and Resource Conservation in Hunter-Gatherer Societies', *Oxford Economic Papers*, 59.1, Jan. 2007, pp. 63–88.

2. Grant Hardin (1968), 'The Tragedy of the Commons', *Science*, 162: 243–48.

3. Susan Jane Buck Cox (1985), 'No Tragedy on the Commons', *Journal of Environmental Ethics*, Vol. 7, Spring 1985, 7 (1):49–61; Daniel W Bromley; Michael M. Cernea (1989), *The management of common property natural resources: some conceptual and operational fallacies*, Washington, DC, The World Bank; Matto Mildenberger (2019), 'The Tragedy of "The Tragedy of the Commons"', Scientific American Blog Network.

4. Elinor Ostrom (2009), Prize Lecture, Nobel Prize, 8 December 2009 at Aula Magna, Stockholm University, *Beyond Markets and States: Polycentric Governance of Complex Economic Systems*; Elinor Ostrom (1990), *Governing the Commons: The Evolution of Institutions for Collective Action*, Cambridge

University Press; The Nobel Prize (2009), The Nobel Foundation, Stockholm, Sweden.

5. David Western et al (2020), 'Conservation from the inside-out: Winning space and a place for wildlife in working landscapes', *British Ecological Society. People and Nature*, 2020; 00:1–13.

6. David M. Anderson (1984), 'Depression, Dust Bowl, Demography, and Drought: The Colonial State and Soil Conservation in East Africa during the 1930s', *African Affairs*, Vol. 83, No. 332 (July, 1984), pp. 321–343; Hughes, 2007: pp. 307–330.

7. Clark C. Gibson (1999), *Politicians and Poachers: The Political Economy of Wildlife Policy in Africa*, Cambridge University Press, pp. 2–3.

8. Steinhart, 2006: p. 161. Most of the rhinos were killed between 1946 and 1948 in Kenya's south-eastern Makueni district, near Tsavo National Park. The land proved to be of little use for intensive agriculture.

9. Noel Simon (1962), pp. 69–70.

10. The reserve, also called Ukamaba, extended for 10,695 sq miles, 27,699 km sq, nearly a third bigger than today's Tsavo national parks, which it stretched across. Simon, 1962: pp. 116–8.

11. John F. Oates (1999), *Myth and Reality in the Rain Forest*, Berkeley, University of California Press, p. 31.

12. National Parks UK, 2020.

13. Steinhart, 2006: p. 1.

14. Roderick P. Neumann (2002), 'The Postwar Conservation Boom in British Colonial Africa', *Environmental History*, Vol. 7, No. 1 (Jan. 2002), pp. 22–47, Oxford University Press.

15. A 1988 study by David Western, quoted by Somerville, *Ivory*, p. 116.

16. Michael Ranneberger, US Ambassador to Kenya (2006), 'Cows Versus Crops: Government Responds to 'Illegal' Pastoralists', Embassy Cable, November 17, 2006.

17. Dan Brockington, Rosaleen Duffy, Jim Igoe (2008), *Nature Unbound: Conservation, Capitalism and the Future of Protected Areas*, London, Earthscan, p. 20.

7. THE BATTLE OF THE BARREN RIVER (HOW TO STOP A WAR)

1. Deo Gumba, Nelson Alusala and Andrew Kimani (2019), 'Vanishing herds—Cattle rustling in East Africa and the Horn', Vol. 10, December 2019, ENACT: Nairobi, pp. 2–6; Human Rights Watch (2002), *Playing with Fire: Weapons Proliferation, Political Violence, and Human Rights in Kenya*, New York: HRW, pp. 11, 16–20.

2. James Bevan (2008), *Blowback—Kenya's Illicit Ammunition Problem in Turkana North District*, Geneva, Small Arms Survey, pp. 20–25.

3. In one raid, some 550 animals were taken by Samburu gunmen. But when the soldiers finished their heavy-handed operation, they returned with 4,000 animals. Identifying where livestock comes from is not difficult, since owners brand or scar their cattle with unique symbols; it was later reported that none of the 4,000 animals were those that had initially been stolen. Ranneberger (2009), 'Government Raids Samburu Cattle, Stage Set For More Tribal Conflict', Embassy Cable, 18 March 2009.

4. Scientists who have studied the bird found it helps cut the time to find a hive by two-thirds. Hussein Isack and Heinz Reyer (1989), 'Honeyguides and Honey Gatherers: Interspecific Communication in a Symbiotic Relationship', *Science*, Vol. 243, No. 4896, pp. 1343–1346.

8. THE MOTHERS OF THE MORANS (HOW THE CONSERVANCIES CAME TOGETHER)

1. David Tillman and John A Downing (1994), 'Biodiversity and Stability in Grasslands', *Nature*, 367 (6461) pp. 363–365; Robert Pringle, Truman Young, Daniel Rubenstein, Douglas J. McCauley (2007), 'Herbivore initiated interaction cascades and their modulation by productivity in an African Savannah', January 2007, *Proceedings of the National Academy of Sciences*, 104: pp. 193–197.

2. Ranneberger (2009), 'Isiolo's Security Problem', Embassy Cable, 23 June 2009.

3. Gumba, Alusala and Kimani (2019), pp. 2–4.

9. JOSEPHINE AND THE GUNMEN (HOW THE MESSAGE SPREAD)

1. Severin Hauenstein, Mrigesh Kshatriya, Julian Blanc, Carsten F. Dormann, Colin M. Beale, (2019), 'African elephant poaching rates correlate with local poverty, national corruption and global ivory price', *Nature Communications*, 10: 2242 (2019); Jason G. Goldman (2019), 'Where Humans Suffer, So Do Elephants', *National Geographic*, 28 May 2019.

2. Wilfrid Odadi, Joe Fargione & Daniel Rubenstein (2017), 'Vegetation, Wildlife and Livestock Responses to Planned Grazing Management in an African pastoral landscape', *Land Degradation and Development*, February 2017; Mohamed Shibia (2011), 'Effects of Grazing Management on forage production and rangeland condition in Il Ngwesi group ranch of Laikipia', MSc, Egerton University, Kenya.

3. Margaret Jacobsohn (2019), *Life is Like a Kudu Horn*, Cape Town, Jacana, p. 8; Garth Owen-Smith (2010), *An Arid Eden: A Personal Account of Conservation in the Kaokoveld*, Jeppestown, Jonathan Ball Publishers.

4. Jeffrey Hackel (1999), 'Community Conservation and the Future of

Africa's Wildlife', *Conservation Biology*, 13 (4), pp. 726–734; Clemens Greiner (2012), 'Unexpected Consequences: Wildlife Conservation and Territorial Conflict in Northern Kenya', *Human Ecology*, Vol. 40, No. 3, June 2012, pp. 415–425.

5. J. Fairhead, M. Leach, and I. Scoones (2012), 'Green grabbing: a new appropriation of nature?', *The Journal of Peasant Studies*, 39(2), pp. 237–261; Brock Bersaglio and Frances Cleaver (2018), 'Green Grab by Bricolage, The Institutional Workings of Community Conservancies in Kenya', *Conservation and Society*, 16(4): pp. 467–480.

6. The Oakland Institute (2021), "Stealth Game 'Community' Conservancies devastate land and lives in Northern Kenya". Oakland, California.

7. John Mbaria and Mordecai Ogada (2016), *The Big Conservation Lie: The untold story of wildlife conservation in Kenya*, Auburn, Lens & Pens Publishing.

10. THE RHINO IN THE SCHOOL (HOW THE BEST SECURITY IS THE COMMUNITY)

1. Iain Douglas-Hamilton (2012), 'Save the Elephants on Ivory and Insecurity: The Global Implications of Poaching in Africa before the Committee on Foreign Relations', U.S. Senate, May 2012.

2. Tom Milliken and Jo Shaw (2012), 'The South Africa—Viet Nam Rhino Horn Trade Nexus', TRAFFIC, Johannesburg, South Africa.

3. The money he got for each horn varied, but Keleshi said he earned between 300,000 and 500,000 Kenyan shillings, roughly, $3–5,000.

12. AN ELEPHANT CALLED POKOT (HOW HUMANS AND WILDLIFE TRUSTED EACH OTHER AGAIN)

1. Joyce Poole (1996), *Coming of Age with Elephants*, London, Hodder & Stoughton, p. 133.

2. Onesmas Kahindi (2001), 'Cultural perceptions of elephants by the Samburu people in northern Kenya', University of Strathclyde, pp. 34–6.

3. G. A. Bradshaw, Allan Schore, Janine Brown, Joyce Poole & Cynthia Moss (2005), 'Elephant Breakdown', *Nature*, 433, 807, 24 February 2005.

4. Y. Niimura, A. Matsui, K. Touhara (2014), 'Extreme expansion of the olfactory receptor gene repertoire in African elephants and evolutionary dynamics of orthologous gene groups in 13 placental mammals', *Genome Res*, 22 July 2014, pp. 1–12.

5. Karen McComb, Lucy Baker, and Cynthia Moss (2006), 'African elephants show high levels of interest in the skulls and ivory of their own species', *Biol. Lett.* (2006), 2, pp. 26–28; Iain Douglas-Hamilton, Shivani

Bhalla, George Wittemyer, Fritz Vollrath (2006), 'Behavioural reactions of elephants towards a dying and deceased matriarch', *Applied Animal Behaviour Science*, 2006, Elsevier, pp. 1–16; Shifra Goldenberg, George, Wittemyer (2020), 'Elephant behavior toward the dead: A review and insights from field observations', *Primates*, 61, pp. 119–128 (2020).

6. Such accounts are common in northern Kenya. Another herder, in Sere Lepi, described waking after a drink too many at a wedding party in a dry riverbed, where he had laid down for a snooze on the way home, to find three elephants covering him in branches. When he got up in the light, he knew it was not a firewater dream of drink because the branches were still piled up protecting him. See also Douglas-Hamilton (1975), pp. 240–1; Cynthia Moss (1988), *Elephant Memories: Thirteen Years in the Life of an Elephant Family*, Chicago: University of Chicago Press, p. 270; Poole (1996), pp. 132–135.

7. Daphne Sheldrick (2013), *An African Love Story: Love, Life and Elephants*, London, Penguin, pp. 229–331.

8. Over 70 percent cited economic gain as the primary reason. Sera Wildlife Conservancy (2011), 'Management Plan for the Reintroduction of Black Rhino', February 2011.

9. The cost of setting up the sanctuary, including all the infrastructure and the complex translocation of the rhinos, plus annual running costs for the first five years, totalled $3 million. Donors included the Netherlands government, Zoos South Australia, San Diego Zoo, Fauna & Flora International, and The Nature Conservancy.

13. THE ELEPHANT ROADS (HOW DATA HELPS IT WORK)

1. 'Vulnerability Impact and Adaptation Assessment in Northern Kenya Rangelands' (2018), CARE International, USAID Kenya, NRT.

2. Ihwagi F.W., Wang T., Wittemyer G, Skidmore A.K., Toxopeus A.G., Ngene S., et al. (2015), 'Using Poaching Levels and Elephant Distribution to Assess the Conservation Efficacy of Private, Communal and Government Land in Northern Kenya', PLoS ONE 10(9), pp. 1–17.

3. Douglas-Hamilton (1992), *Battle for the Elephants*, London, Doubleday.

4. *Great Elephant Census*, 2016.

5. Jake Wall et al (2014), 'Novel opportunities for wildlife conservation and research with real-time monitoring', *Ecological Applications*, 24(4), 2014, pp. 593–601.

6. David O'Connor, Jenna Stacy-Dawes, San Diego Zoo Global.

7. N Gravett et al. (2017), 'Inactivity/sleep in two wild free-roaming African elephant matriarchs', PLoS ONE 12(3), pp. 1–33.

8. Joseph Soltis et al (2012), 'Accelerometers in collars identify behavioral

states in captive African elephants', *Loxodonta Africana, Endangered Species Research*, 2012: 18, pp. 255–263; Max Graham et al. (2019), 'The movement of African elephants in a human-dominated land-use mosaic', *Animal Conservation*, 12, 2009, pp. 445–455; F. Ihwagi et al. (2019), 'Poaching Lowers Elephant Path Tortuosity: Implications for Conservation', *The Journal of Wildlife Management*, 2019, pp. 1–10.

9. Gary Haynes (2012), 'Elephants (and extinct relatives) as earth-movers and ecosystem engineers', *Geomorphology*, 2012:157–158, pp. 99–107; George Monbiot (2015), 'Thinking Like an Elephant', *BBC Wildlife Magazine*, June 2015.

10. William Newmark (1987), 'A Land-Bridge Island Perspective on Mammalian Extinctions in Western North American Parks', *Nature*, 325 (6103), pp. 430–432.

11. One British officer, Lieutenant Colonel C.H. Stockley, reported in 1942 seeing buffalo as high as 14,000 feet, while elephants were seen grazing at 11,000 feet. Quoted in Mohamed Amin et al. (1991), *On God's Mountain, The Story of Mount Kenya*, Nairobi, Camerapix, p. 95.

12. Maurice Nyaligu and Susie Weeks (2013), 'An Elephant Corridor in a Fragmented Conservation Landscape: Preventing the Isolation of Mount Kenya National Park and National Reserve', *Parks*, Vol 19.1 March 2013; Sian Green et al. (2018), 'Do wildlife corridors link or extend habitat? Insights from elephant use of a Kenyan wildlife corridor', *Afr J Ecol*, 2018;56: pp. 860–871.

14. THE RAREST ANTELOPE ON EARTH (HOW IT WORKS IN DIFFERENT ECOSYSTEMS)

1. Andanje, S., Davey, K., Ogwoka, B., Agwanda, B., Ali, A., Bruce, T., Wacher, T., Amin, R. (2015), 'Mammal Diversity Surveys in the Coastal Forests: Kenya, 2010–2011', The Zoological Society of London.

2. International Union for Conservation of Nature (2012), 'A sanctuary for Hirola', November 2012 IUCN: SOS—Save Our Species.

3. P. L. Sclater (1889), 'Description of Hunter's antelope', *Proceedings of the Zoological Society*, 1889, pp. 372–377.

4. Abdullahi H. Ali (2018), 'Evaluating support for rangeland-restoration practices by rural Somalis: an unlikely win-win for local livelihoods and hirola antelope?' *Animal Conservation*, The Zoological Society of London; James Probert (2011), 'The Tsavo Hirola: Current status and future management', MSc Conservation Science, Imperial College London.

5. Zoo Atlanta (2000), 'Independent Evaluation of Hirola Antelope Beatragus Hunteri Conservation Status and Conservation Action in Kenya: A Report For The Kenya Wildlife Service and The Hirola Antelope

Management Committee', September 2000; Juliet King et al. (2011), 'Aerial survey of Hirola (Beatragus hunteri) large mammals in south-east Kenya', Northern Rangelands Trust; Kenya Wildlife Service, University of Wyoming; Zoological Society of London.

6. The High Court of Kenya, Civil Case No. 2959:1996: Abdikadir Sheikh Hassan & 4 Others vs. Kenya Wildlife Service, 29 August 1996.

7. Kimberly Medley (1993), 'Primate Conservation along the Tana River, Kenya: An Examination of the Forest Habitat', *Conservation Biology*, 7: pp. 109–121; David N.M. Mbora, Douglas B. Meikle (2004), 'Forest fragmentation and the distribution, abundance and conservation of the Tana river red colobus (Procolobus rufomitratus)', *Biological Conservation* 118 (2004) pp. 67–77; Thomas Butynski, Geoffrey Mwangi (1994), *Conservation Status And Distribution Of The Tana River Red Colobus And Crested Mangabey*, Zoo Atlanta, Kenya Wildlife Service.

8. Gilchrist, H., Rocliffe, S., Anderson, L.A. (2020), 'Reef fish biomass recovery within community-managed no take zones', *Ocean and Coastal Management*, 192. 1 July 2020, 105210.

9. Oliver T.A., Oleson K.L.L., Ratsimbazafy H., Raberinary D., Benbow S., Harris A. (2015), Positive Catch & Economic Benefits of Periodic Octopus Fishery Closures: Do Effective, Narrowly Targeted Actions 'Catalyze' Broader Management? PLoS ONE 10(6).

15. FROM THE SACRED MOUNTAIN (HOW IT OFFERS HOPE FOR OUR FUTURE)

1. In 1925, Kenya's population was around 2.5 million people, growing to some 4 million in 1950, and to over 40 million by 2011. Daniel Branch (2011), *Kenya, Between Hope and Despair, 1963–2011*, New Haven, Yale University Press, p. 17. By 2019, the UN estimated the population to be around 50 million people.

2. Gerardo Ceballos el al. (2020), 'Vertebrates on the brink as indicators of biological annihilation and the sixth mass extinction', *PNAS*, 2020, pp. 1–7.

3. United Nations Environment Programme (2018), 'South Sudan: First State of Environment and Outlook Report', MoAF & UNEP: Juba; Harum Mukhayer and Hassan Abdirizak (2016), *Somalia National Action Programme for the United Nations Convention to Combat Desertification*, Mogadishu, UNDP.

4. World Meteorological Organization and Food and Agriculture Organization of the United Nations (2016), *Weather and Desert Locusts*, Geneva: WMO, pp. 27–28.

5. Dickson Kaelo; Daniel Sopia; Damian Bell; Richard Diggle and Fred

Nelson (2020), 'From crisis to solutions for communities and African conservation', *Mongabay*, 20 May 2020; Richard Damania et al. (2019), *When Good Conservation becomes Good Economics: Kenya's Vanishing Herds*, Washington, DC, World Bank.

INDEX

INDEX